GDP GROWTH AND POVERTY

An Analytical Study of Poverty Reduction Strategies and Achievements during Plans in Indian States

GDP GROWTH AND POVERTY

An Analytical Study of Poverty Reduction Strategies and Achievements during Plans in Indian States

DR. MANISH DEV

DEEP & DEEP PUBLICATIONS PVT. LTD.
F-159, Rajouri Garden, New Delhi - 110 027

GDP GROWTH AND POVERTY
An Analytical Study of Poverty Reduction Strategies and Achievements during Plans in Indian States

ISBN 978-81-8450-369-2

Typeset by RAHUL COMPOSERS
358, Pocket-B, Phase-2, Sector-16B, Dwarka, New Delhi - 110 075

Printed in India at MAYUR ENTERPRISES
WZ Plot No. 3, Gujjar Market, Tihar Village, New Delhi - 110 018

Published by DEEP & DEEP PUBLICATIONS PVT. LTD.
F-159, Rajouri Garden, New Delhi - 110 027 • Phone : 25435369, 25440916
E-mail : ddpubs@gmail.com • ddpbooks@yahoo.co.in
Showroom :
2/13, Ansari Road, Daryaganj, New Delhi - 110 002 • Telefax : 23245122

Contents

Preface

Higher growth rates of Gross Domestic Product is fundamental for the eradication of poverty. But, the real impact of growth does not produce the desired results if the growth is not inclusive. Poverty has many dimensions which requires a multi-dimensional approach to eliminate it on a sustainable basis. Various committees, appointed by the international organisations and the Government of India, and several economists and researchers have developed their own methodologies for the measurement and estimation of quantum and severity of poverty. It made the issue more complex. "Growth mediated Approach", "Capability Approach", "Safety-net Approach" and alternatively the "Area Specific Approach" have been adopted for the eradication of poverty. Several policies and programmes have been implemented to combat it. Despite this, more than 400 million persons live in conditions of extreme poverty earning income less than US $ 1 a day. 37.2 per cent population in India is still living below poverty line. India ranks 67th in Global Hunger Index developed by International Food Policy Research Institute.

Public policies, adopted for the eradication of poverty during the last three decades, still needs an optimal mix of strategies involving higher growth rate and initiation of direct poverty alleviation programmes designed and implemented on the theories of convergence. The concept of inclusive growth, as enunciated in Eleventh Five Year Plan, seems a balanced approach as it emphasises that the poor should have enough opportunities to reap the benefits from the growth. Empowerment of deprived sections of the society especially the SCs, STs, nomedic tribes and the women, will definitely bring them out of the vicious circle of 'Unemployment—poverty—malnutrition—illiteracy'.

This book examines various concepts and dimensions of poverty. The book explores indepth the characteristics and trends in poverty in India. It also discusses the impact of growth on poverty alongwith the functioning of various poverty alleviation programmes. The book gives enough space to policies and programmes for creating physical infrastructure and human development. Inclusive growth, investment in social infrastructure, empowerment of deprived sections of the society and last but not the least the governance have been given due thrust in the book.

In bringing out this book I have received help and guidance from various quarters. I am highly thankful to Dr. J.S.P. Dwivedi, Principal, Narain College, Shikohabad; Dr. Anil Kumar Thakur, Honorary Secretary and Treasurer of Indian Economic Association; Dr. Manoj Kumar Rawat, Principal, Agra College, Agra; Dr. Deepa Rawat, Head, Department of Economics, Agra College, Agra; Dr. Ravi Kauf, RBS College, Agra; Dr. Alok Kumar, St. John's College, Agra; Dr. K.P. Singh, RBS College, Agra; Dr. Gunjan Dhakney, Institute of Life Science, Dr. B.R. Ambedkar University and Dr. Deepti, Government Engineering College, Jhalawar, for their valuable suggestions to make the book more useful.

I am fortunate enough to recall the contribution of my father Dr. Shyam Sunder Singh Chauhan, Associate Professor and HOD, Department of Economics, Government Girls P.G. College, Sirsaganj, my mother Smt. Rani Singh, my sisters Mrs. Madhulika Singh and Dr. Deepankar Singh, my brother-in-laws—Er. Ajay Pundeer and Subodh Solanki. This book would have not come to this stage unless my wife Mrs. Radha Parmar had not helped me. I am thankful to her for her valuable suggestions.

Mr. G.S. Bhatia and the entire staff of M/s. Deep and Deep Publications Pvt. Ltd., New Delhi deserve my gratitude and thanks to bring out this book in a very short span of time.

DR. MANISH DEV

Abbreviations

BIMARU	:	Bihar, Madhya Pradesh, Rajasthan, Uttar Pradesh
BPL	:	Below Poverty Line
CSCS	:	Community Based Convergent Services
CCA	:	Child Care Activities
CEO	:	Chief Executive Officers
CPI-AL	:	Consumer Price Index for Agricultural Labourers
CPI-IW	:	Consumer Price Index for Industrial Workers
CPI-UNMW	:	Consumer Price Index for Urban Non-Manual Workers
DPAP	:	Drought Prone Area Programme
DDP	:	Desert Development Programme
DWCRA	:	Development of Woman and Children in Rural Areas
EAS	:	Employment Assurance Scheme
FCI	:	Food Corporation of India
GDP	:	Gross Domestic Product
GKY	:	Ganga Kalyan Yojna
GOI	:	Government of India
HDI	:	Human Development Index
HPI	:	Human Poverty Index
HRD	:	Human Resources Development
HUDCO	:	Housing and Urban Development Corporation

IAY	:	Indira Awas Yojna
IBRD	:	International Bank of Reconstruction and Development
ICOR	:	Incremental Capital-Output Ratio
IDA	:	International Development Agency
ILO	:	International Labour Organisation
IMR	:	Infant Mortality Rate
IRDP	:	Integrated Rural Development Programme
JGSY	:	Jawahar Gram Samridhi Yojna
JRY	:	Jawahar Rozgar Yojna
LEI	:	Life Expectancy Index
MFAL	:	Marginal Farmers and Agricultural Labourers Programme
MMR	:	Maternal Mortality Rate
MRP	:	Mixed Recall Period
NCAER	:	National Council of Applied Economic Research
NMBS	:	National Maternity Benefit Scheme
NSAP	:	National Social Assistance Programme
NSS	:	National Sample Survey
NSSO	:	National Sample Survey Organisation
NREGS	:	National Rural Employment Guarantee Scheme
NREP	:	National Rural Employment Programme
NRY	:	Nehru Rozgar Yojna
NSS	:	National Sample Survey
PCME	:	Per Capita Monthly Expenditure
PCTE	:	Per Capita Total Expenditure
PDS	:	Public Distribution System
PESA	:	Panchayat Raj Extension in Scheduled Areas
PG	:	Poverty Gap
PLBs	:	Poverty Line Baskets
PMIUPEP	:	Prime Minister's Integrated Urban Poverty Eradication Programme
PMRY	:	Prime Minister's Rozgar Yojna
RBI	:	Reserve Bank of India
RLLEGP	:	Rural Landless Labourers Employment Guarantee Programme

SEEUY	:	Self-Employment to the Educated Unemployed Youth
SEPUP	:	Self-Employment Programme for Urban Poor
SFDA	:	Small Farmers' Development Agency
SGDP	:	State Gross Domestic Product
SGSY	:	Swaranjayanti Gram Swarozgar Yojna
SITRA	:	Supply of Improved Tool-kits to Rural Artisens
SJSRY	:	Swaranjayanti Shahri Rozgar Yojna
SPG	:	Squared Poverty Gap
TPMY	:	Tribal Project Management Unit
TRYSEM	:	Training of Rural Youth for Self Employment
TSP	:	Tribal Sub-Plan
UK	:	United Kingdom
UNDP	:	United Nations Development Programme
UNESCO	:	United Nations Educational Scientific and Cultural Organisation
UNICEF	:	United Nations Children Emergency Fund
UNO	:	United Nations Organisation
URP	:	Universal Recall Period
USA	:	United States of America
UBSP	:	Urban Basic Services for Poor

CHAPTER

1 Introduction

CHAPTER

1

Introduction

Indian economy has grown at an average rate of 6.0 per cent during the last 20 years in general and 8.6 per cent plus during the last four years, in particular. In per capita terms, income growth has accelerated from the 'Hindu rate' of less than 1 per cent prior to 1980s, to 3.8 per cent per annum since 1980-81. However, the performance is considerably different on the flip side of growth, poverty levels, and changes in the levels of poverty. Now, it has been accepted at policy formation and implementation levels that the advantages of so-called high growth rates of GDP could not percolated downward. There is a raging controversy about whether poverty levels in India have increased in the late 1990s, a period coincident with ushering in of major economic reforms. India, containing the large number of poor in the world, is an obvious test case for whether economic liberalization works, whether reforms had a human face, etc.? Hence, the debate on Indian reforms, and Indian poverty levels, is as good academic as practical.

Poverty alleviation is still the greatest challenge of Indian Economy. Considerable efforts have been done to understand the various dimensions of poverty and the design and implementation of public policies to combat it. Despite this, almost 443.56 million persons (2004-05), in India live in conditions of poverty receiving income between Rs. 404.79 to Rs. 687.30 per month in rural areas and Rs. 506.17 to Rs. 745.73 in urban areas. The proporition of people living in extreme poverty is about 18-19 per cent. Thus, more than a third of the Indian population is living in condition of poverty. The optimal mix of strategies involving accumulation of growth and the initiation of direct anti-poverty intervention through employment generation and introduction of 'safety nets', reduced the incidence of poverty from 54.9 per cent in 1973-74 to 27.5 per cent in 2004-05. The incidence of poverty is not universally distributed throughout the country. Poverty ratio is as high as 46.4 per cent in Orissa, 41.4 per cent in Bihar, 40.3 per cent in Jharkhand, 39.6 per cent in Uttar Pradesh to merely 5.4 per cent in Jammu & Kashmir.[1,2]

An Expert Group to review the methodology for estimation of poor, under the Chairmanship of Prof. S.D. Tenduklar has suggested a new methodology to arrive at Statewise and all India rural and urban poverty lines for 2004-05, the latest available major National Sample Survey (NSS) round on household consumer expenditure that provides the data base for the calculation of poverty estimates by the Plan panel.

Whereas the 61st Round of NSS estimates state that 27.5 per cent people in the country were living below the poverty line (BPL) with the rural area poverty at 28.3 per cent and urban areas at 25.7 per cent, the new methodology has raised the all India poverty headcount ratio to 37.2 per cent of the population—with the rural area poverty at a sharper 41.8 per cent and urban area poverty at 25.7 per cent.

The point to ponder upon is that while the all India poverty ratio has edged up from a level 27.5 per cent to 37.2 per cent for the year 2004-05, the urban area poverty stays put at 25.7 per cent in both the estimates. The worrisome feature is, however, the rural area poverty, which has shot up sharply from a level of 28.3 per cent to 41.8 per cent, reflecting the inescapable point that even the gradualist economic reforms have bypassed the vast swathe of rural India.

The distressing aspect to the rural scenario continues to be the parlous state of affairs in the so-called BIMARU States comprising Bihar, Madhya Pradesh, Rajasthan and Uttar Pradesh where rural poverty is at its worst at 55.7 per cent, 53.6 per cent, 35.8 per cent and 42.7 per cent respectively, with some modicum of relief only in Rajasthan. For Bihar, the urban poverty is 43.7 per cent while its aggregate poverty level is at 54.4 per cent, the second in the list of home to maximum percentage of poor people. The worst hit State remains Orissa, whose rural poverty is 60.8 per cent, urban poverty is 37.6 per cent and aggregate percentage of poverty is 57.2 per cent, earning the dismal distinction of being the number one State at an all India level for being home to the highest percentage of people below the poverty line.[3]

It is also interesting to note that even as the new methodology has moved away from the calorie intake norms, the new poverty lines have been arrived at after assessing the adequacy of private household expenditure on education and health—the two crucial aspects of well-being—that the earlier calorie anchored poverty lines did not explicity account for.

Be that as it may, any assessment of the extent of poverty beyond the latest period of 2004-05 needs to reckon the subsequent measures the UPA government took, including National Rural Health Mission, Bharat Nirman and National Rural Employment Guarantee Scheme, in its earlier dispensation, which are being continued and scaled up.

At the same time, it cannot be gainsaid that despite the accent being on rural development, inclusive growth and raft benign welfare schemes specifically tailed to address the rural areas, the percentage of people continuing to eke out their lives on the edges of existence, with health and education concerns not duly factored in, show the vast ground that remains to be covered.

Policy analysis contend the fact that close to 42 per cent of the rural population in the country is trapped in poverty needs to be reckoned so that effective intervention measures are mooted and implemented on a war footing, even as India is striving to become a developed country from its emerging economy status before long.

The approaches to reducing poverty over the last six decades, has evolved in response to a variety of experiences in different parts of the world and deepening of understanding of the complexity of development process itself. During 1950s and 1960s, development of key and heavy industries was seen as the prime means of development with a limited positive impact on the poverty reduction through 'trickling down' affect. The 1970s underlined the primacy of investing in human development—health and education, 1980s, saw the active intervention of the state in the form of so many poverty alleviation programmes in rural and urban areas. Greater emphasis on poverty alleviation programmes along with the massive reduction in social spending to bring down fiscal deficit was the policies adopted during 1990s and onwards. Now the concept of 'inclusive growth' and 'growth with equity' has acquired the centre stage in Eleventh Five Year Plan.

It is now being recognized that the growth impulsive from inward-looking policies was inadequate to reduce poverty with a reasonable time period. More importantly policies and institutions evolved in the backdrop of such a development strategy had perverse incentives, constrained development and provided avenues for rent-seeking. The growth rate during Sixth and Seventh Five Year Plan showed a significant acceleration and with this there was significant reduction in poverty as well. Market-based economic reforms during 1990s, accelerated the growth rate further but there have been serious questions on its impact on poverty. The data of 61st Round of NSSO shows that employment intensity in growth has declined during 1993-94 to 2004-05. The NSSO data for the last decade suggests that there is an inverse relationship between income growth and poverty reduction—as growth accelerated upward, poverty reduction hurtles downward. NSSO 'findings' assume significance because since post-reforms initiated in 1991, the Indian economy has witnessed accelerated economic growth from 3 per cent in 1970s to 5.5 per cent in 1980s, and 6.0 per cent plus in post-reform period. But, the one is confronted with a bizarre situation of accelerated growth, higher per capita income and an increase in an absolute poverty to levels observed in the early 1980s. Of course, the issue of impact of liberalization led high growth rate on poverty is far from being settled, the debate has helped to refocus attention on the identification of appropriate strategy for improving the living conditions of the poor.

Growth performance in India is not evenly distributed throughout the country and so is the case with reduction in poverty. Less developed regions including the north-eastern states, Orissa and the heartland states of Bihar, Uttar Pradesh and Madhya Pradesh have generally recorded growth rates below the all India average during 1980s, 1990s and the current decade. States like Maharashtra, Tamilnadu, Gujarat, Karnataka, Goa, Rajasthan, West Bengal, Kerala recorded an higher growth rate during the same period. But the impact of growth on poverty reduction is not in the same way as was perceived. The available data on growth rate and poverty reduction shows that the average annual decline in the incidence of poverty in India was highest during 1977-78 to 1983-84 despite a low average annual growth rate of GNP. The next highest decline in the poverty incidence was during 1983-84 to 1987-88 and the average annual growth rate of GNP during the same period was 4.61 per cent. Period from 1993-94 to 2004-05 saw ever highest growth rate of GNP, but the average annual decline in the incidence of poverty had remained in the order of 0.86 per cent to 0.96 per cent. *Prima-face,* it shows that high growth rate across the country could not result into corresponding decline in poverty incidence. The story is almost same in many fast developing states. One of the fastest growing state Maharashtra, still has 38.1 per cent population living below poverty line. Hundreds of debt ridden farmers have ended their lives by committing suicides in the rapidly growing states of Maharashtra, Karnataka and Andhra Pradesh. On the other hand, state like Kerala, with moderate growth rate has recorded steep decline in the incidence of poverty. So is the case with Jammu & Kashmir with lowest poverty incidence in the country.

Many studies on the impact of growth on poverty in India show that the gap between rich and poor has widened in the last 25 years. With the rich and the poor gap becoming wider, the overall gains on poverty reduction have not translated into much touted 'inclusive' growth. Planning and economic policies have failed to produce inclusive growth to enable substantial parts of the country to get the benefits of development.

The gap between the highest and lowest per capita income has increased from 4.09 times to 6.57 times between 1993-94 and 2004-05. In absolute terms, the per capita income gap between the highest and lowest per capita income has increased from Rs. 11782 to Rs. 21024 during the same period.

In this scenario, it is a matter of serious concern that the benefits of higher growth rate are not percolating downward. India's growth rate over the past decade has not greatly reduced social inequalities. For emerging economies such as India, the stakes are high in terms of translating the aspirations of millions of young people into concrete opportunities for advancement, even as the authorities wrestle with endless problems—poverty, illiteracy, poor health status and crumbling infrastructure.

Thus, the situation like this requires further deep investigation as to why the high growth rate of the GDP is not helping the poor to cross over the poverty line? The study is broad-based covering the trends in all the states and UTs. Although a lot of work has been done on the impact of poverty alleviation programmes on poverty-reduction, yet a little has been tried to examine the impact of growth on the poverty reduction on regional or state basis. Thus, the outcome of the study would definitely help the students, policy-makers and researchers in particular and common men in general.

Notes and References

1. Government of India (2008) : Tenth Five Year Plan (2002-07), Planning Commission, Vol. III, p. 97.
2. http://pib.nic.in.
3. Planning Commission (2009) : Report of the Expert Group to Reviews the Methodology for Estimation of Poverty, pp. 17-18.

CHAPTER 2

Concepts of Poverty

- Historical Background
- Income Poverty
  - (i) Absolute Poverty
  - (ii) Relative Poverty
- Types of Poverty
  - (i) Mass Structural Poverty
  - (ii) Destitution
  - (iii) Conjunctural Poverty
- Human Poverty

CHAPTER

2

Concepts of Poverty

Various concepts and definitions exist for well-being and its counterpart the poverty. The most important aspects of well being or the poverty are following:

- *First,* it addresses what is typically referred as *poverty,* that is, whether individuals or households possess enough resources or abilities to meet their current needs. This definition is based on a comparison of individual's income, consumption, education and skill, or other attributes with some defined threshold below which individuals are considered as poor in that particular attribute.
- *Second,* the focus is on inequality that persists in the distribution of income and wealth, consumption or other attributes across the population. This is based on premise that the relative position of the individuals or households in society is an important aspect of their welfare.
- *Third,* the vulnerability dimension of well-being, which is defined as the probability or risk today of

being in poverty—or falling deeper into poverty—at some point in future. It is a key element of well-being, since it affects individual's behaviour and their perceptions of their own situation.

Poverty, as generally conceived, is a situation under which an individual is not capable enough to generate that much amount of money (income) which is required to purchase basket of goods and services necessary for the survival of him and his family.

Is poverty simply about the level of income obtained by the households or individuals? Is it about lack of access to social services? Or is it more correctly understood as the inability to participate in the society, economically, socially, culturally or politically? World-wide the following terminology is being used to define or understand the concept of poverty:

- Income or consumption poverty,
- Human Poverty in terms of Human (under) Development,
- Social exclusion,
- Ill beings,
- (lack of) Capability and Functioning,
- Vulnerability,
- Inequality of income and consumption,
- Livelihood Unsustainability,
- Lack of basic human needs,
- Violation of basic human rights,
- Relative deprivation, and
- Lack of dignity, self-respect, security and justice.

All the above factors can be used individually or collectively to identify the poor in the society. However, it is rather difficult to use them simultaneously because of the subjective nature of some of them. The complexity of measurement mirrors the complexity of definition, and the complexity increases where participatory methods are used and people define their own indicators of poverty.[1]

HISTORICAL BACKGROUND

Poverty is blessed with a rich vocabulary, nationally as well-internationally, throughout the history. Basically it was Rowntree, who published perhaps for the first time the estimates of poverty in Yorks in 1901. Rowntree's estimates were based on nutritional and other requirements of individuals and households.[2] In the 1960s, the main focus was on the level of income, reflected in macro-economic indicators like Gross National Product per head. This was associated with an emphasis on growth. In the 1970s, poverty gained prominence as a result of Robert MacNamara's celebrated speech to the World Bank Board of Governors in Nairobi in 1973, and the subsequent publication of *"Redistribution with Growth"*. Two other factors played a part, first, there was greater emphasis on relative deprivation, inspired by work in the UK by Runciman and Townsend. Townsend, in particular, redefined poverty not just as a failure to meet minimum nutrition or subsistence levels, but rather as a failure to keep up with the standards prevalent in the society.

The second shift was to broaden the concept of income poverty, to a wider set of 'basic needs' including those provided socially. Thus, following ILO's pioneering work in the mid-1970s, poverty came to be defined not just as lack of income enough to meet the nutritional requirement, but also as lack of access to health, education, clean and wholesome drinking water, adequate shelter and clean environment, etc. The concept of basic human needs inspired policies and programmes like minimum needs programme (MNP) and integrated rural development.[3] Its influence continues to be seen in current debates about human development. The core objective of Eighth Five Year Plan in India was Human Development.[4]

New layers of complexity were added in the 1980s. These were following:

(i) Non-monetary aspects of poverty were incorporated, particularly as a result of Robert Chamber's work on powerlessness and isolation. Because of this greater attention was being given to 'participation'.[5]

(ii) Vulnerability and its counterpart security, associated with better understanding of seasonality and of the impact of natural disasters such as drought, floods, cyclone, earthquacks, etc. were also added to the concept of poverty. As a result assets got importance as buffers, and more emphasis was given to issues like moral economy and social capital. It led to new work on 'Coping Strategies'.

(iii) 'Livelihood' a broader concept of poverty was adopted by the 'Brundtland Commission on Sustainability and Environment'. It popularised the term 'sustainable livelihood'.

(iv) Noble Laurate Prof. Amartya Sen, who eartier contributed the notion of food 'entitlement' or 'food access', emphasised that income was only valuable in so far as it increased the 'capabilities' of individuals and thereby 'functioning' in the society.[6]

(v) Finally, gender and poverty became the hot debate on poverty during 1980s. The debate moved from a focus on women alone (Women in Development), to a wider gender relations (Gender and Development).

The 1990s saw further development of the concept of poverty. The idea of 'well-being' came to act as a metaphor for the absence of poverty, with concomitant emphasis on how poor people themselves view their situations. Simultaneously, UNDP, inspired by Prof. Amartya Sen, coined the idea of 'human development', "the denial of opportunities and choices . . . to lead a long, healthy, creative life and to enjoy a decent standard of living, freedom, dignity, self-esteem and the respect of others. . ."[7]

The developed rich countries moved further in this direction and conceptualized the term 'social exclusion', which focuses not only on multiple deprivation (low income, poor housing, poor access to education and health), but also on the process by which multiple deprivation occurs. The key areas for exclusion include democratic and legal system, markets, welfare state provisions, and family and community rights, resources and relationship, etc.

The participatory approach, emerged recently to describe the poverty, is really not a way of conceptualising poverty/ deprivation. It argues that conceptualisation of poverty and deprivation must follow an interactive process involving Participatory Poverty Assessment (PPA) facilitator and local people engaged as participants in dialogue. It is an example of social deprivation. Elements of deprivation which often figure prominently in Participatory Approach in lack of dignity, self-respect, security, justice, etc.[8]

Vulnerability is alwo regarded a form of poverty. However, it often results into poverty or falling into greater poverty. The emphasis on vulnerability is very closely linked with the recent change in thinking about poverty.[9] Inequality has been 'rediscovered' in recent years as an indicator of poverty because of following reasons :

(i) Research results affirms that on an average, the rate at which growth reduces poverty, the lower the level of inequality.[10]

(ii) A growing, though still inconclusive, body of evidence suggesting the higher inequalities reduces the rate of growth.[11]

(iii) The fact that some social ills, such as crime and conflicts, appear to be a function of inequality and not 'absolute' poverty levels.[12]

(iv) The rapid rise in inequality in some developed, transition and developing countries in recent years.[13]

Reduction in inequality and poverty is often seen as the core objective of growth with human face.

The conceptualisation of poverty as the violation of basic human rights has received attention recently due largely to the efforts of UNDP and other agencies of UNO and human rights organisation. Poverty is the denial of an entitlement, a right which is unfulfilled.[14]

INCOME POVERTY

Poverty is a state of deprivation. In absolute terms it reflects the ability of an individual to satisfy certain basic minimum needs for a sustainable healthy and reasonably productive living.[15] Conceptually, any attempt to quantify the incidence of poverty in any society requires taking into account the level and pattern of an individual's personal consumption expenditure (or income), as well as their access to social transfers and public provisioning. The proportion of population not able to earn that much of amount is segregated as poor. However, it is not easy to measure with consumption share of an individual in the publicly provided goods and services or the benefit he or she derives from the overall social context, for often it is not possible to price them or they are provided free of charge, even though it all adds up to the well being of the concerned individual.[16] Since all indicators of poverty except income, are subjective in nature and hence hard to express them in monetary terms, so it is the income or consumption expenditure which has been accepted world-wide to assess the incidence of poverty.

Income poverty has two concepts :

(i) Absolute Poverty

Absolute income poverty, as a definition, is based on what human beings require as a minimum to survive. This definition uses the arbitrary concept of 'Absolute Poverty' to suggest that there are certain absolute standards that can be identified; the most frequently used absolute measurement is income—personal or family income falling below a certain level indicated as essential to maintain an appropriate standard of living can be used to define poverty. Other forms of absolute measurements for poverty resolve around concepts of basic needs and evaluate whether the households and/or individuals are covering those needs or not.

Absolute poverty, measured by the Head Count Ratio (HCR) is about the magnitude of the population consumption below a certain absolute level of income.[17] This level of income is derived not by the estimates of income, but in terms of consumption. Often, survey data are available for income, although consumption, because it better reflects 'permanent income', is preferred.

The World Bank used a figures of $US 1 per day (in 1985 purchasing power dollars) for absolute poverty, while in India the accepted, and official, definition of poverty is consumption of goods worth Rs. 49 (per person) per month in the rural areas and Rs. 57 in the urban areas according to 1973-04 prices. These figures have been updated for subsequent years by using national deflator. The government of India conducts, via the National Sample Surveys (NSS), annual surveys of the consumption expenditure of Indian households. Every five years, a five times larger sample size (approximately 1,25,000 households) is used. The government agencies as well as individual economists and researchers estimated the incidence of poverty in the country by using these sets of data.[18]

(ii) Relative Poverty

The other definition of poverty is relational in nature—relative poverty—and is based on the position of a person or family in relation to others in the community or to a standard considered necessary for living in the society. Thus, the positions of different individuals and groups are considered in relation to others in a specific universe. Under this perspective, it is clear that persons who can be classified as poor in some countries or regions may have higher income or greater comfort that some groups not considered poor in other less developed countries.

Relative poverty does not consider the income or standard of living of individuals in absolute terms, rather than it observe them in relativity. It trys to assess their standard of living in terms of position they held in the society. It means how they are better-off or worst-off than the others. Two persons, with the same level of income, living in different countries with varied economic condition may not have to same level of well-being. Both of them may be poor? None of them is poor? One of them may be poor than other. Then it seems justified that the policies of poverty removal should consider the relative income poverty rather than absolute poverty.

In an another form, relative poverty is said to be related to property rights and distributional aspects.[19] From this point of view relative poverty is not only a problem of the third world, but also that of the developed countries where private ownership of property and inequality in wealth exist.

In this context its is worth mentioning here that absolute poverty and relative poverty may co-exist in a society. For example, primitive societies and population living in slums reveal a low standard of living with a total lack of basic amenities to survive and develop and hence poverty and distress in absolute sense. But with the evolution of modern society, standard of living improved in general and private property rights evolved growth could heal absolute poverty, leaving behind traces of relative poverty, as in the cases of advanced countries. But the myth of growth and non-sustainability of poverty in absolute terms broke as per the backward countries. Here, relative poverty feeds absolute in the term gets fed by it thereby generating a vicious circle of poverty where the backward economy gets entrapped.[20]

TYPES OF POVERTY

Last two and half decades, particularly the post-reforms period, have been marked by intensive growth with a secular rise in per capita incomes as the growth of GDP outstripped that of population. There has been a dispute over the advantage of this high performance of the economy to the common man, especially the poor. Whether such rise in the per capita income played any significant role to alleviate the poverty, that is whether the fruits of intensive growth have 'trickled down' and alleviated the poverty.

Prof. Deepak Lal (James S. Coleman, Professor of International Development Studies, University of California, Los Angeles) tried to answer the above questions. In doing so he analysed the poverty in three types.[21]

(i) Mass Structural Poverty

Mass Structural Poverty has for most of history been mankind natural state. It is most common in agricultural economies, or what the economic historian E.A. Wringley has called 'Organic Economies', whose growth was ultimately bounded by productivity of land. In such an economy there is a universal dependency on organic raw materials for food, clothing, housing and fuel. Their supply in long-run inevitably constrained by the fixed factor—land. Law of diminishing return took its inexorable toll in these economies where the growth of population remained rather high. With diminishing returns to land, conjoined to the Malthusian principle of population, a long-run stationary state where the mass of people languished at a subsistence standard of living seemed inevitable.

Even in an organic economy there is some hope for intensive growth as is the case with Indian economy, but with a limited success. The productivity and subsequently the returns of land increased considerably during the era of 'Green Revolution' (1968 and onward). But many studies revealed that the gains of green revolution have limited to large farmers and that too in the states of Punjab, Haryana, Western Uttar Pradesh, a part of Madhya Pradesh, Tamil Nadu and Karnataka. Because of the irrigational facilities and their exploitation, Modern farming technologies have been adopted in these areas and results were impressive. It increased the per capita income and thereby per capita consumption leading to decline in poverty incidence in rural areas. But the relatively higher growth of population continuously put pressure on labour force which increased by leaps and bounce. The industrial development, started with fanfare during Second Five Year Plan, could not absorb the addition in labour force in rural areas, as was expected under Mahalonobis model, thus, the unemployment, especially the disguised unemployment increased in rural areas, causing stagnation in wages. Because of this peculiar phenomenon more than a third of population in India is still living below poverty line. The poverty in India is, thus, mass structural poverty.

A crude measure of the extent of mass structural poverty is the so-called 'head count ratio' of the proportion of the population below some national but time invariant real poverty line. Using the measure the Lal and Myint found that there was a clear effect of per capita income growth on mass poverty redressal in all their countries over the period of study (1950-85).[22] Whlist Gary Field for the same study found for a larger sample that, in most but not all cases poverty tends to decrease with growth, and that where poverty tends to decrease most the more rapid is economic growth.[23]

Tendulkar and Jain have examined the effects of growth on poverty alleviation in India for the period 1970-71 to 1988-

89—taking account of alternative social welfare ordering. It was concluded in that study that in comparison to the 1990s, the doubling of annual growth rate of per capita GDP in 1980s was associated with improvement in both the poverty and social welfare situation.[24] Prof. Lal is of the firm view that in India as elsewhere growth does thus alleviate mass structural poverty. But the latest data of NSS' 61st round do not corroborate the story. The latest preliminary estimates of poverty in India would seem to suggest a mixed picture of its magnitude 15 during years into reforms. The data compiled by NSSO and Planning Commission of those living below poverty (BPL) either present a grim picture or a happy one depending on the context one places the figures in. No doubt, there has been a decline in the proportion of those living below poverty line from 36 per cent in 1993-94 to 27.5 per cent in 2004-05 as per 30 days URP (Universal Recall period).

Another estimates, which include expenditure on infrequently purchased items like clothing, footwear and consumer durables also and then uses a 365 day recall period called Mixed Recall Period (MRP)—shows that poverty levels have declined from 26.1 per cent in 1999-2000 to 21.8 per cent in 2004-05.[25]

This suggests that the series of poverty alleviation programmes undertaken by the government between 1993-94 and 2004-05 have had only a minimal impact on the real economic situation of a larger section of the population.[26] Data regarding poverty are not comparable over the time. Even than NSS gamely holds on to its conclusion of a decline in poverty. To its credit it does acknowledge that in terms of absolute numbers the reverse is the case and that is cause enough for alarm.

To understand just how alarming it is one should consider the pattern of the country's growth process over the last twenty years. While manufacturing has grown rapidly, in double digits some years, the rural sector has not gone beyond 2-3 per cent. While a small segment of the economy has contributed the largest share of GDP (services, that is) and thus enjoyed a spurt in jobs and incomes, the farm sector, with the lowest growth in decades, has the largest numbers of mouths to feed and few resources to do its with. If employment is the best antidote to poverty then the situation in rural areas can be said to be worst. Over 190 million rural people below the poverty line have no access to jobs. It resulted into higher levels of migration of unskilled workers from rural areas to urban areas where the population below the poverty line has risen from 7.63 crore to 8.08 crore between 1993-94 and 2004-05 (URP) and from 6.7 crore to 6.82 crore between 1999-2000 and 2004-05 (MRP).[27]

In relative terms, the proportion of rural poor has fallen sharply from 37.3 to 28.3 per cent between 1993-94 and 2004-05 (URP) and from 27.1 to 21.8 per cent between 1999-2000 and 2004-05 (MRP). The decline is much less in respect of urban poverty ratio from 32.4 to 25.7 per cent between 1993-94 and 2004-05 (URP) and from 23.6 to 21.7 per cent between 1999-2000 and 2004-05 (MRP). This is the net result of a massive distress induced migration, so much so that the poor are relocating to cities from rural areas.

The other phenomenon of mass structural poverty is the geographical concentration of poverty. BIMARU States (Bihar, Madhya Pradesh, Rajasthan and Uttar Pradesh) plus Orissa, Jharkhand and Chhattisgarh have a higher incidence of poverty than Punjab, Haryana and Southern States as do the scheduled castes and backward classes in them. The geographical concentration of poverty is a result of the skew in investments and job opportunities not be mention the basic amenities of life.

(ii) Destitution

Another form of poverty is destitution which is a situation of almost total lack of basic amenities required for the survival. Non-availability of food leads to death due to starvation as has happened in Orissa some years ago. Although the famine like situation does not occur now-a-days because of fast movement of food items in times of scarcity and active involvement of international agencies.

With mass structural poverty ubiquitious till recently, the problem of 'poverty' has historically been confined to destitution. Most of these traditional organic economies were labour scarce and land abundant. But the labour, the destitute, lacked physical power and skill to do the work in farms. The productivity was low because of primitive nature of farming. This remains a major source of destitution in land-abundant parts of Africa. Destitution is a common phenomenon in countries like Ethopia, Somalia, etc.

With population expansion and the emergence of land scarce economies in Europe and in many parts of Asia, there arose the poverty of the able bodied who lacked land, work, or wages adequate to support the dependents who were partly responsible for their poverty.[28]

So far as the India is concerned no estimates of destitution are available officially or otherwise. However, there are scarce reports of destitution in the states of Orissa and in some parts of Rajasthan. Recently, some cases of deaths due to starvation have been reported from Bundelkhand region of U.P. also.

(iii) Conjunctural Poverty

Finally the famine is the dramatic manifestation of long lasting destitution. In organic Agraian economies, climatic crises or political turmoil are the principal causes of famine like situations which are the examples of conjunctural poverty. Conjunctural poverty may also be a result of business cycles in a market economy. A large scale unemployment may cause havoc for the mass because of sever depression in the economy. In an agrarian economy like Indian economy, the seasonal unemployment of landless labourers in rural areas is likely to be of greater importance than urban industrial unemployment.

Thus, the majority of countries of the third world including India are facing the problem of mass structural poverty of which degrees may be varied. A small portion of the poor might be living under destitution but the conjunctural poverty or the famine like situation is not found anywhere.

HUMAN POVERTY

The meaning and concept of poverty may be different for different people but in more specific terms it implies the deprivation of the necessities of material well-being and the denial of opportunities for living a tolerable life. If in any way the life is prematurely shortened or made difficult, painful and hazardous, or is deprived of knowledge and communication, or is robbed of dignity, confidence and self-respect. it is full of poverty. With the aim of establishing the welfare state, almost all the countries of the world have shown keen interest in alleviating the poverty. For the purpose of the measurement of success in this direction, the concept of poverty line in terms of purchasing power, millions of the people have crossed the poverty line with the help of the programmes launched by the Governments, but the situation is still grim, if these achievements are assessed in terms of the availability of opportunities and necessities which are essential for the overall well-being of the mankind.

Recently the concept of human poverty has gained prominence amongst the economists and human rights activists as they have taken the serious view of all factors which prevent or may prevent a person to lead a healthy and dignified life. This concept has been used by UNDP in its Human Development Report, 1997.

Human poverty is defined by impoverishment in multiple dimensions—deprivations in a long and healthy life, in knowledge, in a decent standard of living, in participation. The concept of human poverty sees lack of adequate income as an important factor in human deprivation, can all improvement be reduced to income. If income is not the sum total of human lives, lack of income cannot be the sum total of human deprivation.[29]

In a more meaningful manner, human poverty means the denial of fundamental human rights. To promote social progress and raise the standard of living within the wider concept of freedom, International Human Rights laws as enshrined in the U.N. Charter, the Universal Declaration of Human Rights and other treaties and declarations—recognise economic and social rights, with the aim of attacking poverty and its consequences.

Thus, human rights, having direct bearing on the poverty, are[30]:

- Right to a standard of living adequate for the health and well-being of himself and of his family, including food, clothing, housing and medical care and necessary social services, and the right to security in the event of unemployment, sickness, disability, widowhood, old age or other lack of livelihood in circumstances beyond his control.
- Motherhood and childhood are entitled to special care and assistance. All children, whether born in or out of wedlock, shall enjoy the same social protection.
- Right to education which shall be directed to the full development of the human personality and to the strengthening of respect for human rights and fundamental freedom. It shall promote understanding, tolerance, and friendship among all nations racial or religious groups.
- Right to work, to free choice of employment to just and favourable conditions of work and to protection against employment.
- Right to equal pay for equal work.
- Right to just and favourable remuneration for all those work to ensure for them and their family and existence worthy of human dignity.
- Right to freedom of opinion and expression.
- Right to freedom of thought, conscience and religion.

If in any manner these rights are denied to people they may result into human poverty. Human poverty also exist in those sections of the society where human development is inadequates. Human development is the process of enlarging people's choices, by expanding human functioning and capabilities. Human development thus also reflects human outcomes in these functioning and capabilities. It represents a process as well as an end.

At all levels of development the three essential capabilities are for people to lead a long and healthy life, to be knowledgeable and to have access to the resources needed for a decent standard of living. But the realm of human development extends further other areas of choice highly valued by people include participation, security, sustainability, guaranteed human rights—all needed for being creative and productive and for enjoying self-respect, empowerment and a sense of belonging to a community.[31]

Thus, income poverty is defined by deprivation in a single dimension—income because it is believed either that this is the only impoverishment that matters or that any deprivation can be reduced to a common denominator. Human poverty relates to the lack of opportunities for the survival and development in a dignified manner.

Notes and References

1. Maxwell, Simon : "The Meaning and Measurement of Poverty", Overseas Development Institute, pp. 1-2.
2. World Bank (2000-01) : World Development Report, 2000-01, Oxford University Press, New Delhi, p. 17.
3. GOI (1980) : Sixth Five Year Plan, 1980-85, Planning Commission, New Delhi.
4. GOI (1992) : Eighth Five Year Plan, 1992-97, Planning Commission, New Delhi.
5. Chambers, Robert (1995) : "Poverty and Livelihoods : Whose Reality Counts?", Institute for Development Studies Discussion paper 347. Sussex University, Brighton, p. 19.
6. Sen, Amartya (1984) : "Poor Relatively Speaking". In Amartya Sen (ed.), Resources, Values and Development, Basil Blackwell, New York, p. 97.
7. UNDP (1997) : Human Development Report, 1997, Oxford University Press, New Delhi.
8. Shaffer, Paul (2008) : New Thinking on Poverty : Implications for Globalisation and Poverty Reduction Strategies", DESA Working Papers, UNO, No. 65, February, p. 5.
9. *Ibid.*, p. 6.
10. Ravallion, Martin (1997) : *op. cit.*
11. Aghion, P. and others (1999) : Inequality and Economic Growth : The Perspection of New Growth Theories, *Journal of Economic Literature*, 37, December.
12. Bourguignon, F. (1998) : "Crime as a social cost of poverty and inequality : A Review focusing on development countries', Background paper for World Development Report, 1998, Oxford University Press.

13. Cornia, G. (1999) : Liberalisation, gloablisation and income distribution, WIDER Working paper 167, *World Institute for Development Economic Research*, Helsinki.
14. UNDP (2000) : Human Development Report, Oxford University Press, Oxford.
15. Reddy, S. Sudhakar, S. Gulab, P. Padmnabha Rao (2003) : "Trend and Determination of Poverty : 1973-79 to 1999-2000", *Economic and Political Weekly*, March 22-29.
16. Ravallion, M. (2001) : "What is needed for a more pro-poor growth process in India", *Economic and Political Weekly*, Bombay, Vol. 35, No. 12.
17. (i) Bhalla, Surjit, S. (2006) : "Growth and Poverty in India : Myth and Reality" in M. Govind Rao's (ed.), Development, Poverty and Fiscal Policy, Oxford University Press, New Delhi, p. 16.
    (ii) Bhalla, Surjit, S. (2006) : Growth and Poverty in India : Myth and Reality", In M. Govind Rao (ed.) "Development, Poverty and Fiscal Policy", Oxford University Press, New Delhi, pp. 19-21.
18. *Ibid.*, p. 19.
19. Gupta, Sunita Das and Ramesh Kumar Roy (2003); "The Economy of Dependency and Sustained Poverty", Conference Volume, Indian Economic Association, Shivaji University, Kolhapur, pp. 168-70.
20. *Ibid.*, p. 171.
21. Lal, Deepak (1998) : "Economic Reforms and Poverty Alleviation in Isher Judge Ahluwalia and I.M.D. Little eds., *India's Economic Reforms and Development : Essays for Manmohan Singh*, Oxford University Press, New Delhi.
22. Lal, Deepak and H. Myint (1996) : "The Political Econmy of Poverty, Equity and Growth—A Comparative Study", Oxford, Clarendon Press, p. 45.
23. Fields, Gray (1991) : "Growth and Income Distribution" in G. Psacharopoulos (ed.) (1993), Quoted in India's Economic Reforms and Development, *op. cit.*, p. 236.
24. Tendulkar, S.D. and L.R. Jain (1995) : Economic Growth and Equity : India 1970-71 to 1988-89, *Indian Economic Review*, Vol. XXX, No. 1, pp. 19-49.
25. (http://www.financialexpress.com/fe-full-story.php).
26. Mukherjee, Ambarish (2006) : 23 crore People still below Poverty Line; *Business Line*, New Delhi, 15 June, 2006.
    (i) *Business Line*, New Delhi, 25th June, 2006.
    (ii) *Business Line*, New Delhi, 22nd March, 2007.

27. *Ibid.*
28. Iliffe, J. (1987) : The Agrican Poor, Cambridge University Press, pp. 5-6.
29. UNDP (2000) : Human Development Reports, 2000, Oxford University Press, New Delhi, p. 17.
30. *Ibid.*, pp. 14-15.
31. UNDP (2003) : Human Development Report, 2003, Oxford University Press, New Delhi.

CHAPTER 3

Measurement of Poverty

A Theoretical Perspective

- Perspectives on Poverty
- Measurement of Incidence, Depth and Severity of Poverty
  - (1) Income Poverty
    - Poverty Line
    - Poverty Gap
    - Squared Poverty Gap
    - Subjective Measurements of Poverty
  - (2) Human Poverty
- Some Other Aspects of Poverty

CHAPTER

3

Measurement of Poverty
A Theoretical Perspective

Concerns with identifying people affected by poverty and the desire to measure it have at times obscured the fact that the poverty is too complex to be reduced to a single dimension of human life. In its true sence poverty has many dimensions. Income is one of them. It has become common practice for countries to establish an income-based or consumption-based poverty line. Although income focuses on an important dimension of poverty, it gives only a partial picture of the many ways human lives can be blighted.

The present chapter gives a brief account of various concepts of poverty and the methods to measure them.

PERSPECTIVES ON POVERTY

Over the years the concepts of poverty has been defined in different ways. These are followings[1] :

(i) Income Perspective

A person is poor, if and only if, his or her income level is below the defined poverty line. Many countries have adopted income poverty lines to monitor progress in reducing the poverty incidence. Often the cut-off poverty line is defined in terms of having enough income for a specified amount of food.

(ii) Basic Needs Perspective

Poverty is deprivation of material requirements for minimally acceptable fulfilment of human needs including food. This concept of deprivation goes well beyond the lack of private income. It includes the need for basic health and education and essential services that have to be provided by the community/state to prevent people from falling into poverty. It also recognises the need for employment and participation.

(iii) Capability Perspective

Poverty represents the absence of some basic capabilities to function—a person lacking the opportunities to achieve some minimally acceptable levels of these functionings. These functionings relevant to this analysis can vary from such physical ones as being well nourished, being adequately clothed and sheltered and available preventable morbidity, to more complex social achievements such as participating in the life of the community. The capability approach, reconciles the notions of absolute and relative poverty; since relative deprivation in incomes and commodities can lead to absolute deprivation in minimum capabilities.

MEASUREMENT OF INCIDENCE, DEPTH AND SEVERITY OF POVERTY

(1) Income Poverty

The most acceptable and objective measurement of the poverty is to measure the number of poor in the society, and their percentage to the total population by using either their income or consumption. These estimations are done by constructing a *Poverty Line.*

(A) Poverty Line

Poverty line is an imaginary cut-off mark of the income

or expenditure below which the persons are treated as poor. Thus, poverty lines are cut-off points separating the poor from the non-poor.

They can be monetary (for example, a certain level of consumption) or non-mometary (for instance, a certain level of literacy). The use of multiple lines can help in distinguising among different levels of poverty. There are two main ways of setting poverty lines-relative and absolute.

- *Relative poverty lines* : These are defined in relation to the overall distribution of income or consumption in a country;
- *Absolute poverty lines* : These are anchored in some absolute standard of what households should be able to count on in order to meet their basic needs. For monetary measures, these absolute poverty lines are often based on estimates of the cost of basic food needs, that is, the cost of a nutritional basket considered minimal for the survival and health of a typical family, to which a provision is added for non-food requirements. [Considering that large parts of the populations of developing countries survive with the bare minimum or less, reliance on an absolute rather than a relative poverty line often proves to be more relevant].

Sometimes alternative poverty lines are also used. They can be set on the basis of subjective or self-reported measures of poverty. Moreover, absolute and relative poverty lines can be combined. This technique allows for taking into account inequality and the relative position of households while recognizing the importance of an absolute minimum below which livelihood is not possible. When deciding on the weight to give to the two lines when combining them, one can use information contained in the consumption or income data and information from qualitative data (if the qualitative data show that people consider a specific good to be a basic need, the elasticity of ownership of that good to income can be used.[2]

The choice of a poverty line is ultimately arbitrary. In order to ensure wide understanding and wide acceptance of a poverty line, it is important that the poverty line chosen resonate with social norms, with the common understanding of what represents a minimum.

Some of the other poverty lines are also useful to assess the real impact of poverty in the community. These may be the following[3] :

- *Health and nutrition poverty* : The health status of household members can be taken as an important indicator of well-being. Analysts could focus on the nutritional status of children as a measure of outcome as well as the incidence of specific diseases (tuberculosis, diarrhea, malaria, respiratory diseases) or life expectancy of life at birth for different groups within the population. If data on such health outcomes are unavailable, input proxies could be used, such as the number of visits an individual makes to hospitals and health centers, access to specific medial services (such as pre- and post-natal care), or the extent to which children receive vaccinations in time as an input for their future health status.
- *Education poverty* : In the field of education, one could use the level of literacy as the defining characteristic and some level judged to represent the threshold for illiteracy as the poverty line. In countries where literacy is nearly universal, one might opt for specific test scores in schools as the the relevant outcome indicator to distinguish among different population groups. Another alternative would be to compare the number of years of education completed to the expected number of years that, in principle, should be completed.
- *Composite indexes of wealth* : An alternative to using a single dimension of poverty could be to combine the information on different aspects to poverty. One possibility is to create a measure that takes into account income, health, assets, and education. It is also possible that information on income is unavailable though other dimensions are covered. It

is important to note that a major limitation of composite indexes is the difficulty of defining a poverty line. Analysis by quintile or other percentile remains possible, however, and offers important insights into the profile of poverty.

Choosing and Estimating Poverty Measures

The poverty measure itself is a statistical function that translates the comparison of the indicator of household well-being and the chosen poverty line into one aggregate number for the population as a whole or a population subgroup. Many alternative measures exist, but the three measures described below are most commonly used[4] :

> *Incidence of poverty (headcount index)* : This is the share of the population whose income or consumption is below the poverty line, that is, the share of the population that cannot afford to buy a basic basket of goods. An analyst using several poverty lines, say, one for poverty and one for extreme poverty, can estimate the incidence of both poverty and extreme poverty. Similarly, for non-monetary indicators the incidence of poverty measures the share of the population that does not reach the defined threshold (for instance, the percentage of the population with less than three years of education).

(B) Poverty Gap (Depth of Poverty)

This provides information regarding how far-off households are from the poverty line. This measure captures the mean aggregate income or consumption short-fall relative to the poverty line across the whole population. It is obtained by adding up all the shortfalls of the poor (assuming that the non-poor have a shortfall of zero) and dividing the total by the population. In other words, it estimates the total resources needed to bring all the poor to the level of the poverty line (divided by the number of individuals in the population). This measure can also be used for non-monetary indicators, provided that the measure of the distance is meaningful. The poverty gap in education could be the number of years of education needed or required to reach a defined threshold. In some cases, though, the measure does not make sense or is not quantifiable (for example, when indicators are binary, such as literacy, in which case only the concept of the headcount can be used). The poverty gap can be used as a measure of the minimum amount of resources necessary to eradicate poverty, that is, the amount that one would have to transfer to the poor under perfect targeting (that is, each poor person getting exactly the amount he/she needs to be lifted out of poverty) to bring them all out of poverty.

(C) Squared Poverty Gap (Poverty Severity)

This takes into account not only the distance separating the poor from the poverty line (the poverty gap), but also the inequality among the poor. That is, a higher weight is placed on those households further away from the poverty line. As for the poverty gap measure, limitations apply for some of the non-monetary indicators.

All of these measures can be calculated on a household basis, that is, by assessing the share of households that are below the poverty line in the case of the headcount index. However, it might be better to estimate the measures on a population basis—in terms of individuals—in order to take into account the number of individuals within each household.

The measurement of depth and severity of poverty are important complements of the incidence of poverty. It might be the case that some groups have a high poverty incidence but low poverty gap (when numerous members are just below the poverty line), while other groups have a low poverty incidence but a high pyoerty gap for those who are poor (when relatively few members are below the poverty line but with extremely low levels of consumption or income).

Depth and severity might be particularly important for the evaluation of programmes and policies. A programme might be very effective at reducing the number of poor (the incidence of poverty) but might do so only by lifting those who are closest to the poverty line out of poverty (low impact on the poverty gap). Other interventions might better address the situation of the very poor but have a low impact on the overall incidence (if it brings the very poor closer to the poverty line but not above it).

(D) Subjective Measurement of Poverty

Subjective perceptions can be used to measure poverty. Such measurement of poverty are based on questions to households about (a) their perceived situation, such as "Do you have enough?" "Do you consider your income to be very low, rather low, sufficient, rather high, or high?" (b) a judgment about minimum standards and needs, such as, "What is the minimum amount necesary for a family of two adults and three children to get by?" or "What is the minimum necessary for your family?" or (c) poverty rankings in the community, such as "Which groups are most vulnerable in the village?" On the basis of the answers to these questions, poverty lines can be derived. Answers to the second group of questions could provide a line for different types of reference households, and answers to the first group of questions can be compared with actual income to infer the income level that households judge to be sufficient. This income level could then be used as the poverty line.[5]

Subjective measures can be used not only to assess the situation of a particular household but also to set or inform the choice of poverty lines. equivalence scales, economies of scale, and regional cost of living differences. It can also be useful to compare subjective and self-reported measures of well-being to objective measures based on observed income and consumption data.

Self-reported measurement have improtant limitations, however, subjective measures might reproduce existing discrimination or exclusion patterns if these patterns are perceived as normal in the society. This might be the case in discrimination against girls or other particular groups in society. Subjective assessments could then fail to capture discrimination, which should be addressed by public policy. More generally, the observed perceptions of poverty need not provide a good basis to establish priority public actions. This may be the case if policy-makers have a different time horizon or a different understanding of the determinants of social welfare from the population providing the subjective measurement of poverty. It might also be the case that people perceive the elderly to be those most in need, but that public policy aimed at improving nutrition practices or providing preventive health care would have a higher impact on poverty.[6]

Methods of Setting Absolute Poverty Lines

Different methods have been used to define absolute poverty lines.[7] The choice of method can greatly affect poverty estimates and who is considered poor. It is important to derive poverty lines that provide consistency in welfare measurement in space and time; two people with the same real consumption should be considered either poor or non-poor. As discussed in Ravallion and Bidani (1994) and Wodon (1997), the food energy intake method defines the poverty line by finding the consumption expenditure or income level at which a person's typical food energy intake is just sufficient to meet a predetermined food-energy requirement. If applied to different regions within the same country, the underlying food consumption pattern of the population group consuming only the necessary nutrient amounts will vary. This method can thus yield differentials in poverty lines in excess of the cost-of-living differential facing the poor. An alternative is the cost of basic human needs method, where an explicit bundle of goods typically consumed by the poor is first valued at local prices. To this a specific allowance for non-food goods, consistent with spending by the poor, is added. However, defined poverty lines will always have a high arbitrary element; for example, the calorie threshold underyling both methods might be assumed to vary with age. Ordinal ranking of welfare crucial for the poverty profile—is more important than cardinal ranking, with one household above and another below the line. For comparisons over time, however, the stability and consistency of the poverty line need to be ensured.

Poverty Line—India

Several economists and individual researchers and the Planning Commission of Government of India have constructed their own poverty lines. All of these poverty lines are based on monthly average per capita consumption expenditure required enough for the survival of the mankind. Some of the poverty lines are given below.

(A) Planning Commission

The Planning Commission of Government of India constituted four task forces to estimate the poor in the country. The first one was under the chairmanship of Prof. Y.K. Alagh (1979). This group accepted the calorie intake norms recommended by the Nutritional Expert Group (1968) according to the age sex categories. The census-based activity pattern, according to age and sex (differing for rural and urban populations) was superimposed on the projected rural and urban populations. This provided the sex-age activity specific composition of the rural and urban populations. The specific calorie norms consumed to be uniform for the rural and urban populations) were then weighted by the corresponding compositions of the rural and urban populations separately to derive the rural and urban average uniform calorie norms.[8] Thus, 2400 calorie intake of food per capita per day for rural areas and 2100 calorie intake of food per capita per day for urban areas were taken as the calorie norms to define the poverty line.

In determining poverty lines in monetary terms, the task force recognised that human beings required not only the food, but other goods and services also for the survival. Since there is no priori norms for these goods and services, the task force felt that the actual expenditure of households, selected as poor on the basis of calorie intake of food should form the basis for estimating the necessary expenditure on these goods and services, so that arbitrariness could be avoided. The task force calculated the average calorie intake of every expenditure class, norms, identify the lowest expenditure class, which consumed the calorie norms and used the per capita total expenditure of that class as the poverty line.[9]

Based on these norms poverty lines for rural and urban areas were determined for the 28th round of NSS consumption expenditure data for the year 1973-74. These came out to be Rs. 49.09 per capita monthly expenditure in rural areas and Rs. 56.64 in urban areas. These lines have not been changed over the years. Another Expert Group, under the Chairmanship of Prof. D.T. Lakdawala (1993) also accepted these poverty lines. The expert group, additionally, constructed state specific poverty lines for different states, keeping in view the vast variations in the consumption patterns of the people living in the states.

Poverty lines, thus arived, have not changed over the years. Planning Commission has been measuring absolute poverty in the consumption dimension, keeping aside other dimensions of poverty, as discussed in 1993 Expert Group Report headed by Professor D.T. Lakdawala.[10] Absolute (private) consumption poverty line is taken to convey the inability of an individual or a household to afford a socially perceived normative minimal basket of basic human needs that is expected to be reflected in some normative minimal standard of living that should be assured to every individual/ household. 2008 Expert Group headed by Prof. S.D. Tendulkar identified three major criticisms of poverty lines suggested by 1993 Expert Group.[11]

(i) The consumption patterns underlying the rural and urban Poverty Line Baskets remained tied down to those observed more than three decades ago in 1973-74 and hence had become outdated. Changes in the income consumption pattern during the last three decades did not reflect in these poverty lines.

(ii) Crude price adjustment for prices was leading to implausible results such as proportion of total urban population below poverty line being higher than its rural counterpart in certain major states.

(iii) Private consumption on health and education was not taken into accounts with the assumption that these are public goods and thus available free of cost.

In view of the above criticisms of 1993 Expert Groups Methodology, 2008 Expert Group departured at least in four following ways:[12]

- The 2008 Expert Group moved away from caloric

anchor but test for the adequacy of actual food expenditure near the poverty line to ensure certain aggregate nutritional outcomes.

- The Expert Group (2003) did not discriminate between rural and urban population and recommended a uniform Poverty Line Basket.
- The Expert Group (2008) suggested a price adjustment procedure that is predominantly based in the same data set that underlines the poverty estimation.
- The Expert Group (2008) incorporated an explicit provision in price indices for private expenditure on health and education keeping in mind its rising trend.

The Expert Group (2008) accepted official estimate of poverty for urban population because 25.7 per cent poverty Head Cout Ratio is less countroversial in terms of the broad order of magnitude of extent of urban poverty detials of new methodology have been presented in Chatper 4.

Poverty Line—The World Bank's Approach

The World Bank has been estimating global income poverty figures since 1990. The latest round of estimation, in October 1999, used new sample survey data and price information to obtain comparable figures for 1987, 1990, 1993, 1996, and 1998 (the figures for 1998 are preliminary estimates). The method is the same as in past estimates.[13]

Consumption : Poverty estimates are based on consumption or income data collected through household surveys. Data for 96 countries, from a total of 265 nationally representative surveys, corresponding to 88 per cent of the developing world's people, are now available, up from only 22 countries in 1990. Of particular note is the increase in the share of people covered in Africa from 66 to 73 per cent, a result of extensive efforts to improve household data in the region.[14]

Consumption is conventionally viewed as the preferred welfare indicator, for practical reasons of reliability and because consumption is thought to better capture long-run welfare levels than current income. Where survey data were available on incomes but not on consumption, consumption was estimated by multiplying all incomes by the share of aggregate private consumption in national income based on national accounts data. This procedure, unchanged from past exercises, scales back income to obtain consumption but leaves the distribution unchanged.

Prices : To compare consumption levels across countries, estimates of price levels are needed, and the World Bank's purchasing power parity (PPP) estimates for 1993 were used. These estimates are based on new price data generated by the International Comparison Programme (ICP), which now covers 110 countries, up from 64 in 1985, and a more comprehensive set of commodities.

Poverty Lines : The 1990 calculations of the international poverty lines had to be updated using 1993 price data and the 1993 PPP estimates. In 1990 national poverty lines for 33 countries were converted into 1985 PPP prices, and the most typical line among the low-income countries for which poverty lines were available was selected. In 1999 the same lines were converted into 1993 PPP prices and the new line was obtained as the median of the 10 lowest poverty lines. That line is equal to $ 1.08 a day in 1993 PPP terms (referred to as "$ 1 a day" in the text). This line has a similar purchasing power to the $ 1 a day line in 1985 PPP prices, in terms of the command over domestic goods. The upper poverty line (referred to as "$ 2 a day") was calculated by doubling the amount of the lower poverty line as in1990, reflecting poverty lines more commonly used in lower middle income countries.[15]

Country Specific Poverty Line : The $ 1 and $ 2 a day poverty estimates, as developed by World Bank here are useful only as indicators of global progress, not to assess progress at the country level or to guide country policy and programme formulation. Country specific poverty lines, reflecting what it means to be poor in each country's situation and not affected by international price comparisons, are used in country level analysis. Most of the countries, initiating policy measures for poverty alleviation, have developed their own poverty lines.

Measurement of Poverty

Poverty Headcount : This is the share of the population

that is poor, that is, the proportion of the population for which consumption or income y is less than the poverty line z. Suppose we have a population of size n in which q people are poor. Then the headcount index is defined as

$$H = \frac{q}{n} \text{ or } H = \frac{q}{n} \times 100 \text{ (if it is expressed in percentage)}$$

Poverty Gap : The poverty gap, which is calculated to estimate the depth of poverty, is the mean distance separating the population from the poverty line, with the non-poor being given a distance of zero. The poverty gap is a measure of the poverty deficit of the entire population in which the notion of 'poverty deficit' captures the resources that would be required to lift all the poor out of poverty through perfectly targeted cash transfers. It is defined as follows :

$$PG = \frac{1}{n}\sum_{i=1}^{q}\left[\frac{z - y_i}{z}\right]$$

Alternatively it can also be calculated as :

PG Index = Poverty Ratio

$$\times \frac{\text{Poverty line} - \begin{array}{l}\text{Per capita consumption}\\ \text{of the poor}\end{array}}{\text{Poverty line}} \times 100$$

where, y_i is the income of individual i, and the sum is taken only on those individuals who are poor (in practice, we often work with household rather than individual income, but individual income can still be defined as being equal, say, to the per capita income of the household). The poverty gap can be written as being equal to the product of the income gap ratio (I) and the headcount index of poverty (H) where the income gap ratio is itself defined as

PG = I × H, with

$I = \frac{z - y_q}{z}$ where $y_q = \frac{1}{q}\sum_{i=1}^{q} y_i$ is the average income of the poor.

It must be emphasized here that the income gap ratio I in itself is not a good measure of poverty. Assume that some households or individuals who are poor but close to the poverty line are improving their standards of living over time and, thereby, become non-poor. The income gap ratio will increase because the mean distance separating the poor from the poverty line will increase (this happens because some of those who were less poor have emerged from poverty—so that those still in poverty are, on average, farther away from the poverty line), suggesting a deterioration in welfare, while nobody is worse off and some people are actually better-off. Although the income gap ratio will increase, the poverty gap PG will decrease, because the headcount index of poverty will decrease, suggesting an improvement toward poverty reduction. The problem with the income gap ratio is that it is defined only on the population that is poor, while the poverty gap is defined over the population as a whole.

The poverty gap is a useful statistic to assess how many resources would be needed to eradicate poverty through cash transfers perfectly targeted to the poor. Assume, for example, that the poverty gap is equal to 0.20. This means that, on an average, the cash transfer needed to lift each poor person out of poverty represents 20 per cent of the poverty line. If the mean income in the country is equal to twice the poverty line, the cash transfer would represent 10 per cent of the country's mean income. If the mean income of the non-poor equals twice the poverty line, and if half the population is poor, it can be shown that the tax rate that would have to be imposed on the nonpoor to lift the poor out of poverty with perfectly targeted transfers again would be 20 per cent. If the mean income of the nonpoor is equal to four times the poverty line, under the same assumption the necessary tax rate would be 10 per cent. Such simple simulations can be used to communicate intuitively the meaning of the poverty gap. In practice, however, given that perfectly targeted cash transfers to eradicate poverty are neither feasible nor necessarily a good thing (high tax rates could stifle economic growth and, thereby, future poverty reduction), one must be careful with their use.

Squared Poverty Gap Index : This is often described as a measure of the severity of poverty. While the poverty gap index takes into account the distance separating the poor from the poverty line, the squared poverty gap index takes the square of that distance into account. When using the squared poverty gap index, the poverty gap index is weighted by itself, so as to give more weight to the very poor. In other words, the squared poverty gap takes into account the inequality among the poor. It is obtained as follows :

$$p^2 = \frac{1}{n}\sum_{i=1}^{q}\left[\frac{z-y_i}{z}\right]^2$$

The headcount index, the poverty gap index, and the squared poverty gap index are the first three measures of poverty incidence in a country. The general formula for these poverty measures depends on a parameter, which takes a value of zero for the headcount, one for the poverty gap, and two for the squared poverty gap in the following expression :

$$p^\alpha = \frac{1}{n}\sum_{i=1}^{q}\left[\frac{z-y_i}{z}\right]^\alpha$$

In simple words :

Poverty incidence (Head Count Index) $= \frac{1}{\text{n}}\sum_{i=1}^{q}\left[\frac{z-y_i}{Z}\right]^0$

Poverty Gap Index $= \frac{1}{\text{n}}\sum_{i=1}^{q}\left[\frac{z-y_i}{Z}\right]^1$

Squared Poverty Gap Index $= \frac{1}{\text{n}}\sum_{i=1}^{q}\left[\frac{z-y_i}{Z}\right]^2$

It is important to use the poverty gap or the squared poverty gap in addition to the headcount for evaluation purposes, since these measures present different aspects of income poverty. Indeed, basing an evaluatiion on the headcount ratio would consider as more effective those policies that lift the richest of the poor (those close to the line) out of poverty. On the basis of the poverty gap PG and the squared poverty gap, on the other hand, the emphasis is put on helping those who are farther away from the line, the poorest of the poor.

(2) Human Poverty

Poverty of lives and opportunities—or human poverty—is multi-dimentional in character and diverse rather than uniform in content. Poverty, in the human development approach draws on each of the perspectives of the poverty, but drows particularly on the capability perspective.

In the capability concept the poverty of a life lies not merely in the impoverished state in which the person actually lives, but also in the lack of real opportunity—due to social constraints as well as personal circumstances—to lead valuable and valued lives.

In the capability concept the focus is on the functionings that a person can or cannot achieve, given the opportunities one has. Functionings refer to the various valuable things a person can do or be, such as living long, being healthy, being well nourished, mixing well with others in the comunity and so on.

Human poverty, a subjective concept in general form, can be quantified by using certain monetary as well as non-monetary indicators such as per capita income, longevity in the form of expectancy of life at birth and literacy rate, etc.

United Nation Development Programme (UNDP) developed the following measures to assess the human poverty in the country.[16]

1. *Human Development Index (HDI)*

The HDI is a summary measure of human development. It measures the average achievements in a country in three basic dimensions of human development—

- A long and healthy life, as measured by life expectancy at birth.
- Knowledge, as measured by the adult literacy rate (with two-third weight) and the combined primary, secondary and tertiary gross enrolment ratio (with one-third weight).
- A decent standard of living, as measured by GDP per capita (PPP US$).

Before the HDI itself is calcualted, an index needs to be created for each of these dimensions. To calculate these dimension indices—the life expectancy, education and GDP indices—minimum and maximum values (goal posts) are chosen for each underyling indicator.

Performance in each dimension is expressed as a value between 0 and 1 by applying the following general formula :

$$\text{Dimension index} = \frac{\text{Actual value} - \text{minimum value}}{\text{maximum value} - \text{minimum value}}$$

The HDI is then calculated as a simple average of the dimensions indices.

Goalposts for Calculating the HDI

Indicator	*Maximum value*	*Minimum value*
Life expectancy at birth (years)	85	25
Adult literacy rate (%)	100	0
Combined gross enrolment ratio (%)	100	0
GDP per capita (PP US$)	40,000	100

The construction of HDI for India during 2004 can be understood with the following data[17] :

Life expectancy at birth (year)	63.6	(2004)
Adult literacy rate (%)	61.0	(2004)
Combined gross enrolment ratio (%)	67.0	(2004)
GDP per capita (PPP $ US)	3139.0	(2004)

Let us now calculate

(A) Life Expectancy Index

$$\text{LEI} = \frac{\text{Actual value} - \text{minimum value}}{\text{Maximum value} - \text{minimum value}}$$

$$= \frac{63.6 - 25}{85 - 25}$$

$$= \frac{38.6}{60.0}$$

$$= 0.64$$

(B) Education Index

The education index measures a country's relative achievement in both adult literacy and combined primary, secondary and tertiary gross enrolment. First, an index for adult literacy and one for combined gross enrolment are calculated. Then these two indices are combined to create the education index, with two-third weight given to adult literacy and one-third weight to combined gross enrolment.

$$\text{Adult Literacy Index} = \frac{61-0}{100-0}$$

$$= \frac{61}{100}$$

$$= 0.61$$

$$\text{Gross Enrolment Index} = \frac{62-0}{100-0}$$

$$= \frac{62}{100}$$

$$= 0.62$$

$$\text{Education Index} = \frac{2}{3}(\text{Adultg literacy index}) + \frac{1}{3}(\text{Gross enrolment index})$$

$$= \frac{2}{3} \times 0.61 + \frac{1}{3} \times 0.62$$

$$= 0.406 + 0.206$$

$$= 0.612$$

(C) GDP Index

The GDP index is calculated using adjusted GDP per capita (PPP US$). In the HDI income serves as a surrogate for all the dimensions of human development not reflected in a long and healthy life and in knowledge. Income is adjusted because achieving a respectable level of human development does not require unlimited income. Accordingly, the logarithm of income is used.

$$\text{GDP} = \frac{\log(3139) - \log(100)}{\log(40{,}000) - \log(100)}$$
$$= 0.58$$

Calculating the HDI

Once the dimension indices have been calculated, determining the HDI is straightforward. It is a simple average of the three dimensions indices.

HDI = 1/3 (life expectancy index) + 1/3 (education index) + 1/3 (GDP index)
= 1/3 (0.64) + 1/3 (0.58) + 1/3 (0.61) = 0.611

2. *Human Poverty Index*

UNDP introduces a human poverty index (HPI) in an attempt to bring together a composite index the different features of deprivation in the quality of life to arrive at an aggregate judgement on the extent of poverty in a community. Human Development Report 1996 attempted this through a particular version of the "capability poverty measure". The HPI pursues the same approach, focusing on a broader and more representative set of variables, in a consistent relationship to the human development index (HDI).[18]

Like many other concepts, human poverty is larger than any particular measure, including the HPI. As a concept, human poverty includes many aspects that cannot be measured—or are not being measured. It is difficult to reflect them in a composite measure of human poverty. Critical dimensions of human poverty excluded from the HPI for these reasons are lack of political freedom, inability to participate in decision-making, lack of personal security, inability to participate in the life of a community and threats to sustainability and inter generational equity. The nature of the main deprivations varies with the social and economic conditions of the community in question. The choice of indicators in the HPI cannot but be sensitive to the social context of a country. For example, an index that concentrates on illiteracy and premature mortality may be able to discriminate between Pakistan and Sri Lanka more easily than it can between, say, France and Germany.[19]

Issues of poverty in the developing countries involve hunger, illiteracy; epidemics and the lack of health services or safe water—which may not be so central in the more developed countries, where hunger is rare, literacy is close to universal, most epidemics are well controlled, health services are typically widespread and safe water is easy to tap. Not surprisingly, studies of poverty in the more affluent countries concentrate on such variable as social exclusion. These can be forceful deprivations and very hard to eliminate in all countries. But they take on relatively greater prominence in the affluent ones. There is no real possibility of constructing an index of human poverty that would be equally relevant in the different types of countries.

Given the pervasiveness of poverty in poor countries, the HPI developed is aimed as that context and the variables chosen reflect that. The nature of poverty in rich countries deserves a specialized study—and a more specialized index—focusing on those deprivations particularly relevant for those countries.

The three indicators of the human poverty index :

> The HPI as developed by UNDP concentrates on the deprivation in three essential elements of human life. These have been reflected in the HDI—longevity, knowledge and a decent living standard.[20]

(i) The first deprivation relates to survival—the vulnerability to death at a relatively early age—and is represented in the HPI by the percentage of people expected to die before age 40.

(ii) The second dimension relates to knowledge—being excluded from the world of reading and communication—and is measured by the percentage of adults who are illiterate.

(iii) The third aspect relates to a decent standard of living, in particular, overall economic provisioning. This is represented by a composite of three variables—the percentage of people with access to health services and to safe water, and the percentage of malnourished children under five.

A few observations must be made about this last variable and about why income does not figure in the HPI. The logic underlying the construction of the economic provisioning variable is that the GNP included in the HDI is actually an amalgam of private and public facilities, since public services are paid out of aggregate national income.

Private income could not be an adequate indicator of an individual's economic facilities, which also include crucial public services (such as health care arrangements and a safe water supply). But why is private income not chosen to supplement the information on public facilities?

A more practical possibility is to be less ambitious and focus on material deprivation in hunger and malnutrition, not on income. A very high proportion of personal income goes to food and nourishment, especially for poor people in poor countries.

For this we can use information on food intake, which relates to personal incomes. Alternatively, there are estimates of malnutrition, but these are influenced by a number of variables, such as metabolic rate, climatic conditions, activity patterns and epidemiology. Since our concern is with the lives that people can lead, there is a case for going straight to the prevalence of malnutrition, and this is what is done in the HPI, concentrating specifically on the malnutrition of children, which is relatively easier to measure and for which usable data are more uniformly available.

For public provisions, access to health services and to safe water were chosen. Combining these two access variables with the prevalence of malnutrition gives a fairly broad picture of economic provisioning—private and public—to supplement the information on survival and literacy.

These are the basic informational ingredients of the HPI. It must be emphasized that there is some inescapable arbitrariness in any such choice. The choice was made on the basis of balancing considerations of relevance on the one hand, and the availability and quality of data on the other. There are inevitable compromises made, and it would be idle to pretend that even the variables that have been included have high-quality data for every country. There has been an attempt, in these selections, to strike a balance between the demands of relevance and the need for tolerably usable data, and these choices would certainly remain open to criticism and public scrutiny.

Calculating the HPI-1 (for developing countries) is more straightforward than calculating the HDI. The indicators used to measure the deprivations are already normalized between 0 and 100 (because they are expressed as percentages), so there is no need to create dimension indices as for the HDI.

Originally, the measure of deprivation in a decent standard of living also included an indicator of access to health services. But because reliable data on access to health services are lacking for recent years, deprivation in a decent standard of living is measured by two rather than three indicators—the percentage of the population without sustainable access to an improved water source and the percentage of children under weight for age.

Calculating the HPI-1

1. Measuring Deprivation in a Decent Standard of Living

An unweighted average of two indicators is used to measure deprivation in a decent standard of living.

Unweighted average = 1/2 (population without sustainable access to an improved water source) + 1/2 (children under weight for age)

A Sample Calculation : India

Population without sustainable access to an improved water source = 14%

Children under weight for age = 47%

Unweighted average = 1/2 (14) + 1/2 (47) = 30.5%

2. Calculating the HPI-1

The formula for calculating the HPI-1 is as follows :

$$HPI-1=\left[1/3\left(P_1^{\alpha}+P_2^{\alpha}+P_3^{\alpha}\right)\right]^{1/\alpha}$$

where;

P_1 = Probability at birth of not surviving to age 40 (times 100)

P_2 = Adult illiteracy rate

P_3 = Unweighted average of population without sustainable access to an improved water source and children under weight for age

α = 3

(i) Probability at birth of not surviving to age 40 (% of cohort) (P_1) = 16.6

(ii) Adult illiteracy rate (P_2) = 39.0

(iii) Unweighted average of population without sustainable access to an improved waier source and children under weight for age (P_3) = 30.5.

(iv) α = 3

HPI (India) $= \left[1/3\left(P_1^{\alpha}+P_2^{\alpha}+P_3^{\alpha}\right)\right]^{1/\alpha}$

$= [1/3\ (1.6^3 + 39.0^3 + 30.5^3)]^{1/3}$

$= [1/3\ (4574.296 + 59319.00 + 28372.625)]^{1/3}$

$= [1/3\ (92265.921)]^{1/3}$

$= [30755.307]^{1/3}$

$= 31.33$

The Human Poverty Index for Selected OECD Countries (HPI-2)

The HPI-2 measures deprivations in the same dimensions as the HPI-1 and also captures social exclusion. Thus, it reflects deprivations in four dimensions:

- A long and healthy life—vulnerability to death at a relatively early age, as measured by the probability at birth of not surviving to age 60.
- Knowledge—exclusion from the world of reading

and communications, as measured by the percentage of adults (aged 16–65) lacking functional literacy skills.

- A decent standard of living—as measured by the percentage of people living below the income poverty line (50% of the median adjusted household disposable income).
- Social exclusion—as measured by the rate of long-term unemployment (12 months or more).

Calculating the HPI-2

The formula for calculating the HPI-2 is as follows :

$$HPI-2=\left[1/4\left(P_1^{\alpha}+P_2^{\alpha}+P_3^{\alpha}++P_4^{\alpha}\right)\right]^{1/\alpha}$$

P_1 = Probability at birth of not surviving to age 60 (times 100),

P_2 = Adult lacking functional literacy skills,

P_3 = Population below income poverty line (50% of median adjusted household disposable income), and

P_4 = Rate of long-term unemployment (lasting 12 months or more)

α = 3

A sample Calculation : United Kingdom

P_1 = 8.9%

P_2 = 21.8%

P_3 = 12.5%

P_4 = 1.3%

$$\text{HPI–2 } [1/4(8.9^3 + 21.8^3 + 12.5^3 + 1.3^3)]^{1/3} = 14.8$$

why α = 3 in calculating the HPI-1 and HPI-2.

The value of a has an important impact on the value of the HPI. If a = 1, the HPI is the average of its dimensions. As a rises, greater weight is given to the dimension in which there is the most deprivation. Thus as an increases towards infinity, the HPI will tend towards the value of the dimension in which deprivation is greatest.

Human Development Report 2003 and onward used the value of α as 3 to give additional but not overwhelming weight to areas of more acute deprivation.[21]

SOME OTHER ASPECTS OF POVERTY

The "sustainable livelihood approach" to the study of poverty has particularly emphasized the need for local participation. In this approach each community can define criteria of well-being and the key elements of deprivation as they appear in the local context. This process brings out the concerns and worries of vulnerable people that are persistently neglected in national statistics and in many studies of poverty. These criteria of ill-being drawn from various participatory studies, were used by local people in Asia and Sub-Saharan Africa,[22] are following.

For defining poverty and ill-being.

- Being disabled (for example, blind, crippled, mentally impaired, chronically sick).
- Lacking land, livestock, farm equipment, a grinding mill.
- Being unable to decently bury their dead.
- Being unable to send their children to school.
- Having more mouths to feed, fewer hands to help.
- Lacking able-bodied family members who can feed their families in a crisis.
- Having bad housing.
- Suffering the effects of destructive behaviours (for example, alcoholism).
- Being "poor in people", lacking social support.
- Having to put children in employment.
- Being single parents.
- Having to accept demeaning or low status work.
- Having food security for only a few months each year.
- Being dependent on common property resources.

In the 1970s the concept of social exclusion came into the literature to analyse the condition of those who are not necessarily income-poor—though many are that too—but who are kept out of the mainstream of society even if not income-poor. The inadequacy of traditional definitions of poverty, based on incomes and consumption, was widely acknowledged to explain these new concerns.

Notes and References

1. UNDP (1997) : Human Development Reort, 1997, Oxford University Press, New Delhi, pp. 2-4.
2. Madden, D. (2000) : "Relative or Absolute Poverty Lines : A New Approach", *Review of Income and Wealth Series,* 46, No. 2 (June), 18-99.
3. Coudouel Aline, Jeski, S. Hentschel, and Quentin, T. Woden (1997) : "Core Techniques and Cross Cutting Issues", World Bank Assisted Project, pp. 29-33 (http://poverty2.porumone.com/files/5467-chapter I).
4. *Ibid.,* pp. 33-35.
5. Goedhart, T.V., Herberstadt, A. Keptyn and M.B.S. VanPrag (1977) : "The Poverty Line : Concept and Measurement", *Journal of Human Resources,* 12(4) : 503-20.
6. Pradhan, M. and M. Ravallion (2000) : "Measuring Poverty Using Qualitative Perceptions of Welfare", *Review of Economics and Statistics,* 82(3) : pp. 62-71.
7 (i) Deatom, A. (1997) : "The Analysis of Household Surveys : A Micro-Econometric Approach to Development Policy", Baltimore, John Wopkins University Press, pp. 44-45.
  (ii) Ravillion, M. and B. Bidani (1994) : "How Robust is a Poverty Profile"? *World Bank Economic Review,* 8(1) : 75-102.
  (iii) Ravillion, M. (1994) : "Poverty Comparisions", Chur, Harward Academic Publishers, Swikzerland.
  (iv) Wodon, Q. (1997) : "Food Energy Intake and Cost of Basic Needs: Measuring Poverty in Bangladesh", *Journal of Development Studies,* 34(2) : 66-101.
8. Dubey, A. and S. Gangopadhyay (1998) : Counting the Poor : Where are the Poor in India Development of Statistics, GOI, New Delhi, Survekshan Analytical Report No. 1.
9. Sen, Pranab (2005) : "Of calories and Things : Reflections on Nutritional Norms, Poverty Lines and Consumption Behaviour in India", *Economic and Political Weekly,* Oct. 22, pp. 4611-18.
10. Planning Commission (2009) : Report of Expert Group to Review The Methodology for Estimation of Poverty, p. 3.
11. *Ibid.,* p. 4.

12. *Ibid.*, p. 6.
13. (i) World Bank (1990) : World Development Report 1990 : Oxford University Press, New York, pp. 10-16.
    (ii) World Bank (1996): Poverty Reduction and the World Bank : Progress and Challenges in 1990s, Washington D.C., pp. 28-33.
14. World Bank (2001) : World Development Report, 2000/2001 : Attacking Poverty, Oxford University Press, New York, p. 17.
15. Chen, Shaohua and Martin Ravillion (2000) : "How Did the World's Poorest Fare in the 1990s"? Policty Research Working Paper, World Bank, Washington D.C., pp. 4-9.
16. UNDP (2006) : Human Development Report, 2006, Oxford University Press, New York, pp. 157-61.
17. *Ibid.*
18. UNDP (1996) : Human Development Report, 1996, Oxford University Press, New York, pp. 19-27.
19. *Ibid.*
20. *Ibid.*
21. UNDP (2004) : Human Development Report, 2003, Oxford University Press, New York, pp. 67-99.
22. *Ibid.*, p. 110.

CHAPTER 4

Estimation of Poverty in India and Elsewhere
Trends and Regional Variations

CHAPTER

4

Estimation of Poverty in India and Elsewhere

Trends and Regional Variations

Poverty alleviation has been a core issue of developmental planning in India since independence. The official approach to define and measure poverty for policy formation, programme implementation and evaluation and monitoring of the poverty alleviation programmes has been based upon monthly per capita expenditure required for the consumption of goods and services essentially required for the survival. It has provided much of the impetus for academic as well as policy-related studies on issues concerned with definition, measurements, interpretation, policy choice and evaluation. In the initial phase of economic planning much of the emphasis had been placed on a subsistence minimum level of diet in terms of calorie intake per capita per day. This had been regarded the base not only for the estimation of poverty but also for the total eradication of poverty.

ESTIMATION OF POVERTY IN INDIA : PLANNING COMMISSION'S METHODOLOGY

A decade prior to India's independence, the National Planning Committee in 1936 under the Chairmanship of Pandit Jawaharlal Nehru made an economic review and recognized that "there was lack of food, of clothing, of housing and of every other essential requirement of human existence."[1] In view of this assessment, the Committee declared that the development policy objective should be to "ensure an adequate standard of living for the masses, in other words, to get rid of the appalling poverty of the people". Towards this end, the Committee defined goals for the total population in terms of nutrition (involving a balanced diet of 2400 to 2800 calories per adult worker), clothing (30 yards per capita per annum) and housing (100 sq. ft. per capita).

The question of defining the poverty line was first mooted by the Indian Labour Conference in 1957. A distinguished Working Group was set-up by the Planning Commission, Government of India, in July, 1962, to deliberate on the question of what should be regarded as the nationally desirable minimum level of consumption expenditure. The Working Group took into account the recommendation of balanced diet made by the National Advisory Committee of the Indian Council of Medical Research in 1958, and came to the view that in order to provide the minimum nutritional diet in terms of calories intake, and to allow for a modest degree of items other than food, the national minimum consumption expenditure per household of 5 persons should not be less than Rs. 100 per month at 1960-61 prices, i.e., Rs. 20 per capita per month. The Group suggested that for urban areas, the minimum should be raised to Rs. 25 per capita in view of the higher cost of living there. By implication, this mean that the corresponding amount in the rural areas would work out to Rs. 18.9.[2]

V.M. Dandekar and Neelkanth Rath (1971), attempted, perhaps for the first time, to define an income/consumer expenditure norm for poverty with reference to an explicit average daily per capita calorie intake norm of 2250 kcals for both rural and urban areas. On the basis of NSS data on consumer expenditure, the study revealed that an average annual per capita expenditure of Rs. 170.8 or equivalently Rs. 14.2 per capita per month at 1960-61 prices would suffice to meet these calorie requirements in the rural areas. The corresponding figures in the urban area were Rs. 271.7 and Rs. 22.6 at 1960-61 prices. Referring to the recommendations of the Working group set-up by the Planning Commission, it was observed that the rural minimum determined by them was considerably below that proposed by the Group, while the urban minimum determined by them was little above that recommended by the Group. In view of this they decided to revise their rural minimum slightly upwards to Rs. 180 per annum or Rs. 15 per month. Similarly, they rounded-off the urban minimum to Rs. 270 per annum or Rs. 22.5 per month, both at 1960-61 prices.[3]

Reviewing the recommendations made by the Working Group that a per capita monthly consumption expenditure of Rs. 20 (at 1960-61 prices) should be deemed to be a national minimum, Dandekar and Rath observed that the "basis of this determination is not known. Apparently, the study group also did not make a distinction between rural and urban level costs". As far as Dandekar and Rath study is concerned their basis to arrive at the adequacy of 2250 calories per person per day both for rural and urban areas is not clearly spelt out. This was the lower limit of the range of 2250 to 2300 kcals per capita per day on the average at retail level.[4] They do not seem to have taken into account the fact that nutritional requirements in terms of calories are at least age, sex, and occupation-specific. And, as such, they are likely to vary sizably between rural and urban areas especially because population in the former, proportionately speaking, is likely to be more engaged in manual activities.

Task Force on Projections of Minimum Needs and Effective Consumption Demand (1979)

The Planning Commission, GOI, set-up a task force on 'Projections of Minimum Needs and Effective Consumption Demand' under the Chairmanship of Prof. Y.K. Algah.[5] The Perspective Planning Division, Planning Commission, had completed a study on the poverty line as a part of the work assigned to it by the Task Force after allowing, to the extent available data permitted, for the fact that there are age, sex and occupational differentials in the daily calorie requirements of the population. To estimate daily per capita calorie requirements separately for rural and urban areas, age-sex-activity specific calorie allowances recommended by the Nutrition Expert Group (1968) have been averaged by using estimated age-sex-occupational structure of population for 1982-83 as the weighting diagram.

To work out the monetary counterpart or equivalently, poverty lines of these norms, 28th Round (1973-74) NSS data relating to private consumption both in quantitative and value terms were used. Using appropriate conversion factors, calorie content of food items of each monthly per capita expenditure class had been calculated separately for rural and urban areas.

Applying inverse linear interpolation method to the data on average per capita monthly expenditure and the associated calorie content of food items in the class separately for the rural and urban areas, it was estimated that, on the average, Rs. 49.09 per capita per month satisfied a calorie requirements of 2435 per capita per day in the rural areas and Rs. 56.64 per capita per month satisfied a calorie requirements of 2095 per capita per day in the urban areas respectively, both at 1973-74 prices. These poverty lines work out to Rs. 61.8 per capita per month in the rural areas and Rs. 71.3 per capita per month in the urban area at 1976-77 prices.

Professor P.V. Sukhatme, however, emphasised that the above calorie requirement was the average and not the minimum required for biological existence taking into consideration that there was considerable variation in calorie requirement of individuals depending on age-sex and occupational structure. In view of this he strongly recommended that seventy-five per cent of the above poverty lines can be considered as appropriate cut off point which had been rightly considered in the Draft 1978-83 Plan document. It has been found that calorie requirement at this modest poverty line is very close to that required for biological subsistence.[6]

The methodological details for poverty estimation, viz. (i) integration of estimates of mean consumption from the National Accounts Statistics (NAS) and distribution parameters from the NSS, and (ii) use of implicit private consumption deflator from the NAS to adjust poverty lines for changes in prices in particular,[7] became subjects of considerable academic scrutiny and critique.[8] By using this method the Planning Commission tried to establish the fact that incidence of poverty reduced considerably because of poverty alleviation measures adopted by the government on the one hand and higher growth rate of the economy on the other.

Later on the Planning Commission estimated the incidence of poverty taking into consideration the report of the working group "on the estimation of demand for the minimum requirements and effective consumption pattern (1978), five year surveys of consumption expenditure by NSSO and adjusted data of total private consumption expenditure by CSO. On the basis of these concocted data the then finance minister Dr. Man Mohan Singh claimed in parliament, while presenting the economic survey of 1995-96, that incidence of poverty reduced to 18.96 per cent in 1993-94 from 25.49 per cent in 1987-88. These achievements were significant despite the historical economic crises of 1991-92.[9] Everybody, except the leaders of ruling party and the bureaucrats working under them, refuted the claims of the government. The whole methodology was criticised.

Prof. D.T. Lakdawala Expert Group on Estimation of Proportion and Number of Poor

In 1989 the Planning Commission constituted the Expert Group on Estimation of Proportion and Number of Poor under the chairmanship of Prof. D.T. Lakdawala.[10] The method is known as the Expert Group Method. The Expert Group had recommended that the Task Force Poverty Line should be adopted as the base line. It had disaggregated national poverty line into state-specific poverty lines. The national rural poverty line was disaggregated into state-specific poverty lines by using state-specific price indices of 1973-74 and inter-state price differential. The state-specific price indices were constructed by averaging the state-specific food and non-food price indices of Consumer Price Index of Agricultural Labourers (CPI-AL), while the inter-state price differential was done by using Fisher's Index. These state-specific rural poverty lines were updated taking into consideration the expenditures on food, fuel and light, clothing and footwear, and miscellaneous of CPI-AL.

Like the national rural poverty line, the national urban poverty line was disaggregated into state-specific poverty lines by using state-specific price indices of 1973-74 and inter-state differential. The state-specific price indices were obtained from the Consumer Price Index of industrial workers (CPI-IW) and the inter-state price differential was estimated by using Fisher's Index. The state-specific CPI-IW were done by averaging the CPI of food, fuel and light, housing, clothing, bedding and footwear and miscellaneous with their respective weights in the consumption basket of the poor. Later on, this Expert Group Method was modified by the Planning Commission by dropping the Consumer Price Index of Urban Non-Manual Employees and the method was known as "Modified Expert Group Method". This was because of the fact that rate of increase of the Consumer Price Index of Urban Non-Manual Employees had been faster which in turn resulted in rise in the money value of the poverty line and hence the incidence of urban poverty.

The Expert Group has estimated state-specific poverty lines, but not specifically the national level poverty lines. The national poverty lines are worked out as an interpolated value from the national level expenditure distribution obtained from the NSS data on consumer expenditure. The national level poverty ratio is estimated as an average of state-wise poverty ratios, based on availability of state level prices. The Expert Group has estimated the poverty lines and poverty ratios in rural and urban areas of 18 states and UTs. These were : Andhra Pradesh, Assam, Bihar, Gujarat, Haryana, H.P., J & K, Karnataka, Kerala, M.P., Maharashtra, Orissa, Punjab, Rajasthan, T.N., U.P., W.B. and Delhi. Using neighbouring states' poverty line, the poverty ratios for other states and UTs were estimated.

The main recommendations of the expert group were the following:

- The Poverty Line recommended by the Task Force on projection of minimum needs and effective consumption demand, namely, a monthly per capita total expenditure of Rs. 49.09 (rural) and Rs. 56.64 (urban) rounded of respectively to Rs. 49 and Rs. 57 at all India level at 1973-74 prices be adopted as the base line. This was anchored in the recommended per capita daily intake of 2400 calories in rural areas and 2100 calories in urban areas with reference to the consumption pattern as obtained in 1973-74. These norms may be adopted uniformly for all states.

- Since much systematic work has already been done with the base 1973-74, so this base year might be continued for estimating the poverty line.
- For estimating state specific poverty lines, the standardised commodity basket corresponding to poverty line at the national level should be valued at the prices in each state in the base year, i.e. 1973-74. For updating poverty line to the current prices in a year, there is a need to generate State-specific consumer price index. For this purpose, the consumer price index for the agricultural labourers (rural) and the consumer price index for industrial workers and non-manual employees (urban) should be used.
- It would be most suitable to rely on the disaggregated commodity indices for Consumer Price Index for Agricultural Labourers (CPI-AL) to update the rural poverty line and a simple average of suitably weighted commodity indices of consumer price index for industrial workers (CPI-IW) and consumer price index of urban non-manual employees (CPI-UNM) for updating the poverty line.

The expert group analysed the incidence of poverty in India in two separate period of time. One, covering 14-year period 1973-74 to 1987-88 and another for 1993-94. The revised methodology and thus, derived estimates of poverty has changed the scenario of the incidence of poverty in India.

Since the estimates covering a period of 14 years, were based on the same methodology, hence they were comparable. These estimates revealed that rural poverty ratio had declined from 56.4 per cent in 1973-74 to 39.1 per cent in 1987-88. As compared to this, there was a relatively smaller decline in the urban poverty ratio which came down from 49.2 per cent in 1973-74 to 40.1 per cent in 1987-88. The overall poverty ratio had, therefore, declined from 54.9 per cent in 1973-74 to 39.3 per cent in 1987-88. This implies that during the 14-year period, poverty ratio had declined by 15.6 percentage points in percentage terms, or an annual average decline of about 1.2 per cent.

An important revelation of the study was that for the first time, the urban poverty ratio had been estimated to be higher than rural poverty ratio. In absolute terms, the number of urban poor had risen from 60.3 million in 1973-74 to 83.3 million in 1987-88—an increase of 20 million. It underlines the fact that on account of non-availability of employment due to inadequate expansion of jobs in rural areas, the poor were pushed into the urban areas for search of employment. It implies that the overflow of the rural poor to the urban areas was the principal factor accounting for an increase in urban poverty.

The population of the rural poor which was 261 million in 1973-74 rose to 264 million in 1977-78, but thereafter, the number of the rural poor started declining and was 229 million in 1987-88 (Table 4.1). The five states, viz. Uttar Pradesh, Bihar, Maharashtra, West Bengal and Madhya Pradesh accounted for

TABLE 4.1

Incidence of Poverty in India : Expert Group's (1993) Estimation

Year	*Number of persons living below poverty line (million)*			*Percentage of poulation living below poverty line*		
	Rural	*Urban*	*Total*	*Rural*	*Urban*	*Total*
1973-74	261.3	60.3	321.6	56.4	49.2	54.9
1977-78	264.3	67.7	332.0	53.1	47.4	51.8
1983	251.7	75.3	327.0	45.6	42.2	44.8
1987-88	229.4	83.3	317.7	39.1	40.1	39.3

Source : GOI (1993), Report of the Expert Group on estimation of Proportion and Number of Poor, Planning Commission.

181.4 million poor in 1987-88. In relative terms, 58 per cent of the total poor in India resided in these five states.

Although generally there was a decline in the number of poor but unfortunately, during 1973-74 and 1987-88, there was an absolute increase in the number of poor in Orissa, Bihar, Maharashtra, Assam and Uttar Pradesh. A very distressing fact was that the number of poor in Bihar had increased from 37 million to 44 million during the 14 year period, signifying an increase of 7 million.

The states in which poverty ratio was higher than the all India figure were Orissa (55.6%), Bihar (53.4%), Tamil Nadu (45.1%), West Bengal (44%), Madhya Pradesh (43.4%) and Uttar Pradesh (42%). As against them, the States which had achieved heavy reduction in poverty were Gujarat, Kerala, Andhra Pradesh, Haryana and Punjab.

A comparison of the reduction in poverty ratios during 1973-74 and 1987-88 among the major states of India reveals that whereas at the all India level poverty reduction of the order of 15.6 per cent could be achieved during the 14 year period, there was a wide divergence noticed among the various states. On the one extreme, we observe Bihar to have realised a poverty reduction of the order of 8.5 percentage point only and on the other, Kerala achieved a poverty reduction of the order of 27.6 percentage point. Obviously, poverty eradication programmes and general economic development that occurred in various states, resulted in wide variations in poverty reduction in various states.

Since, March 1997 The Planning Commission has been using the Expert Group Method (Expert Group on Estimation of Proportion and Number of Poor) to estimate poverty). According to this method the estimates of poverty are made from the large sample survey data on household consumer expenditure conducted by the National Sample Survey Organization (NSSO) of the Ministry of Statistics and Programme Implementation. Using this methodology the Planning Commission, in the past, had released poverty estimates for the year 1973-74, 1977-78, 1983, 1987-88 and 1993-94, on 11th March 1997. Subsequently, the poverty estimates for 1999-2000 were released on 22nd February, 2001. While releasing the estimates of poverty for 1999-2000, it had been noted that these estimates were not strictly comparable with the estimates for the previous years because of changes in the pattern of NSS on consumption expenditure.

The Planning Commission had adopted data with two different consumption distributions for the year 2004-05. The first one from the consumption data collected using 30 day recall period (also known as reference period) for all the items. The other distribution is obtained from the consumer expenditure data collected using 365 day recall period for five infrequently purchased non-food items, namely, clothing, footwear, durable goods, education and institutional medical expenses and 30 day recall period for the remaining items. These two consumption distributions have been termed as Uniform Recall Period (URP) consumption distribution and Mixed Recall Period (MRP) consumption distribution respectively. The Planning Commission, using the Expert Group methodology has estimated poverty in 2004-05 using both the distributions.[11]

The state specific percentage and number of poor in rural and urban areas estimated from URP consumption distribution is given in Annexure 4.1 and 4.2. It gives the state specific percentage and number of poor in rural and urban areas estimated from MRP consumption distribution.

The percentage and number of poor in 2004-05 estimated from URP consumption distribution of NSS 61st Round of consumer expenditure data are comparable with the poverty estimates of 1993-94. The percentage and number of poor in 2004-05 estimated from MRP consumption distribution of NSS 61st Round of consumer expenditure data are roughly (but not strictly) comparable with the poverty estimates of 1999-2000.

The URP-consumption distribution data of the 61st Round yields a poverty ratio of 28.3 per cent in the rural areas, 25.7 per cent in the urban areas and 27.5 per cent for the country as a whole in 2004-05. The corresponding figures obtained from the MRP consumption distribution data of the 61st Round are 21.8 per cent in the rural areas, 21.7 per cent in the urban areas and 21.8 per cent for the country as a whole.

The poverty estimates in 2004-05 based on URP consumption distribution (27.5 per cent) is comparable with the poverty estimates of 1993-94, which was 36 per cent. The poverty estimates in 2004-05 based on MRP consumption (21.8

per cent) is roughly (but not strictly) comparable with the poverty estimates of 1999-2000, which was 26.1 per cent.

It is clear from the Table 4.2 that number of poor and their percentage to the total population (incidence of poverty) has declined in rural areas. While in urban areas the number of poor decreased from 25.2 million in 1987-88 to 67.1 million in 1999-2000 but increased to 80.7 million in 2004-05. Even on MRP basis the absolute number of poor in urban areas increased from 67.1 million in 1999-2000 to 68.2 million in 2004-05, but it shows a decline in relative form (from 23.6 per cent to 21.7 per cent during the same period). Two possible explanations can be given for this peculiar phenomenon :

TABLE 4.2

Incidence of Poverty in India During the Era of Economic Reforms

	Number of poor (million)			*Poverty ratio (%)*		
	Rural	*Urban*	*Combined*	*Rural*	*Urban*	*Combined*
1987-88	231.9	75.2	307.1	39.1	38.2	38.9
1993-94	244.0	76.3	320.3	37.3	32.4	36.0
1999-00	193.2	67.1	260.3	27.1	23.6	26.1
2004-05	220.9	80.7	301.7	28.3	25.7	27.5 (URP)
	170.3	68.2	238.5	21.8	21.7	21.8 (MRP)

Sources : (i) GOI (2003), Tenth Five Year Plan (2002-07), Vol. I, Planning Commission, New Delhi.
(ii) http://pib.nic.in/release/

(i) The economic reforms, far from bypassing the country side, have actually brought down poverty levels in rural areas much more than in urban areas.

(ii) The other possibility is massive distress—induced migration, so much so that the poor are relocating to cities.

The behaviour of various measures of poverty has been given above. These measures simply show the absolute number of poor and thus percentage to total population. This ratio, however, makes no distribution with the broad category of the poor depending upon their actual levels of consumption and deprivation. As a result, the poverty ratio fails to capture the depth and severity of poverty in an adequate measure.[12] A measure for capturing the depth of poverty is the Poverty Gap (PG) Index which adjusts the poverty ratio with the difference between the per capita consumption of the poor and the poverty line expressed as a percentage of the poverty line.

$$\text{Poverty gap Index} = \text{Poverty Ratio} \times \frac{\text{Poverty line} - \text{Per capita consumption of the poor}}{\text{Poverty line}} \times 100$$

This is therefore, a measure of the magnitude of the effort that would be required to shift the consumption of all persons below the poverty line to the level of poverty line.

A more comprehensive measure of the severity of poverty is the Squared Poverty Gap (SPG). The SPG is composed of not only the poverty ratio and the poverty gap ratio, but it also captures the consumption distribution of the poor as measured by the coefficient of variation. This measure explicitly takes into account the higher intensity of efforts that are required to address the people who are progressively farther below the poverty norm in order to bring them out of poverty. It is to be noted here that :

(i) Squared Poverty Gap is not PG x PG or PG^2;
(ii) It possesses the properties of both the poverty ratio and poverty gap index, and
(iii) It also captures the extent of variation in the levels of consumption of poor.

The Planning Commission, for the first time, analysed the problem of poverty in India, in more regressively during the course of preparation of the draft of Ninth Five Year Plan. It estimated not only the poverty ratio, but also the Poverty Gap Index, Squared Poverty Gap and Lorenze Ratio for 1973-74, 1977-78, 1983-84, 1987-88 and 1993-94. These have been presented in Table 4.3.

TABLE 4.3
Incidence of Poverty and Inequality in India

Year	Poverty Ratio			Poverty Gap Index			Squared Poverty Gap			Lorenze Ratio	
	Rural	Urban	Total	Rural	Urban	Total	Rural	Urban	Total	Rural	Urban
(1)	(2)	(3)	(4)	(5)	(6)	(7)	(8)	(9)	(10)	(11)	(12)
1973-74	56.4	49.0	54.9	16.56	13.64	15.95	6.81	5.26	6.48	0.27581	0.30125
1977-78	53.1	45.2	51.3	15.73	13.13	15.15	6.68	5.25	6.21	0.33861	0.34481
1984-85	45.7	40.8	44.5	12.32	10.61	11.96	4.78	4.07	4.61	0.29759	0.33027
1987-88	39.1	38.2	38.9	9.11	9.94	9.32	3.15	3.60	3.26	0.29826	0.35369
1993-94	37.3	32.4	36.0	8.45	7.88	8.30	2.78	2.82	2.79	0.28196	0.33940

Note : (i) Poverty Ratios are from Expert Group's Estimates.
(ii) PGI and SPG are computed from the NSS consumption expenditure distribution of respective years and the implicit poverty lines as per expert group.
(iii) Lorenze ratio are computed from the NSS consumption expenditure distribution of the respective years.

Source : Govt. of India (1997), Ninth Five Year Plan (1997-2002); Vol. I, Planning Commission, Nabhi Publication, New Delhi, p. 34.

Following conclusions appear from the above table :

- Annual average rate of decline of the poverty ratio during the period 1973-74 to 1993-94 has been 2.05 per cent in both rural and urban areas, and 2.09 per cent for the country as a whole.
- The poverty gap index during 1973-74 to 1993-94 declined by 3.33 per cent per year in rural areas, 2.71 per cent in urban areas and 3.21 per cent for the country as a whole.
- The SPG declined even faster by 4.38 per cent, 3.07 per cent and 4.13 per cent per year in rural, urban and the country respectively.
- It implies that the depth and severity of poverty in India has reduced faster than the incidence of poverty during the 20 years of span (1973-74 to 1993-94), and that over time there has been a trend towards a greater degree of clustering of the poor around the poverty line leading to a situation where economic growth is likely to have a considerably larger impact on poverty reduction than before. This would of course require that the measures of relative inequality do not deteriorate sufficiently to overcome the trend.
- The behaviour of Lorenze Ratio, the most commonly used measure of relative inequality, of household consumption expenditure shows a very high degree of stability. The near constancy of this measure of inequality for 20 years gives a certain degree of justification to believe that it may continue to remain more or less stable in the future as well.

On the basis of above conclusions and higher growth projections for 9th, 10th and 11th Five Year Plans (6.5 per cent per year, 7.7 per cent per year and 8.1 per cent per year, respectively), it was projected in the draft Five Year Plan of 9th Plan that the incidence of poverty in the terminal year of the Ninth Plan (2001-02) would be 18.61 per cent in rural areas, 16.46 per cent in urban areas and 17.98 per cent for the country as a whole.[13] It proved a distant dream. The incidence of poverty in 2004-05 was 28.3 per cent in rural areas, 25.7 per cent in urban areas and 27.5 per cent for the country as a whole despite an impressive average annual growth rate of about 5.7 per cent in 1980s and about 6.1 per cent in Eighth and Ninth Plan (1992-93 to 1996-97) (6.68 per cent in Eighth Plan and 5.35 per cent in Ninth Plan) and in Tenth Plan, 7.6 per cent (3.8% in 2002-03, 8.5% in 2003-04, 7.5% in 2004-05, 9.0% in 2005-06 and finally 9.2% in 2006-07).

The growth rate of GDP during Tenth Plan had been rather impressive making Indian Economy as one of the fastest growing economies of the world, but the high incidence of poverty 27.5 per cent in 2004-05, makes her a backward economy with poor performance on other indicators of human development such as literacy rate, expectancy of life, IMR and MMR, etc.

CONTROVERSY OVER THE ESTIMATION OF POVERTY BY PLANNING COMMISSION

Estimation of poverty in India has been full of controversies because of the methodology used by different organisation/individual researchers. Even the official organisation have different conclusions regarding the incidence of poverty in the country.

Individual researcher like B.S. Minhas, L.R. Jain and S.D. Tendulkar (1991) are of the opinion, "the massive reduction in the incidence of poverty in 1987-88, as reported by the Planning Commission in 1990, is once again largely a consequence of peculiar statistical artifacts used by the commission. The Planning Commission has continued to indulge in mindless tinkering with the observed NSS size distribution of consumer expenditure for 1987-88 also. Appropriately computed incidence of poverty in 1987-88 (affecting appropriate price adjustment at the state level for the relevant poor population) comes to about 48.7 and 37.8 per cent respectively, in rural and urban India, rather than the artificially low estimates of 37.2 and 19.4 per cent reported to parliament by the Planning Commission in 1990."[14]

According to V.M. Dandekar (1992), "the Planning Commission has used erroneous methods to demonstrate a large reduction of poverty line in the country since 1973-74. It compares the total consumer expenditure as estimated by the NSS consumer expenditure survey with the National Accounts Statistics (NAS) estimate of aggregate consumption for the nearest financial year and seeing that the NSS estimate is lower than the NAS estimate, simply jacks pro-rata the NSS size distribution of consumer expenditure and arrives at the very low estimates 32.7 and 19.4 per cent of population below the poverty line in the rural and urban India, respectively, in 1987-88."[15]

In another study Richard Palmer-Jones and Kunal Sen (2001) observed "It is clear that the Head count ratio obtained from the official poverty line may deviate from poverty line obtained from direct estimate of calorie deficiency if the price deflator used by the Planning Commission does not capture the true change in the prices of the commodities that comprise the household's consumption bundle. However, this line of argument would imply that official price deflators are under scoring the 'true' rate of inflation".[16] Mehta and Venkatraman (2000) are of the firm view that the Planning Commission's estimates of poverty, especially of rural areas, are under reported using recalculated poverty lines based on calorie norms of 2400 calories per capita per day for the rural population and 2070 calories per capita per day for the urban population, Mehta and Venkatraman estimated that rural and urban poverty rates for 1993-94 were 75 per cent and 54.4 per cent respectively and not 37.2 per cent and 32.4 per cent as reported by the Planning Commission."[17]

Expert Group to Review the Methodology for Estimation of Poverty (Tendulkar Committee)

Official estimates of poverty released by the Planning Commission are being criticised on various counts. Three major criticisms of official poverty lines which were originally defined in terms of per capita total consumer expenditure (PCTE) at 1973-74 market prices and adjusted over time and across states for changes in prices keeping unchanged the original 1973-74 rural and urban underlying all India reference poverty line baskets (PLB) of goods and services, are as under[18] :

(i) The consumption patterns underlying the rural and urban PLBs remained tied down to those observed more than three decades ago in 1973-74 despite significant changes in consumption pattern of the society in rural as well as urban areas. Hence, the three decade old PLBs had become outdated.

(ii) Crude price adjustment for prices was leading to implausible results such as proportion of total urban population below poverty line being higher than its rural counterpart in certain major states. Deaton and Drez (2008) has shown that use of CPI-AL for rural population resulted into under estimation of rural poverty.

(iii) The earlier poverty lines assumed that basic social services such as health and education would be supplied by the state, free of cost, and hence no account was taken of either the increase in the proportion of these in total expenditure over time or of their proper representation in available price indices (exclusion of private expenditure on health and education was a serious drawback despite their inclusion in the total monthly per capita expenditure in the base year 1973-74.

In view of serious criticism of Expert Group's approach towards the estimation of poverty line in India, Planning Commission set-up another expert group under the Chairmanship of Professor S.D. Tendulkar to examine the issue and suggest a new poverty line and estimates. Prof. R. Radhakrishna and Prof. Suranjan Sengupta were other members of the group. The expert group has considered the above issues in detail and has suggested new methodology to arrive at state-wise and all India rural and urban poverty lines for 2004-05 by using the latest available major NSS's 61st Round data on household consumer expenditure.

The expert group moved away from anchoring the poverty lines to a calorie intake norm in view of the fact that calorie consumption calculated by converting the consumed quantities in the last 30 days as collected by NSS had not been found to be well corrected with the nutritional outcomes observed from other specialised surveys either over time or across space (i.e. between states or rural and urban areas). Expert group adopted the MRP-based estimates of consumption expenditure as the basis for future poverty lines as against previous practices of using uniform reference period estimates of consumption expenditure in view of NSSO's decision to shift Mixed Reference Period (MRP) for all it consumption surveys in future.

According to Expert Group's observations the estimated urban share of the poor population (described as headcount ratio or poverty ratio) in 2004-05, namely, 25.7 per cent at the all India level, is generally accepted as being less controversial than its rural counterpart at 28.3 per cent that has been heavily criticised as being too low. In the interest of continuity as well as in view of the consistency with broad external validity checks with respect to nutritional, educational and health outcomes, the expert group used MRP equivalent of urban Poverty Line Basket (PLB) corresponding to 25.7 per cent urban poverty ratio as the new reference PLB to be provided to rural as well as urban population in all the states after adjusting it for within-state-urban-relative to rural and rural and urban-relative to all India price differentials.[19]

It is worth mentioning here that although those under the poverty line in urban areas continue to afford the original calorie norm of 2100 per capita per day, their actual observed calorie intake from 61st Round of NSS is 1776 calories per capita per day. This actual intake is very close to the revised calorie intake norm of 1770 per capita per day currently recommended for India by the Food and Agriculture Organisation.[20] Actual observed calorie intake of those near the new poverty line in rural areas (1999 calories per capita) is higher than the FAO norm.

The new poverty lines seeks to enable rural as well as urban population in all the states to afford the recommended all India urban PLB after taking due account of within-state rural-urban and inter-state differentials (rural and urban) incorporating observed consumer behaviour both at the all India and state levels. The Expert Group generated the new poverty lines for all the states including the NE-states. However, in the absence of adequate data, the Expert Group has suggested use of poverty line of the neighbouring states for UTs.

The recommended PLB has following points in support of it :

(i) The new Poverty Line Basket (PLB) recommended by the Expert Group (2009) is in terms of MRP that is regarded as better than earlier URP and is going to be adopted by the NSSO in its future consumer expenditure surveys. The choice of MRP over URP is based on the observation that 365 day recall captures better than 30 days recall, the per capita expenditures on low frequency items especially of those at the lower end of PCTE.

(ii) The new PLB corresponds to the urban All India poverty ratio of 25.7 per cent that is widely accepted as being reasonable.

(iii) The new PLB incorporates the latest available data on observed pattern of consumer behaviour in 2004-05.

(iv) The new PLB covers all the items of privately purchased household consumption of goods and services.

(v) A conscious decision was taken by the Expert Group to move away from anchoring the Poverty Line in calorie norm as in the past because—

  (a) There is overwhelming evidence of downward shift in calorie Engel curves over time, and

  (b) Calorie consumption intake calculated by converting the consumed quantities in the last 30 days as collected by NSS has not been found to be well correlated either over time or across states with the nutritional outcomes observed in other specialised nutrition outcome surveys such as National Family Health Surveys (NFHS).

(vi) The revised minimum calorie norm of India recommended by Food and Agriculture Organisation is currently 1770 per capita per day which is very close to the average calorie intake of those near the new poverty lines in urban areas (1776 calories per capita per day) and higher than the revised FAO norm in rural areas (1999 calories per capita per day) in the 61st Round of NSS.

(vii) The new poverty line happens to be close to, but less than, 2006 PPP US $ 1.25 per day poverty norm used by the World Bank in its latest world poverty estimates.

(viii) The new sets of poverty calculations have been developed by taking 2004-05 as base year. The Expert Group suggested this base year poverty line should be taken for the estimation of poverty in the future. Earlier, 1973-74 had been used for this purpose.

(ix) New poverty line basket also contains the expenditures on health and education which were excluded in the earlier estimates, keeping in consideration the rising private expenditure on these items.

New poverty lines seek to provide the uniform yardstick of recommended (all India, urban) PLB for measuring the extent of poverty of both the rural and urban populations in all the states. As prices differ between rural and urban areas of the same state as across states in a continental country like India, it was found necessary to derive within state rural-relative to urban and state relative to all India prices indices for rural areas separately for each state in order to evaluate PLB.

Instead of using CPI-AL for the rural population and CPI-IW for the urban population, as were frequently used by Expert Group (1993), the Tendulkar Committee used data from the following sources:

(a) The household level unit values (or prices) for the most detailed level of commodity disaggregation derived from the 61st Round of NSS data (2004-05) on Consumer Expenditure Survey for food, beverages and tobacco, fuel and light, clothing and footwear.

$$\text{Unit value} = \frac{\text{Reported value of consumer expenditure}}{\text{Quantity consumed by each sample household}}$$

(b) Private expenditure incurred on education (per school attending child) obtained from 61st Round NSS on employment-unemployment.

(c) Private expenditure on health (non-institutional household expenditure on health incurred per treatment not requiring hospitalisation, from the 60th round of NSS on Morbidity and Health Care.

(d) The above three groups of expenditure account for 90 per cent of the urban PLB excluding taxes, rent and conveyance for which no appropriate deflator was available and this combined item has been adjusted separately at current prices on the basis of the observed state/rural/urban specific consumption share of these items.

Thus, in all 176 items (after excluding 11 for inadequate number of sample observations) aggregated into fifteen commodity group indices—cereals, pulses, milk, oil, egg-fish-meat, vegetables, fresh fruit, dry fruit, sugar, salt-spices, other food, beverages and tobacco, fuel-light, clothing and footwear. One index for data source (b), two indices from data source (c), and five indices from data source (e) have been used for the compilation of a combined index number (Fisher Ideal Index Number).

These 23 indices have been aggregated for each state and sector into a single index using budget shares of these commodity groups around the poverty line MPCE class. The urban-state-relative to all India indices have been applied to the All India Urban PLB (excluding rent and conveyance) to arrive at urban poverty lines (excluding rent and conveyance) to which state specific actual expenditure on rent and conveyance of those around poverty line class has been added to derive the final urban poverty lines. The within-state-rural relative to urban indices have been applied to state level urban poverty lines (excluding rent and conveyance) to get the rural state level poverty lines after adding the actual expenditure on rent and conveyance of those around the poverty line class.

The above methodology adopted by the Expert Group (2009) has the following advantages :

- Price index numbers are based on the same data base from which poverty calculations have been made so that these two get integrally linked. Thus, new methodology avoids the criticism of outdated base in the existing population segment specific consumer prices indices.
- The use of Fisher Ideal Index number saves the new poverty lines from the criticism of the existing procedure (of calculating the official poverty lines) which was unable to make allowance for state specific patterns of consumption in price adjustment.
- The new poverty lines have been derived for all the states including NE-states for which the earlier official procedure had to use the poverty ratios of one of the states—Assam for which CPI-AL and CPI-IW were available.

One may criticise the above procedure on the ground of its complexity with a long chain of calculations, but with easy availability of high speed computers the problem may be sorted out

As per the estimates of Expert Group to Review the Methodology for Estimation of Povertv, 37.2 per cent population of the country was living below poverty line in 2004-05. The poverty ratio for rural areas is 41.8 per cent and for urban areas is 25.7 per cent. The combined all India head count ratio is higher by 15.6 percentage point from the official poverty ratio 21.8 per cent (MRP basis) as has been released by the Planning Commission using the old Expert Group's methodology. Likewise, the rural all India headcount ratio derived as a population weighted average of state level headcount ratios using the new poverty lines is 41.8 per cent compared to 28.3 per cent using the old poverty lines. All the state level rural headcount ratios are higher using the new poverty lines than those in the earlier official estimates.

Poverty lines recommended by Tendulkar Committee have been presented in Table 4.4. It reveals that all India

Table 4.4
Poverty Lines by New Methodology in 1993-94 and 2004-05

States/UTs	Poverty Line (Rs.) (1993-94)		Poverty Line (Rs.) (2004-05)	
	Rural	Urban	Rural	Urban
(1)	(2)	(3)	(4)	(5)
Andhra Pradesh	244.1	282.0	433.43	563.16
Arunachal Pradesh	285.1	297.1	547.14	618.45
Assam	266.3	306.8	478.00	600.03
Bihar	236.1	266.9	433.43	526.18
Chhattisgarh	229.1	283.5	398.92	513.70
Delhi	315.4	320.3	541.39	642.4
Goa	316.2	306.0	608.76	671.15
Gujarat	279.4	320.7	501.58	659.18
Haryana	294.1	312.1	529.42	626.41
Himachal Pradesh	272.7	316.0	520.40	605.74
Jammu & Kashmir	289.1	281.1	522.30	602.89
Jharkhand	227.7	304.1	404.79	531.35
Karnataka	266.9	294.8	417.84	588.06
Kerala	286.5	289.2	537.31	584.70
Madhya Pradesh	232.5	274.5	408.41	532.26
Maharashtra	268.6	329.0	484.89	631.85
Manipur	322.3	366.3	578.11	641.13
Meghalaya	284.1	393.4	503.32	745.73
Mizoram	316.5	355.7	639.27	699.75
Nagaland	381.7	409.6	687.30	782.93
Orissa	224.2	279.3	407.78	497.31
Pondicherry	220.3	264.3	385.45	506.17
Punjab	286.9	342.3	543.51	642.51

(Contd.)

TABLE 4.4 (Contd.)

(1)	(2)	(3)	(4)	(5)
Rajasthan	271.9	300.5	478.00	568.15
Sikkim	266.6	362.2	531.50	741.68
Tamilnadu	252.6	288.2	441.69	559.77
Tripura	275.8	316.6	450.49	555.79
Uttar Pradesh	244.3	281.3	435.14	532.12
Uttaranchal	249.5	306.7	486.24	602.39
West Bengal	235.5	295.2	445.38	572.51
All India			446.68	578.80

Notes : (i) The estimates for Chhattisgarh, Madhya Pradesh, Bihar, Jharkhand, Uttar Pradesh and Uttaranchal for 1993-94 are for states as they exist after bifercation in 2001.

(ii) The estimates for 1993-94 have been calculated from the unit data during district and state boundaries of divided states in 1993-94.

Source : Planning Commission, Govt. of India, New Delhi.

poverty line for both rural and urban areas have shown a rising trend under new methodology as compared to old methodology, but the increase in rural poverty line is more significant than in urban poverty line.

As per new methodology all the states have higher poverty lines for rural areas. But the states like Chhattisgarh, Karnataka, Madhya Pradesh, Maharashtra and Uttranchal have lower urban poverty lines. While the rest of the states have higher urban poverty lines under new methodology.

State-wise poverty ratios (or headcount ratios) have been presented in the Table 4.5. Although, Tendulkar Committee explicitly made it clear that except for the urban-all India head count ratio for 2004-05 which was used to derive the new all India reference poverty line basket, all other head count ratios for 2004-05, i.e. rural-all India and rural and urban statewise- are based on the new reference poverty line basket and new price indices, and hence are not comparable and must not be

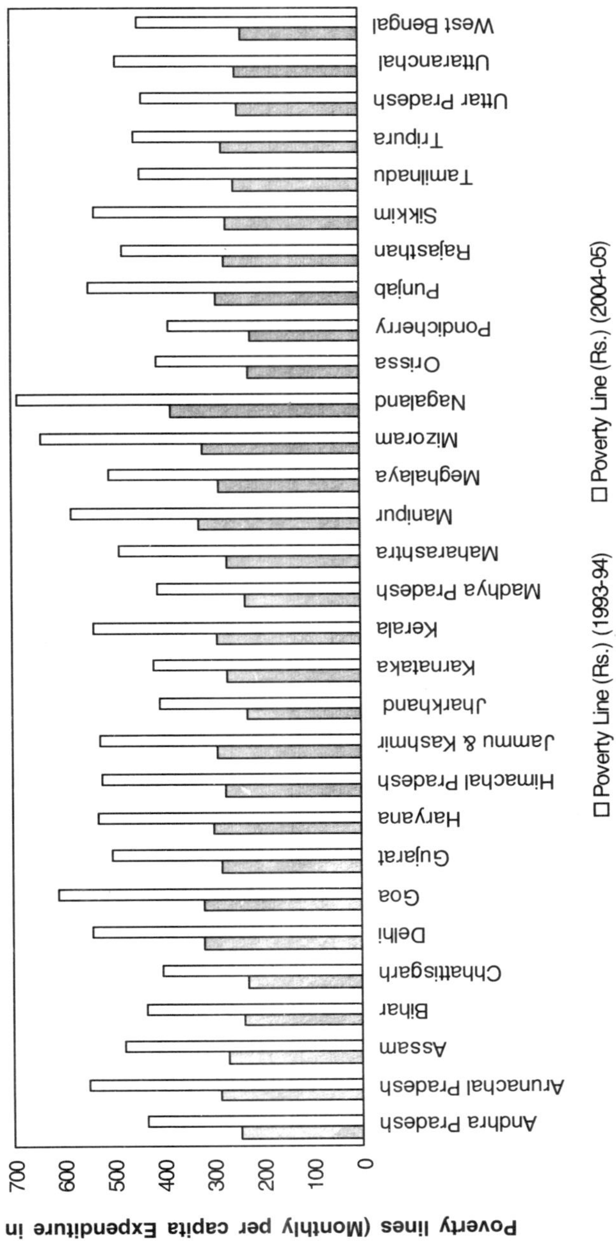

CHART 4.1

State-wise Poverty Lines in Rural Areas (1993-94 and 2004-05) as per Expert Group's (2008) Methodology

CHART 4.2

State-wise Poverty Lines in Urban Areas (1993-94 and 2004-05) as per Expert Group's (2008) Methodology

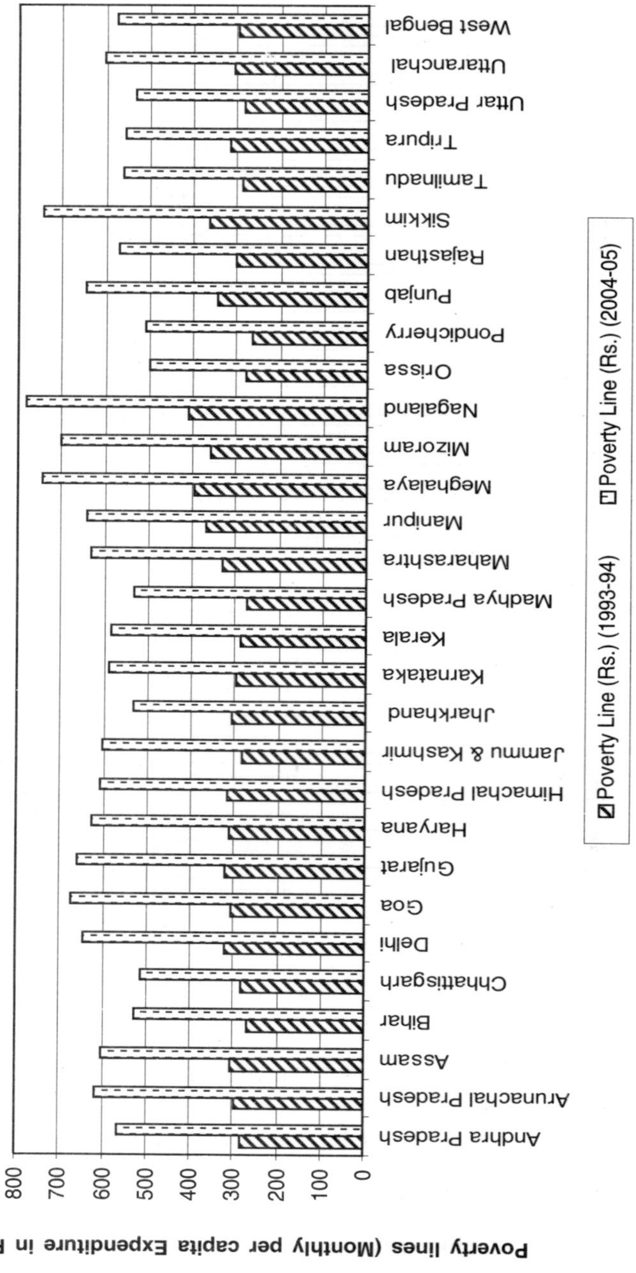

CHART 4.3

State-wise Poverty Lines for Rural and Urban Areas (1993-94) as per Expert Group's (2008) Methodology

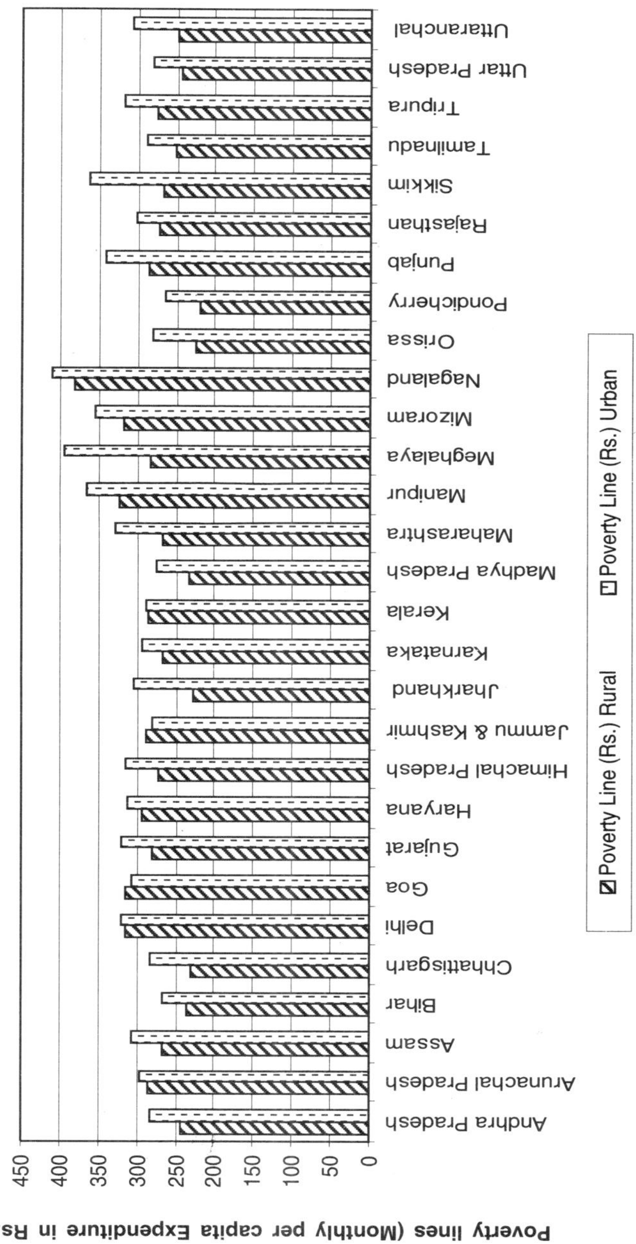

CHART 4.4
State-wise Poverty Lines for Rural and Urban Areas (2004-05) as per Expert Group's (2008) Methodology

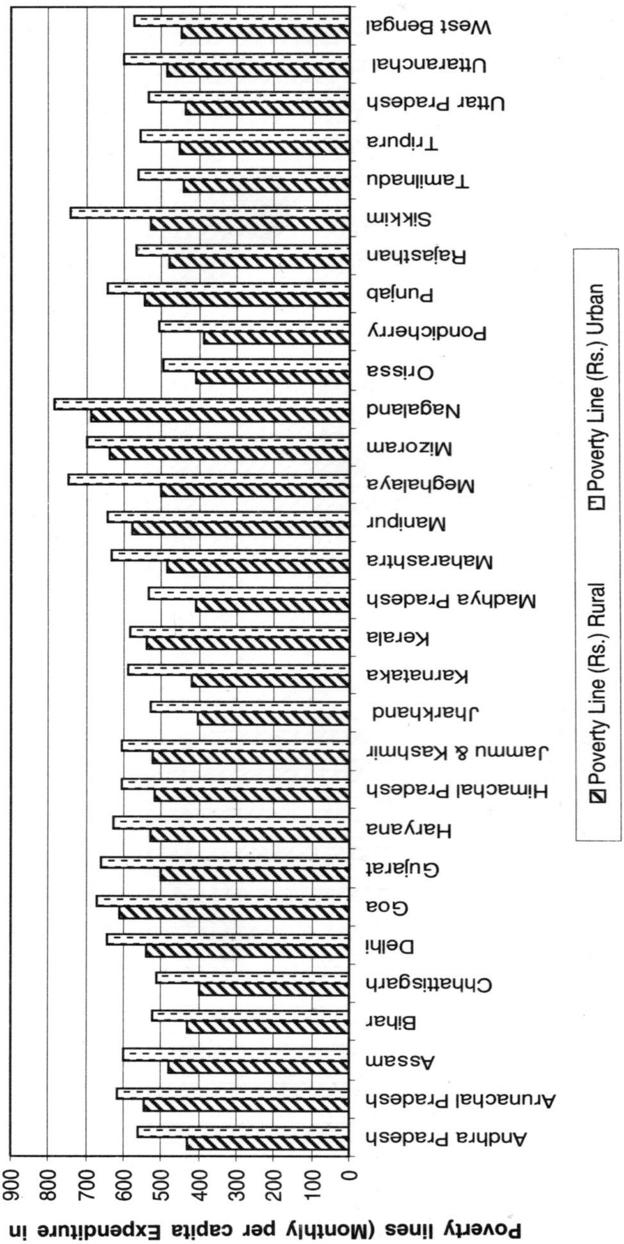

compared with the earlier head count ratios using the old out dated 1973-74 PLB and unsatisfactory price indices.[21] The researcher is also of the view that not only the present data set of poverty is not comparable, but also the other estimates done by various agencies/experts cannot be compared because of serious differences and variations in the base line data and methodology.

However, the Tendulkar Committee did a preliminary exercise, using suggested methodology, for the 50th round of NSS for 1993-94 to facilitate two-time-point comparison of changes in headcount ratios.[22] The poverty ratios, based upon this exercise, have been presented in Table 4.5. The data in Table 4.5 reveals that 45.3 per cent of the population in the country as a whole, 50.1 per cent population in rural India and 31.8 per cent population in urban India were living below the poverty line in 1993-94. This is against official 1993-94 poverty estimates of 36.0, 37.2 and 32.6 per cent respectively. Although, the level of 2004-05 all India poverty ratios based on new PLB appears higher at 41.8 per cent and 37.2 per cent for rural and rural-urban combined populations respectively, than the existing official poverty estimates of 28.3 per cent and 27.5 per cent, the comparable extent of poverty reduction between 1993-94 and 2004-05 is not very much different from that inferred from using old methodology (Table 4.6). The reduction level in rural areas is rather significant as per new methodology between 1993-94 to 2004-05 (8.3 percentage point) as against 5.0 percentage point decline as per old methodology. For urban areas and rural-urban combined the decline is almost the same under both the methodology.

Since the poverty lines for 1993-94 and 2004-05 derived by new Poverty Line Basket, are not comparable with the earlier poverty lines, so the present analysis will be based upon new poverty ratios for India as a whole and various states (Table 4.7). The data presented in Table 4.7 reveals that the pattern of poverty incidence does not show any significant change from 1993-94 to 2004-05. In 1993-94 Manipur was at the bottom with poverty HCR 65.1 per cent followed by Jharkhand (60.7%), Bihar (60.5%), Orissa (59.1%), Arunachal Pradesh (54.5%), Assam (51.8%), Chhattisgarh (50.9%), Karnataka (49.5%) and Uttar Pradesh (48.4%). Various antipoverty

Table 4.5
Poverty Head Count Ratio for 2004-05 as per Lakdawala Committee's and Tendulkar Committee's Recommendations

States	*Lakdawala Committee's Methodology (1993)*						*Tendulkar Committee's Methodology (2008) Poverty Headcount Ratios (%)*		
	Poverty Headcount Ratios (%) MRP-based consumption			*Poverty Headcount Ratios (%) URP-based consumtpion*					
	Rural	*Urban*	*Total*	*Rural*	*Urban*	*Total*	*Rural*	*Urban*	*Total*
(1)	*(2)*	*(3)*	*(4)*	*(5)*	*(6)*	*(7)*	*(8)*	*(9)*	*(10)*
Andhra Pradesh	7.5	20.7	11.1	11.2	28.0	15.8	32.3	23.4	29.9
Arunachal Pradesh	17.0	2.4	13.4	22.3	3.3	17.6	33.6	23.5	31.1
Assam	17.0	2.4	15.0	22.3	3.3	19.7	36.4	21.8	34.4
Bihar	32.9	28.9	32.5	42.1	34.6	41.4	55.7	43.7	54.4
Chhattisgarh	31.2	34.7	32.0	40.8	41.2	40.9	55.1	28.4	49.4
Delhi	0.1	10.8	10.2	6.9	15.2	14.7	15.6	12.9	13.1
Goa	1.9	20.9	12.0	5.4	21.3	13.8	28.1	22.2	25.0
Gujarat	13.9	10.1	12.5	19.1	13.0	16.8	39.1	20.1	31.8
Haryana	9.2	11.3	9.9	13.6	15.1	10.6	24.8	22.4	24.1
Himachal Pradesh	7.2	2.6	6.7	10.7	3.4	10.0	25.0	4.6	22.9
Jammu & Kashmir	2.7	8.5	4.2	4.6	7.4	5.4	14.1	10.4	13.2

Jharkhand	40.2	16.3	34.8	46.3	20.2	40.3	51.6	23.8	45.3
Karnataka	12.0	27.2	17.4	20.8	32.6	25.0	37.5	25.9	33.4
Kerala	9.6	16.4	11.4	13.2	20.2	15.0	20.2	18.4	19.7
Madhya Pradesh	29.8	39.3	32.4	36.9	42.1	38.3	53.6	35.1	48.6
Maharashtra	22.2	29.2	25.2	29.6	32.2	30.7	47.9	25.6	38.1
Manipur	17.0	2.4	13.2	22.3	3.3	17.3	39.3	34.5	38.0
Meghalaya	17.0	2.4	14.1	22.3	3.3	18.5	14.0	24.7	16.1
Mizoram	17.0	2.4	9.5	22.3	3.3	11.6	23.0	7.9	15.3
Nagaland	17.0	2.4	14.5	22.3	3.3	19.0	10.0	4.3	9.0
Orissa	39.8	40.3	39.9	46.8	44.3	46.4	60.8	37.6	57.2
Pondicherry	16.9	18.8	18.2	22.9	22.2	22.4	22.9	9.9	14.1
Punjab	14.3	3.8	5.2	9.1	7.1	8.4	22.1	18.7	20.9
Rajasthan	14.3	28.1	17.5	18.7	32.9	22.1	35.8	29.7	34.4
Sikkim	17.0	2.4	15.2	22.3	3.3	20.1	31.8	25.9	31.1
Tamilnadu	16.9	18.8	17.8	22.8	22.2	22.5	37.5	19.7	28.9
Tripura	17.0	2.4	14.4	22.3	3.3	18.9	44.5	22.5	40.6
Uttar Pradesh	25.3	26.3	25.5	33.4	30.6	32.8	42.7	34.1	40.9
Uttaranchal	31.7	32.0	31.8	40.8	36.5	39.6	35.1	26.2	32.7
West Bengal	24.2	32.0	20.6	28.6	14.8	24.7	38.2	24.4	34.3
All India	21.8	21.7	21.8	28.3	25.7	27.5	41.8	25.7	37.2

Source : Government of India, Planning Commission, New Delhi.

Table 4.6
Reduction in Poverty Incidence Between 1993-94 and 2004-05

(in per cent)

	Lakdawala Committee's Methodology			*Tendulkar Committee's Methodology*		
	1993-94	*2004-05*	*Reduction*	*1993-94*	*2004-05*	*Reduction*
Rural	37.3	28.3	5.0	50.1	41.8	8.3
Urban	32.4	25.7	6.7	31.8	25.7	6.1
Combined	36.0	27.5	8.5	45.3	37.2	8.1

Source : Planning Commission, New Delhi, 2009.

Table 4.7
Poverty Head Count Ratio for 1993-94 and 2004-05

States	*Poverty Headcount Ratios (%)*					
	1993-94			*2004-05*		
	Rural	*Urban*	*Total*	*Rural*	*Urban*	*Total*
(1)	*(2)*	*(3)*	*(4)*	*(5)*	*(6)*	*(7)*
Andhra Pradesh	48.1	35.2	44.6	32.3	23.4	29.9
Arunachal Pradesh	60.0	22.6	54.5	33.6	23.5	31.1
Assam	54.9	27.7	51.8	36.4	21.8	34.4
Bihar	62.3	44.7	60.5	55.7	43.7	54.4
Chhattisgarh	55.9	28.1	50.9	55.1	28.4	49.4
Delhi	16.2	15.7	15.7	15.6	12.9	13.1
Goa	25.5	14.6	20.8	28.1	22.2	25.0
Gujarat	43.1	28.0	27.8	39.1	20.1	31.8
Haryana	40.0	24.2	35.9	24.8	22.4	24.1
Himachal Pradesh	36.7	13.6	34.6	25.0	4.6	22.9
Jammu & Kashmir	32.5	6.9	26.3	14.1	10.4	13.2
Jharkhand	65.9	41.8	60.7	51.6	23.8	45.3
Karnataka	56.6	34.2	49.5	37.5	25.9	33.4
Kerala	33.9	23.9	31.3	20.2	18.4	19.7
Madhya Pradesh	49.0	31.8	44.6	53.6	35.1	48.6

(1)	(2)	(3)	(4)	(5)	(6)	(7)
Maharashtra	59.3	30.3	47.8	47.9	25.6	38.1
Manipur	64.4	67.2	65.1	39.3	34.5	38.0
Meghalaya	38.0	23.0	35.2	14.0	24.7	16.1
Mizoram	16.6	6.3	11.8	23.0	7.9	15.3
Nagaland	20.1	21.8	20.4	10.0	4.3	9.0
Orissa	63.0	34.5	59.1	60.8	37.6	57.2
Pondicherry	28.1	32.4	30.9	22.9	9.9	14.1
Punjab	20.3	27.2	22.4	22.1	18.7	20.9
Rajasthan	40.8	29.9	38.3	35.8	29.7	34.4
Sikkim	33.0	20.4	31.8	31.8	25.9	31.1
Tamilnadu	51.0	33.7	44.6	37.5	19.7	28.9
Tripura	34.3	25.4	32.9	44.5	22.5	40.6
Uttar Pradesh	50.9	38.3	48.4	42.7	34.1	40.9
Uttaranchal	36.7	18.7	32.0	35.1	26.2	32.7
West Bengal	42.5	31.2	39.4	38.2	24.4	34.3
All India	50.1	31.8	45.3	41.8	25.7	37.2

Note : The estimates for Chhattisgarh, Madhya Pradesh, Jharkhand, Bihar, Uttaranchal and Uttar Pradesh are for the states as they exist after bifurcation in 2001. The estimates for 1993-94 have been calculated from the unit data using district and state boundaries of the divided states in 1993-94.

Source : Govt. of India, Planning Commission, New Delhi.

measures brought down the poverty incidence in almost all the states but with varying degree. Smaller states such as Manipur, Arunachal Pradesh, Assam did fairly better and were able to reduce poverty incidence significantly. As a result all these states moved out from bottom ten states list in 2004-05. In 2004-05 Orissa is at the bottom with 57.2 per cent poverty HCR followed by Bihar (54.4%), Chhattisgarh (49.5%), Madhya Pradesh (48.6%) and Uttar Pradesh (40.9%). Goa (25.0%), Madhya Pradesh (48.6%) and Uttaranchal (32.7%) are the only states in India whose poverty HCRs have increased in 2004-05 as compared to 1993-94 (Table 4.7).

WORLD BANK'S ESTIMATE OF POVERTY IN INDIA

The World Bank has also made use of the same procedure as adopted by the Planning Commission. However, the World Bank used an alternative method of estimating poverty proportion applying a deflator series developed by the NSS and the Indian Statistical Institute to calculate updated poverty lines (in current prices) of Rs. 55.2 (rural) and Rs. 68.6 (urban) for 1977-78 and Rs. 89.0 (rural) and Rs. 112.2 (urban) for 1983. The World Bank also worked out the estimate of ultra-poor reckoned at 75% of the expenditure of poverty line. On this basis the proportion of population below poverty line for 1970, 1983 and 1988 has been worked out.[23]

The World Bank's estimates of poverty incidence, poverty gap and squared poverty gap related data reveals that the incidence of poverty in rural areas has increased between 1951 to 1955. Subsequently the incidence of poverty has a fluctuating trend and again a rising trend till 1968. Thereafter, there is a declining trend. But in urban areas the incidence of poverty has a declining trend since 1957 (Table 4.8).

As per latest estimates of World Bank, 24 per cent of all Indians in 2005 lived on average of Rs. 13.14 per day or less (taking the weighted average of the different figures for rural and urban areas). Another 18 per cent lived on an average of between Rs. 16.49 and Rs. 13.14 per day. Thus, 42 per cent of the population (about 460 million people), lived on Rs. 2,50,000 crore, which is barely 10 per cent of total household expenditure in 2005 (the total household expenditure was 60-65 per cent of GDP of India). The world development indicators say that bottom 40 per cent of the population accounted for 19 per cent of household consumption. In fact, there is hardly any country in the world in which the poorest 40 per cent of the population gets less than 10 per cent of total household income. The only major country is Brazil, where poorest 40 per cent population get 9.2 per cent, but the levels of inequality in Brazil are miles ahead of what exist in India. The figures in this respect for China and USA are more unequal than India. China's bottom 40 per cent population accounts for 12.8 per cent of income while that of USA's

TABLE 4.8
Poverty Estimates 1951-97 in India

(in per cent)

NSS Round	*Period*	*Rural*			*Urban*		
		H	*PG*	*SPG*	*H*	*PG*	*SPG*
(1)	(2)	(3)	(4)	(5)	(6)	(7)	(8)
3	Aug. 1951 – Nov. 1951	47.37	16.05	7.53	35.46	11.14	4.82
4	Apr. 1952 – Sep. 1952	43.87	14.64	6.71	36.71	10.91	4.41
5	Dec. 1932 – Mar. 1953	48.21	16.29	7.56	40.14	13.25	5.96
6	May 1953 – Sep. 1953	54.13	19.03	9.12	42.77	13.83	6.29
7	Oct. 1953 – Mar. 1954	61.29	21.95	10.26	49.92	17.24	7.74
8	Jul. 1954 – Mar. 1955	64.24	25.06	12.50	46.19	15.76	7.02
9	May 1955 – Nov. 1955	51.83	18.44	8.80	43.92	14.65	6.40
10	Dec. 1955 – May 1956	48.34	15.65	6.71	43.15	13.34	5.41
11	Aug. 1956 – Feb. 1957	58.86	19.45	8.50	51.45	18.16	8.51
12	Mar. 1957 – Aug. 1957	62.11	21.69	10.01	48.88	16.31	7.25
13	Sep. 1957 – May 1958	55.16	19.01	8.78	47.75	15.95	7.00
14	Jul. 1958 – Jul. 1959	53.26	17.74	7.88	44.76	13.75	5.87
15	Jul. 1959 – Jun. 1960	50.89	15.29	6.13	49.17	15.83	6.75
16	Jul. 1960 – Aug. 1961	45.40	13.60	5.53	44.65	13.84	5.83
17	Sep. 1961 – Jul. 1962	47.20	13.60	5.31	43.55	13.79	6.05
18	Feb 1963 – Jan. 1964	48.53	13.88	5.49	44.83	13.29	5.17
19	Jul. 1964 – Jun. 1965	53.60	16.08	6.60	48.78	15.24	6.38
20	Jul. 1965 – Jun. 1966	57.60	17.97	7.60	52.90	16.82	6.98
21	Jul. 1966 – Jun. 1967	64.30	22.01	10.01	52.24	16.81	7.19
22	Jul. 1967 – Jun. 1968	63.67	21.80	9.85	52.91	16.93	7.22
23	Jul. 1968 – Jun. 1969	59.00	18.96	8.17	49.29	15.54	6.54
24	Jul. 1969 – Jun. 1970	57.61	18.24	7.73	47.16	14.32	5.86
25	Jul. 1970 – Jun. 1971	54.84	16.55	6.80	44.98	13.35	5.35
27	Oct. 1972 – Sep. 1973	55.36	17.35	7.33	45.67	13.46	5.26
28	Oct. 1973 – Jun. 1974	55.72	17.18	7.13	47.96	13.60	5.22
32	Jul. 1977 – Jun. 1978	50.60	15.03	6.06	40.50	11.69	4.53

(*Contd.*)

TABLE 4.8 (Contd.)

(1)	(2)	(3)	(4)	(5)	(6)	(7)	(8)
38	Jan. 1983 – Dec. 1983	45.31	12.65	4.84	35.65	9.52	3.56
42	Jun. 1986 – Jun. 1987	38.81	10.01	3.70	34.29	9.10	3.40
43	Jul. 1987 – Jun. 1988	39.60	9.70	3.40	35.65	9.31	3.25
44	Jul. 1988 – Jun. 1989	39.06	9.50	3.29	36.60	9.54	3.29
45	Jul. 1989 – Jun. 1990	34.30	7.80	2.58	33.40	8.51	3.04
46	Jul. 1990 – Jun. 1991	36.43	8.64	2.93	32.76	8.51	3.12
	Pre-reform Jul. 1989 – Jun. 1991	35.37	8.22	2.75	33.08	8.51	3.08
47	Jul. 1991 – Dec. 1991	37.42	8.29	2.68	33.23	8.24	2.90
48	Jan. 1992 – Dec. 1992	43.47	10.88	3.81	33.73	8.82	3.19
50	Jul. 1993 – Jun. 1994	38.74	9.41	3.27	30.03	7.62	2.76
51	Jul. 1994 – Jun. 1995	41.02	9.29	2.99	35.50	8.38	2.80
52	Jul. 1995 – Jun. 1996	37.15	8.10	2.53	28.04	6.28	2.22
53	Jan. 1997 – Dec. 1997	35.78	8.31	2.76	29.99	7.77	2.73
	Post-reform Jul. 1995 – Dec. 1997	36.47	8.21	2.64	29.02	7.27	2.47

Notes : H : headcout ratio of poverty; PG : poverty gap ratio; SPG : squared poverty gap.

Source : B. Ozler, G. Dutt and M. Ravallion, "A database on Poverty and Growth in India", The World Bank, January 1996, for estimates up to the 48th round: For 50th round, NSS data has been used to calculate the estimates using exactly the same methodology as in the rest of the series. For estimates for 51st round onwards and for pre-reform and post-reform periods, the source is Gaurav Datt, "Has Poverty Declined since economic Reforms?", *Economic and Politcal Weekly*, December 11, 1999.

bottom 40 per cent population accounts for 16.1 per cent income.[24]

What the World Bank has assessed is that 42 per cent of India's population lives on less that US $ 1.25 per day (calculated on the basis of purchasing power parity). On the other hand, World Development Indicators, collectively say that the bottom 20 per cent of the population accounts for 8 per cent of all household consumption, then even their income is higher than the rupee equivalent US $ 1.25 per day. World Bank used income cut off Rs. 21.6 per day in urban areas and Rs. 14.3 per day in rural areas (at 2005 prices) to define who is poor in 2005.

According to the latest World Bank report, the actual number of poor people earning US $ 1.25 a day has increased by 39.8 million in absolute numbers during 1981–2005 coinciding with the reform period and the increase in 9.6 per cent in relative terms (Table 4.9), when the level of income is raised from US $ 1.00 per day to US $ 1.25 per day. In reality 42.2 per cent people in India were lining, below the poverty line in 2005.

TABLE 4.9
Number of Persons with Various Levels of Income

(*US $ per day*) (*million*)

Year	*1981*	*1984*	*1987*	*1990*	*1993*	*1996*	*1999*	*2002*	*2005**
$1/Day	296.1	282.2	285.3	282.5	280.1	271.3	270.1	276.1	266.5**
$1.25/Day	420.5	416.0	428.0	435.5	444.3	441.8	447.2	460.5	455.8
$2.0/Day	608.9	635.6	669.0	701.6	735.0	757.1	782.8	813.1	827.7
$2.5/Day	650.3	686.1	725.0	766.5	808.8	841.1	875.2	914.4	938.0

Note : *India's population was 1080 million in 2005. **All figures are population in millions. One dollar is equivalent to about 40 (Now about Rs. 45).

Source : Nair, K.P. Prabhakaran (2009); Swelling Ranks of the poor, the *Hindu Business Line*, New Delhi, September 23, p. 8.

SOME OTHER ESTIMATIONS OF POVERTY IN INDIA

P.D. Ojha (1986)[25], V.M. Dandekar and Neelkanth Rath (1971)[26], B.S. Minhas (1988)[27], P.K. Bardhan (1993)[28], Montek Singh Ahluwalia (1977)[29], Seventh Finance Commission (1978)[30], S.P. Gupta (1999)[31], etc. have also estimated the poverty in India. Almost all of these studies are based on the data of NSS. However, lately some studies funded by international financial institutions have attempted to prove that incidence of poverty has declined in India during the

1990s. K. Sundaram and Suresh D. Tendulkar found that all the measures of poverty including the size of the poor population and the distribution sensitive measures such as poverty gap and squared poverty gap exhibit a clear and sharp decline in both the rural and urban areas at the level of the country as a whole. Not only this, at the all India level, the overall performance in all dimensions of poverty has been better between 1994 and 2000 than that in the preceding ten-and-a-half years.[32]

In a period of increasing income inequality and growing unemployment, incidence of poverty usually does not fall. Hence if their estimates try to prove the opposite, then both the data base and the methodology become a suspect. There is an added reason for doubting the merit of this study. Sundaram and Tendulkar's study is funded by the World Bank which has vested interest in proving that the neo liberal reforms set by the Washington Consensus are in the best interest of the people of the country. The fact, however, is that "the net effect of the policies set by the Washington Consensus has all too often been to benefit the few at the expense of many, the well-off at the expense of poor.[33]

NCAER'S ESTIMATES OF POVERTY IN INDIA

National Council of Applied Economic Research has been collecting income and expenditure data since 1985 using large sample surveys. Applying to this data Planning Commission's expenditure cut-off for poverty for each and every state (at an all India level, this works out to Rs. 538.6 for urban areas and Rs. 356.3 for rural areas), gives roughly the same poverty levels as the planning commission's earlier estimates (based on Expert Groups', 1993, methodology)—21.8 per cent of rural people and 21.7 per cent of urban people are living below poverty line. According to NCAER data, 21.7 per cent of rural household and 18.7 per cent of urban households were poor in 2004-05 and collectively 20.8 per cent people were living below poverty line in 2004-05.[34] However, if we plug in the higher World Bank income cut-offs used to define poor, the NCAER data shows that around 29.6 per cent of the population is poor—33 per cent in rural areas and 21.6 per cent in urban areas.

But the numbers apart, the real question is whether we should continue to define poverty in terms of calories and the food/income required for this, or whether poverty lines should take into account other aspects of consumption life-styles such as expenditure on education, health and energy?

N.C. SAXENA'S EXPERT GROUP ON THE METHODOLOGY FOR THE BPL CENSUS 2009

While estimations of poverty were done by the Planning Commission on the basis of recommendations of task forces constituted under the chairmanship of Prof. Y.K. Alagh (1979) and Prof. D.T. Lakadawala (1993), a Census to identity the Below Poverty Line (BPL) households has been conducted by the Ministry of Rural Development of Government of India three times (1992, 1997 and 2002) during the last 17 years. The main purpose of conducting such survey was to identify the BPL households that could be assisted under various programmes such as IAY, NSAP, SGSY, TSC, etc. In addition many other Ministries of Government of India use the BPL list so prepared for targeting benefits to them, such a PDS, NMBS, health insurance, scholarships, etc. Some state specific schemes also limit their assistance to this list of the BPL families. Thus, BPL list is an important document as well as parameter that provides a ground for the implementation of various schemes of development so as to make the growth more inclusive and broad-based. The entire exercise is done for rural areas. No such efforts have been done to identify the BPL households in urban areas.

The issue of identification of BPL is highly controversial because of its linkage with the transfer of funds from centre to states. Many state governments criticised the methodology adopted in the previous surveys. In view of the in adequacies pointed out by the state governments and others about the methodology followed in 2002 for identifying the poor, the Ministry of Rural Development constituted an Expert Group in August 2008 under the Chairmanship of Mr. N.C. Saxena to recommend a more suitable methodology to identify the poor in rural areas of India.

The basic criterion adopted by both the task Forces of Planning Commission to identify the poor, hinges upon calorie norms of food adequacies. However, several states have pointed out that the present cut off line for estimation of poverty leaves out a large number of poor households, and thus leads to great dissatisfaction in the rural areas.[35] The committee is of the view that, the poverty lines anchored by the Planning Commission never corresponded to the minimum calorie norm, as according to the NSSO data, to reach at the minimum calorie requirement the poor would need far more consumption expenditure than the monthly cut-off line so arrived at by just adjusting Rs. 49 MPCE for rural areas and Rs. 57 MPCE for urban areas for inflation. For instance, for the year 1999-2000 the monetary cut-off corresponding to the minimum caloric requirements should have been Rs. 565 in rural areas and Rs. 628 in urban areas, whereas by the price updated methodology as used by the Planning Commission the poverty line was Rs. 328 and Rs. 454 respectively.[36] Thus, a large number of rural poor consuming between Rs. 328 and Rs. 565 per month were left-out of the BPL benefits. The above anomaly can be understand more accurately from Table 4.10.

Planning Commission's national poverty line at 2004-05 prices has been fixed as Rs. 356 per capita per month for rural areas and Rs. 539 per capita per month for urban areas. Table 4.10 reveals that this level of income would have permitted both the rural and urban people to consume just 1820 Kcalories, whereas to consume the desired norm of 2400 Kcalories for rural areas and 2100 Kcalories for urban areas, the cut-off line for determining BPL status should have been around Rs. 700 in the rural areas, and Rs. 1000 for the urban areas. Thus, a large number of rural people with consumption in the range Rs. 360 to Rs. 700 have been deprived of the BPL-status. It is worth mentioning here that calorie consumption of the poor has been consistently declining since 1977-78. The calorie intake at the official poverty line was 2170 Kcals in 1977-78, 2060 Kcal in 1983, 1980 Kcal in 1993-94 and 1820 Kcal in 2004-05.[37]

Deaton and Dreze (2008) has shown, with the help of NSSO data, in their study that at any given point of time, the calorie intake of the poorest quartile continues to be 30 to 50

TABLE 4.10
Per Capita Per EDiem Intake of Calorie (Kcal) by MPCE Class

Rural			Urban		
MPCE Class (Rs.)	*Cummu-lative persons as (%) of the total*	*Calorie consum-ption*	*MPCE Class (Rs.)*	*Cummu-lative persons as (%) of the total*	*Calorie consum-ption*
0 - 235	2.88	1376	0 - 335	5.41	1413
235 - 270	5.74	1475	335 - 395	10.70	1608
270 - 320	11.97	1679	395 - 485	21.00	1687
320 - 365	19.18	1800	485 - 580	31.23	1833
365 - 410	26.99	1885	580 - 675	40.03	1856
410 - 455	34.82	1962	675 - 790	48.70	1943
455 - 510	44.00	2042	790 - 930	57.06	2024
510 - 580	54.70	2158	930 - 1100	65.38	2110
580 - 690	67.36	2290	1100 - 1380	75.47	2209
690 - 890	81.41	2380	1380 - 1880	87.06	2341
890 -1155	90.07	2568	1880 - 2540	93.78	2545
>1155	100.00	3018	> 2540	100.00	2839
Average		2047			020

Source : Report of the Expert Group on the Methodology for the BPL Census (2009), Ministry of Rural Development, Govt. of India, New Delhi, p. 5.

per cent less than the calorie intake of the top quartile of the population, despite the poor needing more calories because of harder manual work. Not even this, calorie consumption of the bottom fifty per cent of the population has been consistently decreasing since 1987, which is a matter of concern.

Due to the continuous decline in the calorie consumption, the number of people below poverty norm (2400/2100 Kcals) has consistently increased over the years, and more than 75 per cent of the population in Indian households have per capita calorie consumption less than the norm (Table 4.11).

Table 4.11
Population Living in Households with Per Capita Calorie Consumption below 2400 Kcal in Rural and 2100 Kcal in Urban Areas

(*in per cent*)

	1983	*1987-88*	*1993-94*	*1999-2000*	*2004-05*
Rural areas	66.1	65.9	71.1	74.2	79.8
Urban areas	60.5	57.1	58.1	58.2	63.9
All India	64.8	63.9	67.8	70.1	75.8
NSS Round	38th	43rd	50th	55th	61st

Source : Deaton and Dreze (2008).

In the light of above observations, Dr. Pronab Sen (2005), Chief Statistician and Secretary, Department of Statistics and Programme Implementation, GOI, has commented, "It is undoubtedly true that the per capita calorie intake of the poverty line classes practically all over the country has declined significantly between 1972-73 and 1999-2000. The current value of the poverty line does not permit the poverty line class to consume the calorific norm, and the periodic price corrections that have been carried out to update the poverty lines are inadequate and indeed may be even inappropriate. Consequently, the poverty estimates made in the years after 1973-74 understate the true incidence of poverty in the country.[38]

In view of the above analysis Expert Group on the methodology for the BPL Census (2009), concluded that, "the percentage of rural population that is poor, and is not able to satisfy the minimum required calorie needs, nor is able to consume the minimum cereal required for healthy living, is far greater than the present cut-off line of 28.3 per cent."

The committee recommended that the percentage of people entitled to BPL status should be drastically revised upward to at least 50 per cent, though the calorie norm of 2400 would demand this figure to be about 80 per cent. The figure of 50 per cent in rural areas would correspond to a calories intake of about 2100 Kcal which would imply that whatever calories were considered minimum for a healthy living in urban areas in 1973-74 would now be needed for healthy living in rural areas in view of general reduction in hard manual work (though it can still be argued that such reduction has been only marginal for the rural poor, and that too confined to prosperous regions). Committee's recommendations of 50 per cent of household living BPL is based on a calorie consumption norms of 2100 for rural areas (irrespective of Planning Commission's norm of 2400 calories), as well as on a minimum cereal consumption of 12.25 kg per month, which is still less than what top two quintiles consume despite their sedentary lifestyle and better access to non-cereal food.[39]

Thus, the issue of poverty estimation is highly complex and involves various aspects relating to diet (in terms of calorie intake per diem), consumption expenditure on more than 200 items arranged in 23 subgroups and last but not the least the income of the household. Apart from various estimates of poverty incidence in India by individual researchers, the following three estimates are available officially.

(i) Planning Commission's estimates, based on Lakdawala Committee's methodology earlier and Tendulkar Committee's methodology currently, are official estimates of poverty incidence in the country. As per these estimates 37.2 per cent of the total population is living below poverty line in 2004-05.

(ii) Various programmes provide many types of assistance to rural poor. Delivery of such assistance is based on the concept of below poverty line. The number of persons living BPL is decided through BPL Census which has certain norms and parameters. N.C. Saxena Committee (2008) constituted by Ministry of Rural Development, GOI, recommended that the percentage of people entitled to BPL status should be drastically revised upwards to at least 50 per cent. This recommendations of 50 per cent is based on a calorie consumption norm of

2100 for rural areas, as well as on a minimum cereal consumption of 12.25 kg per month.

(iii) According to World Bank's estimates 42 per cent of India's population lives on less than US $ 1.25 per day (calculated on the basis of Purchasing Power Parity).

Notes and References

1. Nehru, Jawaharlal (1946) : *The Discoverty of India,* The John Day Company, New York, p. 107.
2. Government of India (1962) : "Perspective of Development : 1961-76 : Implications of Planning for a Minimum Level of Living", reprinted to Srinivasan, T.N. and P.K. Bhardhan (eds.) (1974): *Poverty and Income distribution in India,* Statistical Publishing Society, Calcutta, pp. 9-38.
3. Dandekar, V.M. and N. Rath (1971) : *Poverty in India,* Indian School of Political Economy, Lonavala.
4. Sukhatme, P.V. (1965) : *Feeding Indian Growing Millions,* Asia Publishing House, New York, p. 23.
5. Government of India (1979) : *Report of the Task Force on Projections of Minimum Needs and Effective Consumption Demand,* Perspective Planning Division, Planning Commission, New Delhi.
6. Government of India (1981) : *A Technical Note on the Sixth Plan of India (1980-85)*: Perspective Planning Division, Planning Commission, New Delhi.
7. Goverment of India (1986): *A Technical Note on the Seventh Plan of India (1985-90),* Planning Commission, New Delhi.
8. Minhas, B.S., L.R. Jain and S.D. Tendulkar (1991): "Declining incidence of poverty in the 1980s: Evidence *versus* Aretefacts", *Economic and Political Weekly,* Vol. XXVI, Nos. 27 and 28, pp. 1672-82.
9. Government of India (1996) : Economic Survey, 1995-96, Ministry of Finance, New Delhi, p. 168.
10. Government of India (1993): *Report of the Expert Group on Estimation of Proportion and Number of Poor,* Perspective Planning Division, Planning Commission, New Delhi.
11. http://pib.nic.in/relaase/
12. Government of India (1997) : Ninth Five Year Plan (1997-2002), Planning Commission, New Delhi, Vol. I, pp. 34-35.
13. Government of India (1997) : Ninth Five Year Plan (1997-2002), Planning Commission, New Delhi, Vol. I, pp. 35-38.

14. Minhas, B.S., L.R. Jain and S.D. Tendulkar (1991): "Declining Incidence of Poverty in the 1980s : Evidence *Versus* Artefacts", *Economic and Political Weekly*, Mumbai, pp. 1673-82.
15. Dandekar, V.M. (1992) : "Forty years after independence" in Bimal Jalan (ed.) : The Indian Economy—Problems and Prospects, New Delhi, p. 42.
16. Palmer-Jones, Richard and Kunal Sen (2001) : "On Indian Poverty Puzzles and Statistics of Poverty", *Economic & Political Weekly*, Vol. 36, No. 3, pp. 211-17.
17. Mehta, J. and S. Venkatraman (2000) : Poverty Statistics : Bermicide's Feast, *Economic and Political Weekly*, p. 35.
18. Government of India (2009) : Report of the Expert Group to Review the Methodology—For Estimation of Poverty, Planning Commission, November, p. 4.
19. Government of India (2009) : Report of the Expert Group to Review the Methodology—For Estimation of Poverty, Planning Commission, November, p. 2.
20. Food and Agriculture Organisation (2008) : The State of Food Insecurity in the World, FAO, Rome.
21. Government of India (2009), *op. cit.*, p. 14.
22. http://planningcommission.gov.in/eg_poverty
23. Datta, Gaurav (1999) : "Has Poverty Declined Since Economic Reforms", *Economic and Plitical Weekly*, Dec., p. 3517.
24. Hinan, T.H. (2006) : "Poverty in India : Has World Bank Goofed up?", Rediffnews.
25. Ojha, P.D. (1986) : "A configuration of Indian Poverty—Inequality and Levels of Living", In. P.D. Ojha (ed.) Challanges of Poverty in India, p. 40.
26. Dandekar, V.M. and Neelkanth Rath (1971) : "Poverty in India", *Economic and Political Weekly*, Vol. 6, Nos. 1 and 2, Jan. 2 and 9.
27. Minhas, B.S. (1988) : "Validation of Large Scale Sample Survey Data—Case of NSS Estimates of Household Consumption Expenditure", Sankhya A, Series B, Vol. 50, Part 3, Supplement, pp. 1-63.
28. Quoted by Datta and Sandaram, *op. cit.*, p. 326.
29. Ahluwalia, Montek Singh (1977); "Rural Poverty and Agricultural Performance in India", *The Journal of Development Studies*, p. 319.
30. Government of India (1978) : *Report of Seventh Finance Commission*, Ministry of Finance, New Delhi, pp. 56-72.
31. Gupta, S.P. (1999) : "Trickle Down Theory Revisited : Role of Employment and Poverty", V.B. Singh Memorial Lecture, 41st Annual Conference of the Indian Labour Economics, IGIDR, Mumbai, November 18-20.

32. Sundaram, K. and Suresh, D. Tendulkar (2003) : "Poverty has declined in the 1990s : A Resolution of Comparability Problems in NSSS Consumer Expenditure Data", *Economic and Political Weekly*, Mumbai, Jan. 25, pp. 327-37.

33. Stiglitz, Joseph (2002) : Globalisation and its Discountents, London, p. 20.

34. Rao, S.L. and Shukla, Rajesh (2006) : "Er....... Just How Poor is India", September 04, Rediff News.

35. Government of India (2009) : "Report of Expert Group on the Methodology for the BPL Census—2009", Ministry of Rural Development, p. 4.

36. Deaton and Dreze (2008) : *Nutrition in India : Facts and Interpretations*, Princeton University.

37. Goverment of India (2009) : Report of Expert Group on the Methodology for the BPL Census, *op. cit.*

38. Sen, Pranab (2005) : Of Calories and Things : Reflections on Nutritional Norms, Poverty Lines and Consumption Behaviour in India, *Economic and Political Weekly*, Mumbai, 22 Oct., p. 4611.

39. Govt. of India (2009) : *op. cit.*, p. 10.

CHAPTER

5

GDP Growth and Poverty Reduction

- Trends in GDP Growth since 1970-71
- Policies for Pro-Poor Growth
- Growth and Poverty in India : Myth and Reality
- Regional Dimensions of Growth, Poverty and Inequality in India
- Changing Face of Poverty in India

CHAPTER

5

GDP Growth and Poverty Reduction

Growth of the economy at a rapid pace is fundamental for the alleviation of poverty of the masses as well as for overall development of the country. High growth rate of Gross Domestic Product results into improvement of the quality of life of the people. It reflects in the higher value of Human Development Index (HDI) that translates into a developed economy.

India's development strategy, like that of most other developing countries, has evolved over successive plan periods, reflecting the growing strength of its economy, structural transformation taking place in the domestic economy and also developments in the world economy. In the early stages of development, planning, government was viewed as the principal actor in development exercising strict control over private investment and ensuring a dominant role for the public sector in all important sectors of the economy. Import substitution was the main plank of development strategy through inward looking trade policy with a tight control over imports under high tariff regime. The limitations of this strategy became evident by the end of 1970s and early 1980s when it became clear that these policies reduced efficiency and competitiveness and growth was much lower than targeted.[1]

At her independence in 1947, India was already a country with a fair degree of industrialisation under her belt. Textiles and steel were among the many industries that had come up exclusively from market forces and with domestic investment, under a colonial government that certainly had not seen itself as a developmental agency and had therefore, virtually abstained from 'infant industry' protection or promotion. India also enjoyed the presence of an active entrepreneurial class and a modest but definite integration into the world economy. The country was also endowed with a first rate civil services and administrative structure, world class leaders, a democratic form of government with a definite commitment to create a welfare state within a short span of time through economic planning.

But the poverty too was immense, with corresponding standards of living appalling for many, the other parameters of social developments such as illiteracy, IMR, MMR, death rates were abysmal. Although no official data was available regarding the incidence of poverty in the country, but nearly two-third population was living in poverty and at least a quarter of them in destitution.[2]

The key strategy that defined resulting developmental effort was the decision to target efforts at accelerating the growth rate. Given the intensity of poverty, the potential of simple redistribution was considered to be both negligible in its immediate impact and of little sustained value. The central anti-poverty strategy had therefore to be the creation of increasing number of jobs that would draw even more of the underemployment and unemployment into gainful employment. That would yield them both greater incomes and higher standards of living. Accelerated growth was thus regarded as an instrumental variable, a policy outcome that would in turn reduce poverty.

The early strategy of Indian planning was based on the premise that the higher growth will automatically kill poverty through 'trickle-down' effect. For many it was a passive and conservative thought. But these criticisms could not force the government to change her strategy till the end of 1980s.

The growth pattern of 1950s, 1960s, 1970s and 1980s can be summarised as the following:[3]

India had started out in 1950s with :

- High growth rates
- Openness to trade and investment
- A promotional state
- Social expenditure awareness
- Confidence that poverty would be seriously dented by growth
- Macro stability
- Optimism, and hence
- Admiration of the world.

But India ended the 1980s with :

- Low growth rates*
- Closure to trade and investment
- A licence-obsessed, restrictive state
- Inability to sustain social expenditure
- Loss of confidence in the efficacy of growth in reducing poverty
- Macro instability, induced crises
- Pessimism, and therefore
- Marginalistion of India from world affairs.

TRENDS IN GDP GROWTH SINCE 1970-71

The analysis of GDP data highlights important structural changes during the period 1950-51 to 2007-08. Fluctuations in

* The 1980s witnessed higher growth than the "Hindu Growth Rate" of 3.00 to 3.5 per cent during the preceding two decades but, as has been discussed by many, the higher growth of 1980s was based on excess internal spending and both internal and external borrowing, and hence was clearly unsustainable. In fact, it led directly to the huge external crises of 1990-91.

real growth from year to year are common to Indian economy (Table 5.1). Annual fluctuations in GDP growth have been a common phenomenon during the entire period of planned development. Thus, while the standard deviation for the entire period from its trend rate is 3.17, however, it was 2.63 in the first decade, rose to 3.78 in the second decade and touched 4.11 in the third decade. While there was one year of negative growth rate during the first and second decade, there were two negative growth rate years during the third decade. The fluctuations during the first decade ranged between (-)1.4 to 7.7 per cent; during the second decade from (-)3.4 to 8.3 per cent and during the third decade from (-)0.3 to 9.2 per cent.

Indian economy took a positive turn in the early 1970s, when the growth rate of GDP surged to 4.8 per cent in Fifth Five Year Plan. It was for the first time since the commencement of Five Year Plans that the actual growth rate was higher, though marginally, than targeted. From the Fifth Plan to Eighth Plan growth rates achieved were consistently

TABLE 5.1
Growth Rate of Indian Economy during Five Year Plans

(*per cent*)

Five Year Plan	*GDP*		*Per capita NNP*
	Target	*Actual*	
First Plan (1951-56)	3.6	2.1	2.6
Second Plan (1956-61)	4.5	4.5	2.0
Third Plan (1961-66)	2.8	5.6	0.4
Fourth Plan (1969-74)	3.3	5.7	0.8
Fifth Plan (1974-79)	4.4	4.8	2.6
Sixth Plan (1980-85)	5.2	5.7	3.1
Seventh Plan (1985-90)	5.0	6.0	3.3
Eighth Plan (1992-97)	5.6	6.8	4.5
Ninth Plan (1997-2002)	6.5	5.3	3.3
Tenth Plan (2002-07)	7.9	7.7	6.1

Source : *Economic Survey*, 2008-09.

CHART 5.1
Growth Rate of GDP and Per Capita NNP

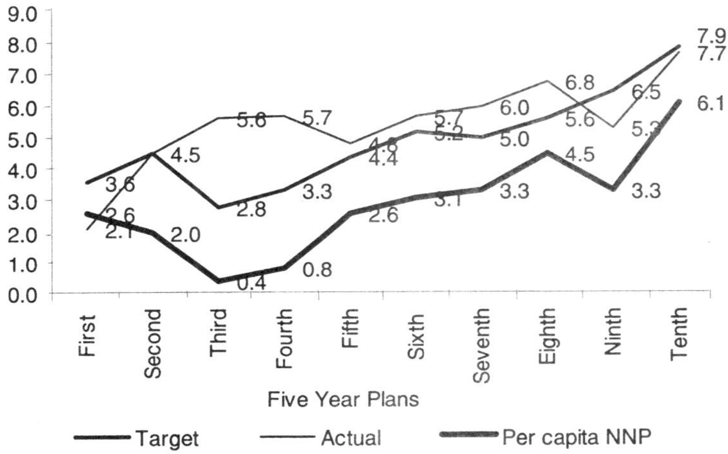

higher than those targeted. This trend had been broken with a shortfall in the actual *versus* targeted growth in Ninth Plan. The GDP of the Economy rose to all time high at 7.7 per cent growth rate during Tenth Five Year Plan against the targeted growth rate of 7.9 per cent (Table 5.1 and Chart 5.1).

Indian economy took almost 'U' turn during 1980s when the annual average growth rate of GDP at factor cost jumped to 5.4 per cent from 3.17 per cent during 1970s. Not even this the standard deviation during 1980s declined to 2.1 from 4.11 during 1970s. Growth momentum continued during 1990s with 5.6 per cent annual average growth rate and a further decline in standard deviation to 1.9 level. Indian economy witnessed 7.69 per cent growth rate during the first decade of new millennium (Table 5.2).

Table 5.2 presents the decadal growth rates observed by different sectors of the economy alongwith those of GDP at factor cost. An examination of these shows that the decadal variations are very specific to agriculture, forestry and fishing, mining and quarrying (Primary) sector. A higher coefficient of variation in this sector confirms the conclusion. Agriculture sector of the Indian economy is highly volatile because of its

TABLE 5.2
Average Decadal Growth Rates, Dispersion in Growth Rates in Real GDP at Factor Cost at 1999-2000 Prices

Decade	*Measurement of dispersion*	*Agriculture, forestry, fishing, mining, etc.*	*Mfg., constrn., elect., gas and water supply*	*Trade, hotels, transport, commn., etc.*	*Financing, insurance, real estates, etc.*	*Public Admn. and Defence*	*Gross domestic product at factor cost*
(1)	*(2)*	*(3)*	*(4)*	*(5)*	*(6)*	*(7)*	*(8)*
1950s	Average*	3.19	6.31	5.39	2.97	3.65	3.93
	S.D.**	4.14	3.99	1.96	1.00	0.80	2.63
	C.V.***	129.79	63.18	36.43	33.77	21.86	67.04
1960s	Average	2.58	5.61	5.01	3.43	5.3	3.78
	S.D.	6.44	2.62	1.59	0.90	1.09	3.28
	C.V.	249.44	46.66	31.65	26.27	20.53	86.79
1970s	Average	1.95	3.96	4.86	4.09	3.98	3.17
	S.D.	8.03	3.67	2.70	2.64	1.32	4.11
	C.V.	16.74	7.64	5.62	5.51	2.76	8.56
1980s	Average	3.83	5.97	5.9	9.09	5.91	5.40
	S.D.	4.97	2.40	0.97	1.72	1.85	2.10
	C.V.	129.85	40.24	16.49	18.96	31.23	38.98

1990s	Average	2.90	5.80	7.70	7.80	6.50	5.60
	S.D.	3.70	3.40	2.70	2.90	3.00	1.90
	C.V.	126.70	60.00	35.40	36.80	46.40	33.70
2000s	Average	3.56	8.34	11.23	9.50	5.69	7.69
	S.D.	4.87	2.93	1.47	2.88	1.31	2.18
	C.V.	5.79	3.49	1.75	3.43	1.56	2.59
1951 and	Average	2.97	5.87	6.44	5.98	5.14	4.78
2008	S.D.	5.61	3.43	2.87	3.41	2.00	3.17
	C.V.	188.87	58.54	44.56	57.09	38.93	66.33

* Average growth rate during decade.
** Standard Deviation in growth rate.
*** Coefficient of variation in growth rate.

Source : GOI (2009), *Economic Survey*, 2008-09; Ministry of Finance.

dependence on monsoon, which has became highly eratic. All the three components of service sector witnessed higher growth rates during 1980s, 1990s and 2000s. The share of service sector in the GDP reached to 55 per cent during 2007-08, while that of primary sector decreased to 17.5 per cent.

As regards to annual average growth rate of per capita NDP at factor cost at constant prices, it remained 2.63 per cent for 1951-52 to 2007-08 with a higher level of fluctuations (3.43 standard deviation and 130.5 coefficient of variation). Annual fluctuations in per capita NDP decreased considerably during 1980s, 1990s and 2000s. Table 5.3 reveals that annual fluctuations in per capita NDP remained higher than in the GNP in almost all the decades.

TABLE 5.3

Decade Variation in Growth Rates of GNP at Factor Cost and Per Capita NDP at Factor Cost (at 1999-2000 Prices)

Decade	*Measurements*	*GNP*	*Per capita NDP*
(1)	*(2)*	*(3)*	*(4)*
1950s	Average	3.93	2.28
	S.D.	2.70	2.89
	C.V.	68.79	126.96
1960s	Average	3.71	1.35
	S.D.	3.51	3.70
	C.V.	94.60	273.78
1970s	Average	3.24	0.70
	S.D.	4.34	4.64
	C.V.	133.84	663.43
1980s	Average	5.24	3.00
	S.D.	2.19	2.42
	C.V.	41.71	80.66
1990s	Average	5.62	3.46
	S.D.	1.92	2.06
	C.V.	34.25	59.64

(1)	(2)	(3)	(4)
2000s	Average	7.81	6.00
	S.D.	2.15	2.36
	C.V.	27.52	39.36
1951-2007	Average	10.36	22.31
	S.D.	21.60	94.42
	C.V.	208.53	423.17

Source : Based on National Account Statistics Data, CSO, 2008-09.

POLICIES FOR PRO-POOR GROWTH

In macro-economic terms economic growth has a positive impact on the reduction of poverty. Economic reforms in India over recent decades has spurred economic growth and contributed to a decline in poverty. Annual per capita income grew from less than 1 per cent during seventies to more than 6 per cent during the first decade of millennium. This implies about more than one-third increase in consumption per capita over the last decade and a 5 to 10 percentage point reduction in national poverty rates, depending on the methodology followed.[4] Empirical studies by Ravillion and Datta (2002, 2006), Tenduklar (2002) and Deaton (2002) highlighted five key statistical regularities that provide an initial basis for evaluating the policy priorities for future pro-poor growth.

(i) Economic growth has been a leading determinant of poverty reduction. Ravallion and Datta (2002 and 2006) reveal an elasticity of (–) 1.2 (regressing the log of the Poverty HCR index against the log of private per capita consumption per capita) by using 23 surveys over 1958-1991 period.[5] Cross country studies on the relationship between growth and poverty reduction provide additional evidence of the key role of growth.[6]

(ii) BIMARU states alongwith Orissa and newly created states Jharkhand (Bihar), Chhattisgarh (MP) and Uttarakhand (U.P.) lagged behind the other major

Chart 5.2
Growth Trend in GNI and Per Capita NDP a Constant Prices

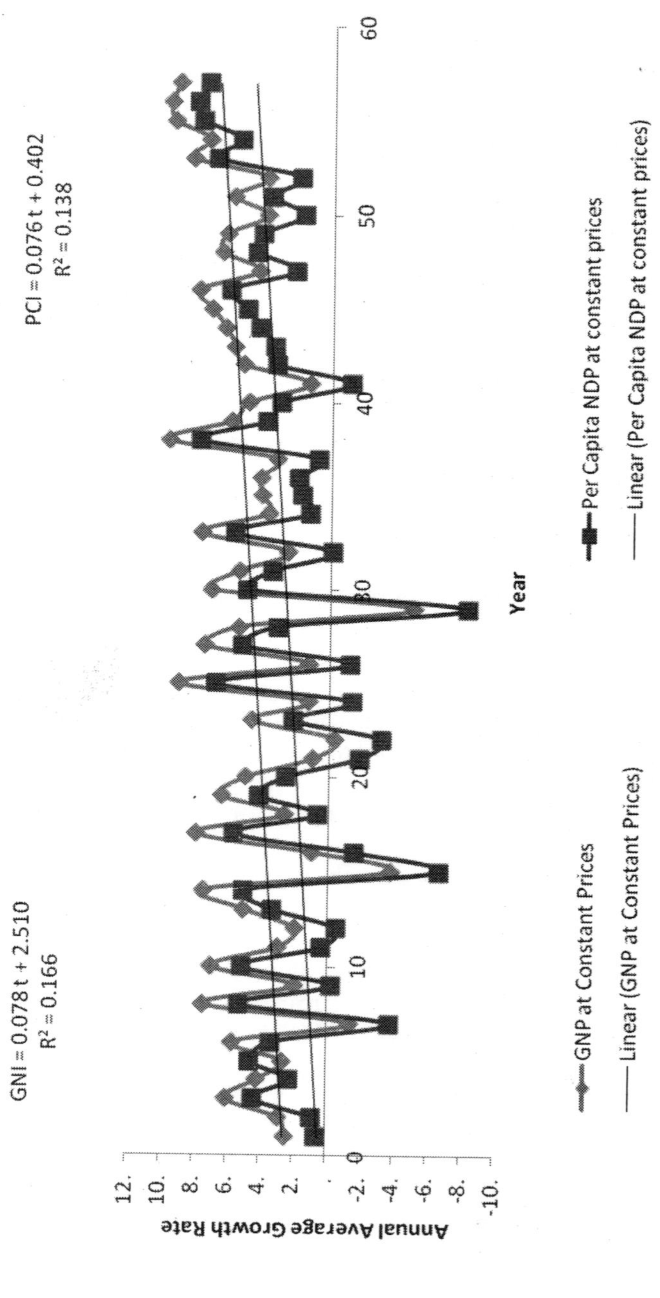

Chart 5.3
Trend of Annual Growth Rate of Real GDP at Factor Cost (at 1999-2000 Price)

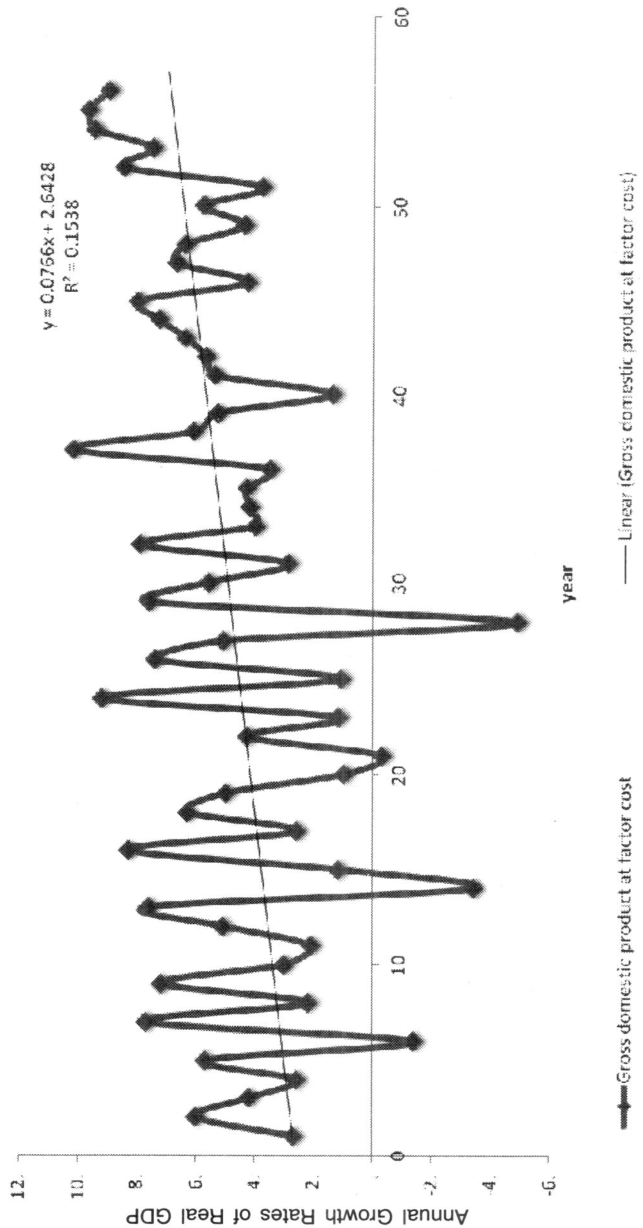

CHART 5.4
Trend in Growth Rates of Agriculture and Allied Sector at Factor Cost (at 1999-2000 Prices)

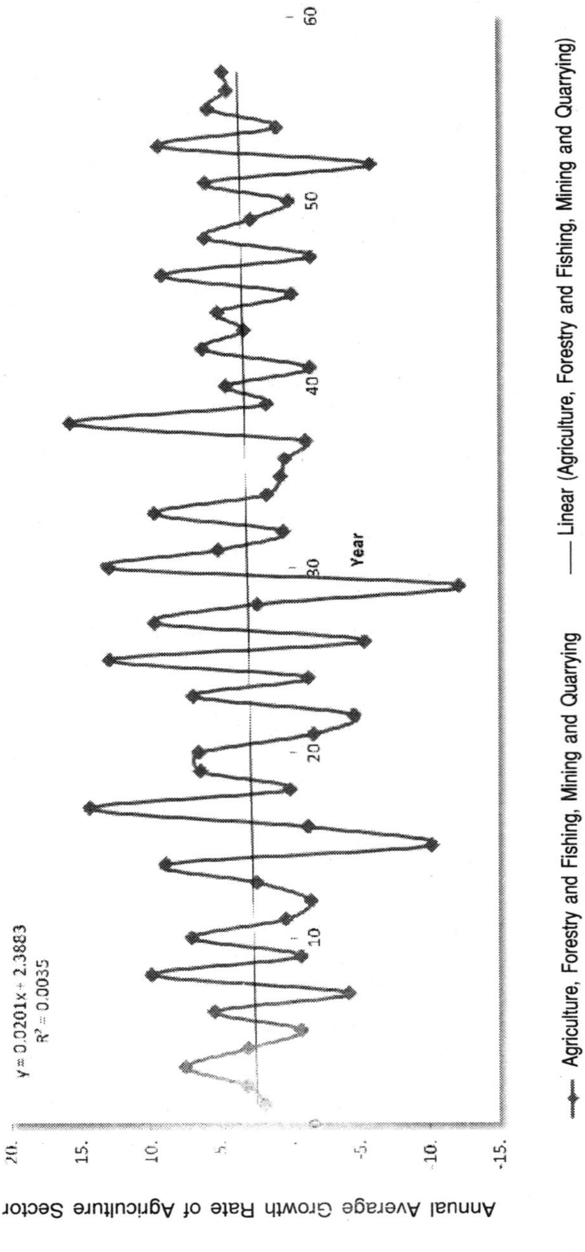

CHART 5.5

Trend in Growth Rate of Manufacturing, Construction, Electricity, Gas and Water Supply at Fator Cost (at 1999-2000 Prices)

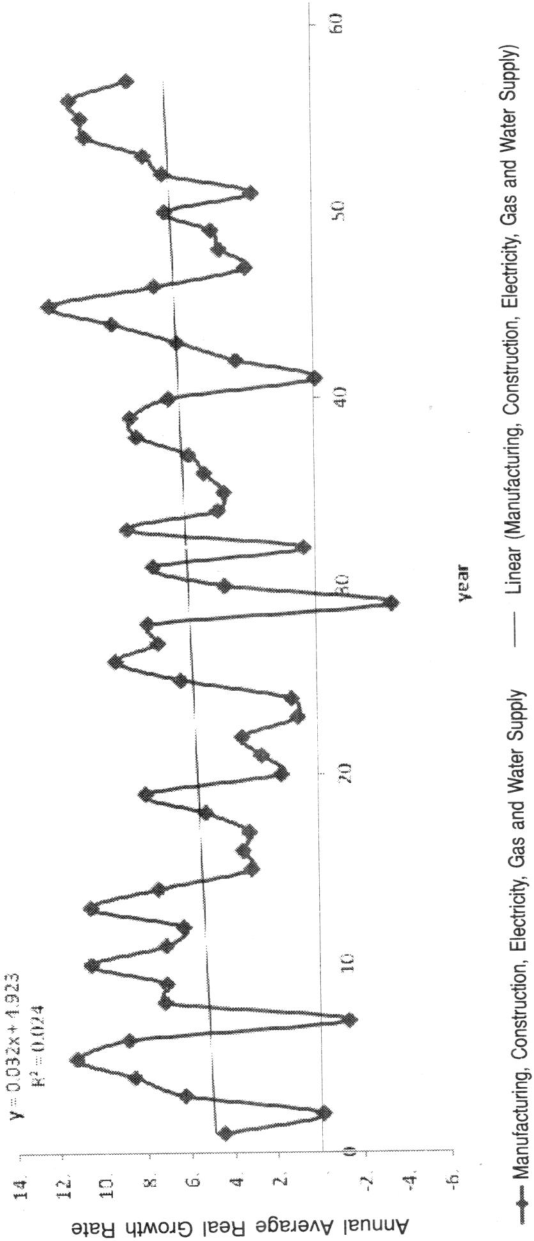

CHART 5.6
Trend in Growth Rate of Manufacturing, Construction, Electricity, Gas and Water Supply at Fator Cost (at 1999-2000 Prices)

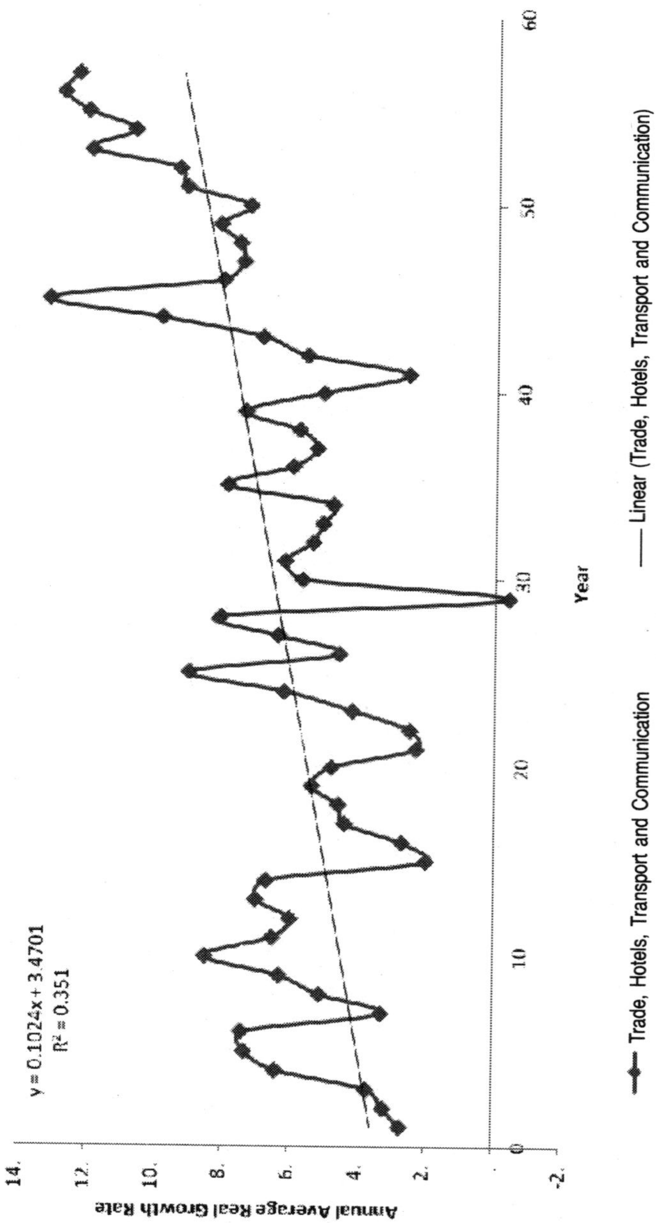

CHART 5.7

Trend in Growth Rate of Financing, Insurance, Real Estate and Business Services at Factor Cost (at 1999-2000 Prices)

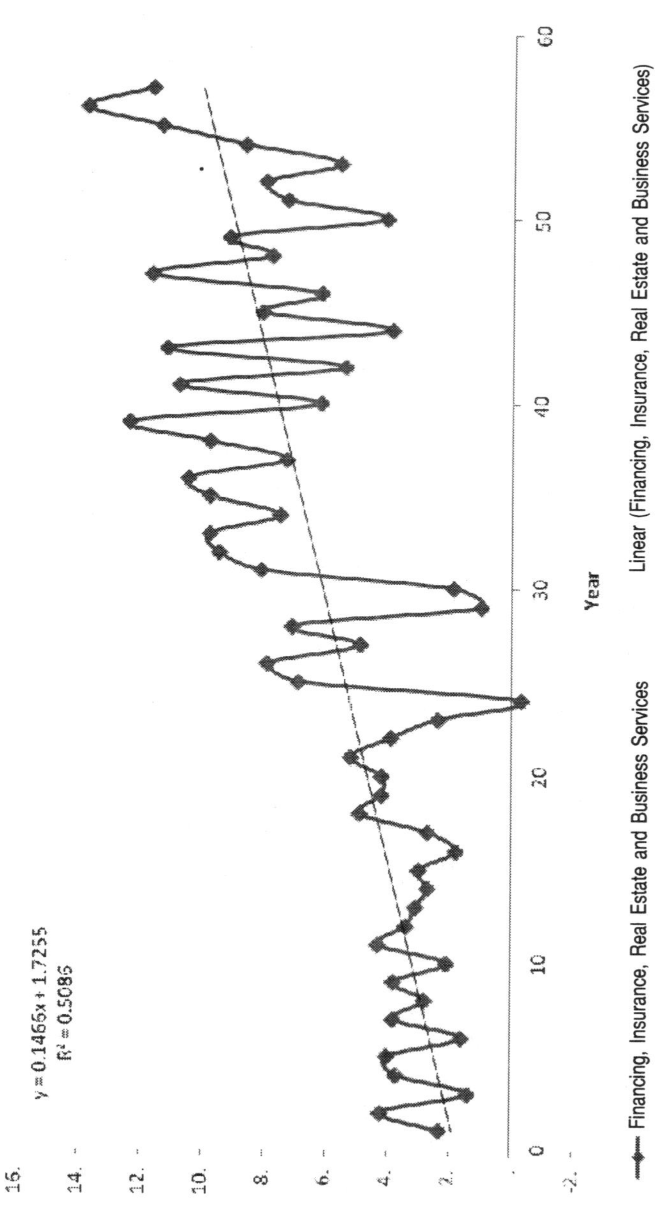

TABLE 5.8

Average Variation in Decadal Growth Rates of GNP at Factor Cost and Per Capita Income

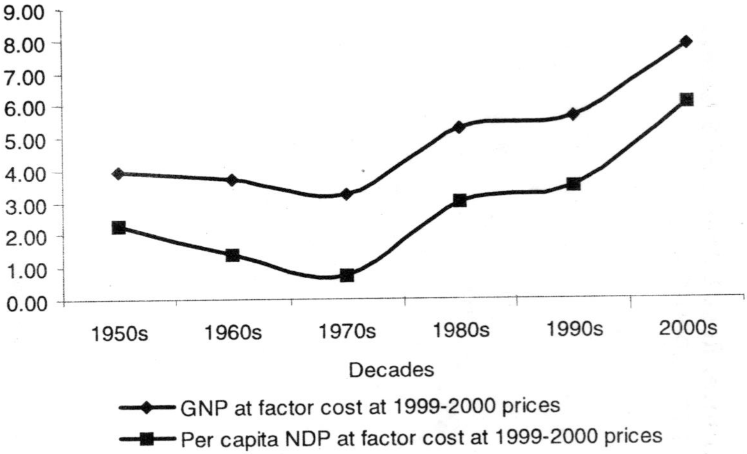

TABLE 5.9

Variation in Standard Deviation of Decadal Growth Rates of GNP at Factor Cost and Per Capita Income

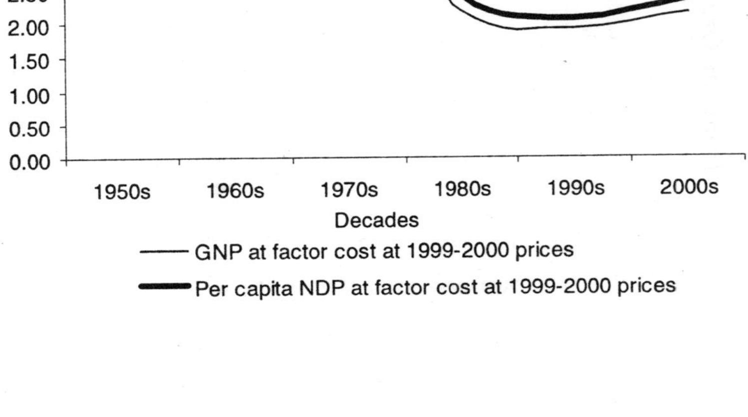

TABLE 5.10
Coefficient Variation of Decadal Growth Rates of GNP at Factor Cost and Per Capita Income

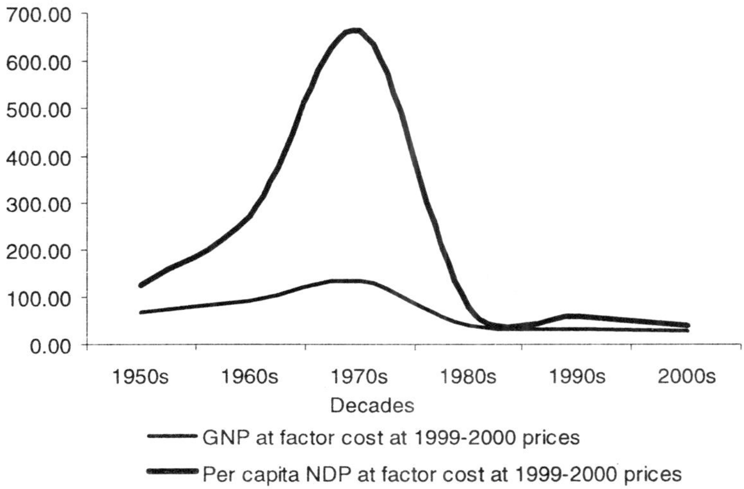

states in lowering poverty incidence. Slow growth in these states could be valid cause of slow progress in poverty reduction in these states.

(iii) The sectoral and urban-rural composition of growth has had an impact on the poverty reducing power of economic growth.[7] Growth in average consumption in rural areas has had a greater impact than growth in urban areas in terms of reducing aggregate poverty incidence.

(iv) Agricultural productivity growth has played a significant role in reducing poverty, directly via higher farm yields to small producers and higher real wages to agricultural labourers.[8]

(v) Non-farm growth has been complementary to agricultural productivity's contribution in poverty reduction. Ravallion and Datta (2001) established that the impact of non-farm growth on poverty reduction had varied strongly across states in India.[9]

However, recent data on growth and poverty at national level as well as regional level, do not confirm the findings (Table 5.4).

TABLE 5.4
Poverty Incidence and Growth of the Indian Economy

Year	Average annual growth rate of real ..... at constant price		Average PCI at constant	Poverty HCR (%)		
	GDP	Per capita NDP	Price*	Rural	Urban	Combined
1973-74	1.73	-0.73	7870	56.44	49.01	54.88
1977-78	4.53	2.43	8639	53.07	45.29	51.32
1983	5.47	3.07	9409	45.65	40.79	44.48
1987-88	6.00	3.57	9978	39.09	38.2	38.86
1993-94	5.83	3.77	12207	37.27 50.10	32.36 31.80	35.97 45.30
1999-00	5.83	3.57	15881	27.09	23.62	26.10
2004-05	6.50	4.87	19331	21.80	21.70	21.8 MRP
				28.30	25.70	27.5 URP
				41.80	25.70	37.2**

* Triennial average for GDP, per capita NDP and per capita income.
** Expert Group (2008) Estimates.
Source : Based on Expert Group for the estimation of poverty (1993).

Table 5.4 reveals that the incidence of poverty at national level has declined from 54.88 per cent in 1973-74 to 21.80 per cent in 2004-05 (Expert Group's 1993 methodology). Ordinary Least Square (OLS) model confirms the observation (Chart 5.11).

In equation form :

$$y_{pov} = -5.649x + 61.65$$
$$R^2 = 0.987$$

Since R^2 in the above model is 0.987 so it is fitted.

TABLE 5.11
Trends in GDP Growth and Poverty HCR (%)

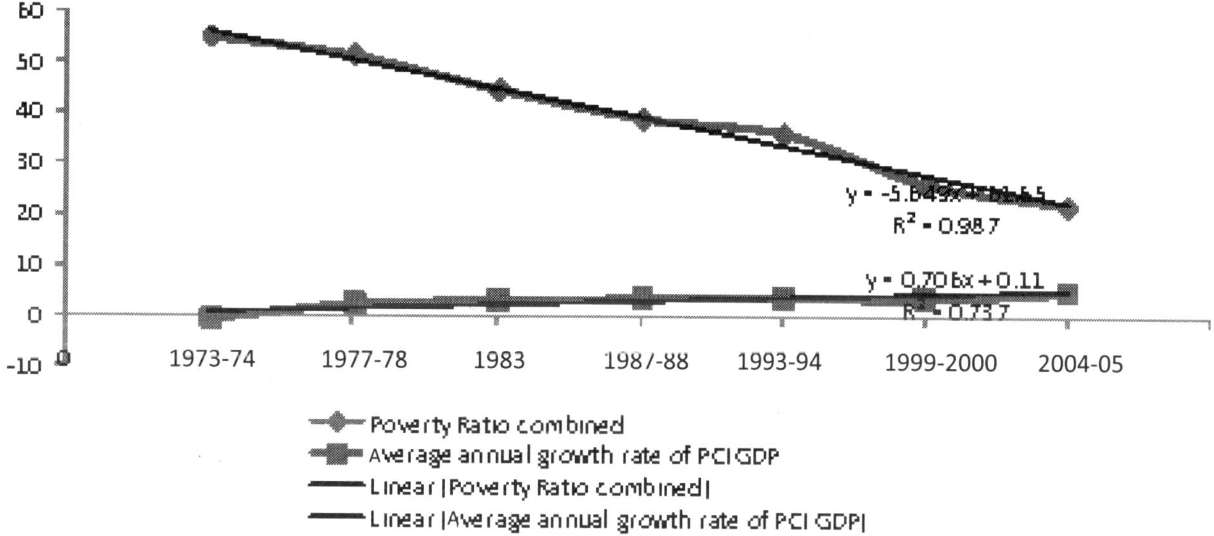

TABLE 5.12

Trends in Growth Rate in Per Capita NDP at Constant Price and Poverty HCR (Old Methodology)

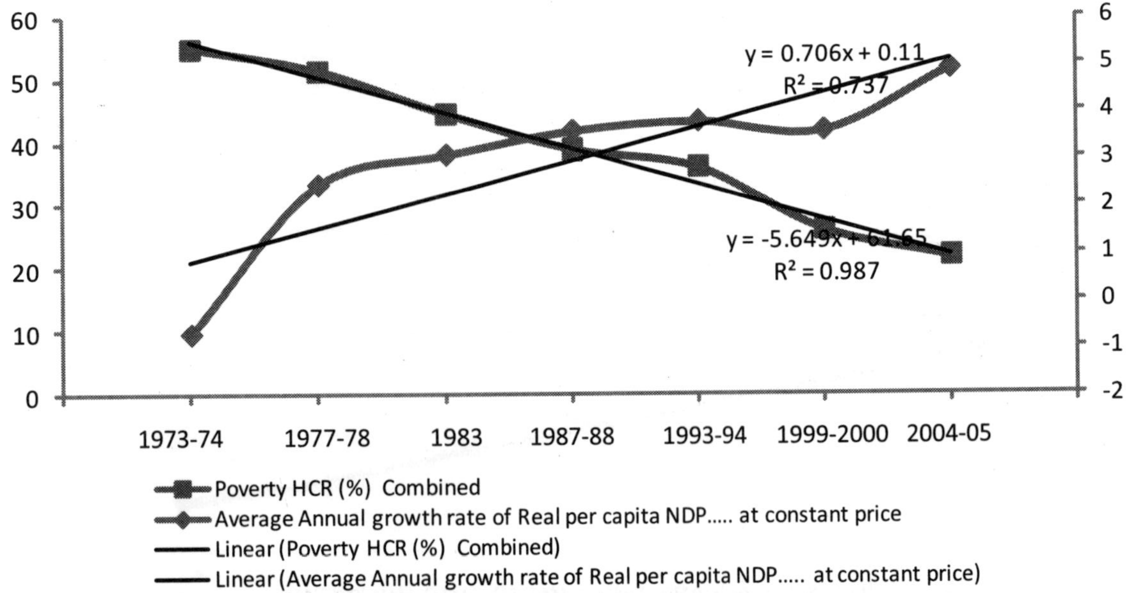

TABLE 5.13
Average Per Capita NDP and Poverty Incidence

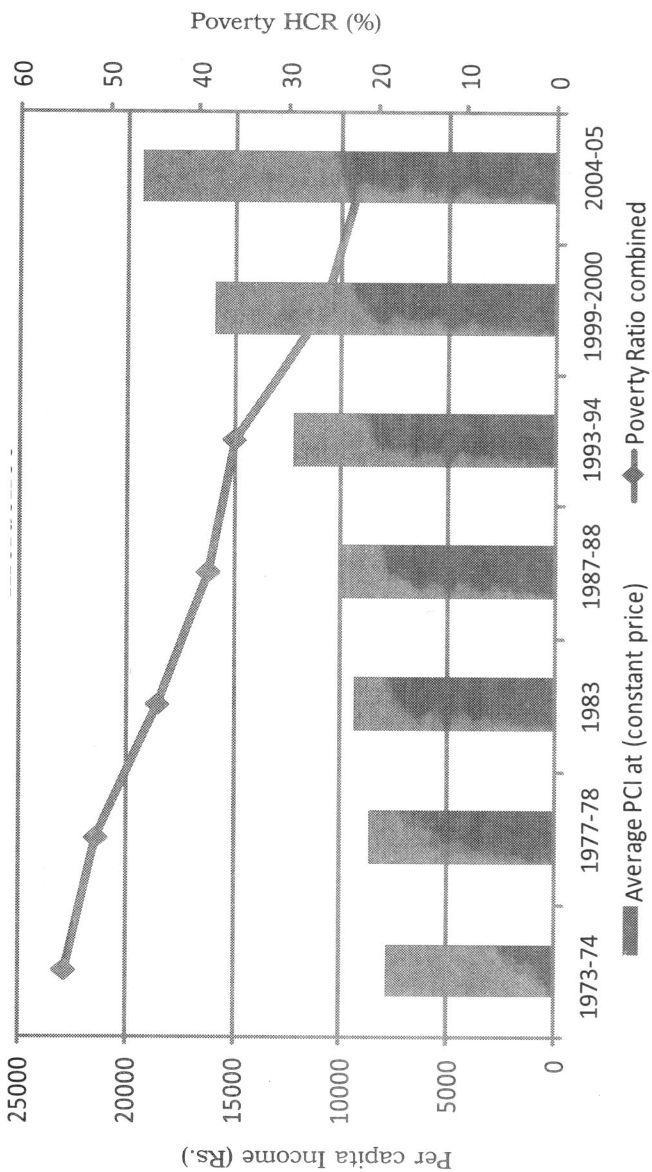

The decline in poverty HCR (%) seems a result of higher growth in GDP and per capita net domestic product for which models are as under :

$$y_{GDP} = 0.616x + 2.66$$
$$R^2 = 0.680$$
$$y_{PCI} = 0.706x + 0.11$$
$$R^2 = 0.737$$

Since R^2 in this case is more than 50 per cent, so the models are fitted.

Coefficient of correlation between real GDP growth and poverty HCR (%) in rural and urban areas and in combined forms are highly negative (Table 5.5) that also confirms hypothesis that higher growth leads to decline in poverty. But the results of Tables 5.4 and 5.5 should be considered cautiously because figures of poverty HCRs for 2004-05 are not strictly comparable with those of 1993-94 and 1999-2000. The poverty estimates in 2004-05 based on URP consumption distribution (27.5 per cent) are comparable with the poverty estimates of 1993-94 (35.97%). The poverty estimates in 2004-05

Table 5.5
Coefficients of Correlation

		With Poverty Incidence		
		Rural	*Urban*	*Combined*
(i)	Average annual growth rate of Real GDP at constant prices (at 1999-2000 prices)	(–)0.795627	(–)0.761729	(–) 0.792684
(ii)	Average annual growth rate of Real per capita real NDP at constant prices (at 1999-2000 prices)	(–) 0.82479	(–) 0.79836	(–) 0.82271
(iii)	Average per capita NDP at constant price (at 1999-2000 prices)	(–) 0.94692	(–) 0.97851	(–) 0.95600

Source : Based on data in Table 5.4.

based on MRP consumption (21.8%) are roughly (but not strictly) comparable with the poverty estimates of 1999-2000 (26.1%). Higher estimates of poverty incidence in 2004-05 by Expert Group (2008) made the whole issue more complicated and it is rather difficult to draw any conclusion, based on poverty data, regarding the exact impact of growth on poverty. However, it is beyond doubt that despite a high growth of real GDP and per capita NDP, more than 40 crore people in India are still living below poverty line.

It is a proven fact that growth is essential for poverty reduction. Experiences of many countries show that they reduced poverty successfully with higher growth rates of national income. But, it is a million dollar question—How can we promote growth in which poor people are able to participate—in other words, pro-poor growth? A strategic policy framework for pro-poor policies can be built upon the twin pillars of improving the investment climate to accelerate growth and empowering poor people to contribute to and benefit from the growth. Investment climate is concerned with the factors that determine the level of current investment, as well as productivity of ongoing investments and the stability of those with returns over the medium-term. The investment climate necessarily involves institutions, rules and governance as well as traditional questions of fiscal policy, public expenditure management and taxation. So far as the eradication of poverty is concerned the role of small and medium sized enterprises is critical. If they grow, it is likely that larger firms will benefit as well.

(i) Macro-economic stability and openness; (ii) Economic governance and institutions, including both implementation of efficiency—enhancing regulation and elimination of regulations that lead to waste and rent-seeking behaviour, and (iii) infrastructure are fundamental for the improvement of climate for investment.

Empowerment is the process that enables people to contribute to and participate in economic growth. Traditional notions of human capital development—notably education and health—are included in this process, as is individuals' ability to influence the public policies that affect them, to build and protect their assets, and to gain access to public and private resources and services.

Macro-stability

RBI's main concern during, 1990s and 2000s has been to keep the inflation and exchange rate of rupee under control. India has made great progress in establishing more stable and positive macro-economic performance during 1990s.[10] Even during the historical global economic crises of 2008 Indian economy has shown the signs of macro-stability. It is to be noted here that macro-economic instability, and in particular high inflation, reduces growth.[11] India has done relatively well in this regards with inflation averaging about 4 per cent over the past two decades with three peak episodes of higher inflation in 1981, 1991 and 2008. Over the nine year span, 2000-01 to 2008-09, inflation remained below 7 per cent except for two breaches. The first breach was in the second half of 2004-05, when the prices of crude oil per barrel rose from US $ 38 in 2004 to US $ 54 in 2005, coupled with an erratic, delayed and uneven spatially spread monsoon. The second breach began from March 2008, prior to the onset of fiscal year. Inflation, which was rising but was in single digit up to end May 2008, reached double digits from June to mid-October, with the price of crude oil touching US $ 147 in July 2008. On both the occasions, inflation in the domestic economy was largely due to developments in the global economy, with the prime movers being the spurt in the prices of crude oil, minerals and metal related products, testifying to the growing connectivity between the domestic and the world economies. In other periods, inflationary pressure were contained below 7 per cent, facilitated not only by the liberalised domestic and foregin trade, which served to foster greater competition, but also due to the reduction and rationalisation of the tax structure, which gave a fillip to cost efficiency.[12]

Indian economy faced a peculier dilema during the last quarter of 2008-09 and in subsequent period of 2008-09, 2009-10 and also 2010-11 when the prices of essential commodities, especially, the primary articles such as cereals, pulses, sugar vegetables and fruits, increased many fold despite a general decline in WPI based inflation. It hurts the poor badly and has made their life difficult.

Trade

Trade is an engine of growth : A lesson of development experience is that rapid overall economic growth depends on rapid export growth. A number of studies, most recently Frankel and Romer (1999);[13] Dollar and Kraay (2001)[14] and World Bank (2002)[15] established that openness to trade and foreign direct investment accelerated growth. Liberalised trade policies, abolition of all types of quantitative restrictions on import, reduced tarriffs spurted the growth of exports that contributed positively in the overall growth of the economy.

The average annual growth rate of exports during 2003-04 to 2007-08 was 25.3 per cent. Export rose from 11.1 per cent of GDP in 2003-04 to 14.1 per cent in 2007-08 and 15.2 per cent in 2008-09 (April-December). Imports, however, grew even faster at an annual average rate of 32.3 per cent during 2003-04 to 2007-08. As a proportion of GDP, imports were 22.00 per cent of GDP in 2007-08 while exports were at 14.2 per cent. Thus, trade deficit widened to 7.8 per cent of GDP in 2007-08.[16]

The surplus in current account, higher capital inflow, and all time high foreign exchange reserves during 2001-02 to 2003-

TABLE 5.6

Foreign Direct Investment : India and Selected Countries

(US $ million)

Year	*India*	*China*	*Malaysia*	*Philippines*	*Thialand*	*Brazil*
1995	2144	35849	4178	1478	2068	4859
1996	2426	40180	5078	1517	2336	11200
1997	3577	44237	5137	1222	3895	19650
1998	2635	43751	2163	2287	7315	31913
1999	2169	38753	3895	573	6213	28576
2000	2315	38399	3788	2029	3366	32779
2006	20336	72715	6060	2921	9460	18822
2007	25127	83521	8401	2916	11238	34585
2008	41554	108312	8053	1520	10091	45058

Source : IMF International Finance Statistics.

04 were the result of liberalised policies. Annual average surplus on current account was 1.4 per cent of GDP during 2001-03, it was because of higher capital inflow.

Foreign Direct Investment is considered to be the most attractive type of capital flow for emerging economies as it is expected to bring latest technology and enhance production capabilities of the economy.

In terms of UNCTAD Survey 2008-10, China is the most preferred investment destination followed by India, US, the Russian Federation and Brazil. While China's export led growth strategy has been based on core policy and economic management decisions that invited foreign investors to provide the capital and expertise to achieve export competetiveness in a wide range of sectors. India's policies towards FDI, are still more ambivalent. On the one hand, the government took all possible policy measures to attract FDI, on the other it maintained significant regulations against full foreign ownership, or insisted on lengthy approval process.

Infrastructure

Highly developed infrastructure—power, road, rail and ports—certainly plays key role in the growth of the economy. India's northern states, where poverty reduction and growth have been lowest, suffered from shortfalls in every infrastructure dimension. This is especially true in rural areas, where water, power, and roads are generally provided without cost or at least with a heavy subsidy, and as a result are in poor shape.

Human Capital Development

Education, health and social 'safety net' programmes—cuts across both the pillars of investment climate and empowerment. Education and health are core factors of human capital development. These not only enhance the capabilities of work force, but also help them to empower themselves to lead a dignified life. In India, states are responsible for much of the delivery of these services, creating a natural experiment for measuring the impact of these policies in affecting pro-poor growth. Ravallion and Datt (2001) had demonstrated that states with lower literacy and poor health status in India have experienced a lower impact on poverty reduction per percentage point in non-farm output.[17]

Government of India, alongwith governments of States, took various measures for the improvement in literacy, health and well being of the people. Following specific programmes were initiated in persuance of policy of universalisation of education :

- Operation Black Board
- Sarva Shiksha Abhiyan
- National Programme for Education of Girls at Elementary Education
- National Programmes of Mid-day Meals in schools
- Kasturba Gandhi Balika Vidyalaya (July 2009)
- Education as a fundamental right (2002)
- Right to Education Act 2009

Likewise, programmes such as National Rural Health Mission and Strenghtening of primary health infra-structure and improving service delivery, Janani Suraksha, Pradhan Mentri Swasthya Surakha Yojana alongwith several national diseases control/eradication programmes have been started to improve the health status of the people. Improvement in health status can be seen in Table 5.7. There has been improvement in the quality of health care over the years, but much more needs to be done.

Apart from these two important segments of social sector, Public Distribution System, Integrated Child Development Services, National Social Assistance Programme (National Old Age Pension Scheme, National Family Benefit Scheme and National Maternity Benefit Scheme), Annapurna Yojna, etc. have been started to provide safety net to the poor. Mahatma Gandhi National Rural Employment Guaranty Scheme (MGNREGA) is a milestone in this direction. MGNREGA provide guaranteed employment for 100 days in a year to poor families in rural areas.

TABLE 5.7
Selected Health Indicators of India

Parameters	*1981*	*1991*	*Current Year*	*Level*
Crude Birth Rate	33.9	29.5	2007	23.1
Crude Death Rate	12.5	9.8	2007	7.4
Total Fertility Rate	4.5	3.6	2006	2.8
Maternal Mortality Rate	NA	NA	2001-04	254
Infant Mortality Rate	110	80	2007	55
Child (0-4) Mortality Rate	41.2	26.5	2006	17
Life Expectancy at Birth (Male)	1981-84 55.4	1989-93 59.0	2002-06	62.6
Life Expectancy at Birth (Female)	1981-85 55.7	1989-93 59.7	2002-06	64.7

Source : GOI (2009) Economic Survey, 2008-09, p. 273.

GROWTH AND POVERTY IN INDIA : MYTH AND REALITY

Indian economy has grown at an average rate of 6.5 per cent during the last twenty years. In per capita terms, income growth has accelerated from the Hindu rate of less than 1 per cent prior to the 1980s, to 3.7 per cent per annum since 1980-81.

In more specific terms the growth rate of GDP has reached to 9 per cent plus level during 2005-06 to 2007-08. Even during the era of historic global recession in 2008-09 Indian economy grew by an impressive rate of 6.7 per cent in comparison to negative growth rates in many developed countries. These achievements present a rosy picture of Indian economy.

However, the acceptance is considerably different on the flip side of growth, poverty levels and changes in the levels of poverty. The definitional aspect in itself is a complicated issue. The accepted and official, definition of poverty in India, based on the recommended methodology of Expert Group (1993)—

consumption of goods worth Rs. 49 (per capita per month) in the rural areas and Rs. 57 in urban areas according to 1993-94 prices—has been rejected by another Expert Group (2009) appointed by Planning Commission under the Chairmanship of Prof. S.D. Tendulkar, Ex-Chairman of Prime Minister's Advisory Council. As per the recommendations of Tendulkar Committee the all India rural poverty head count ratio is 41.8 per cent in 2004-05 (at 2004-05 prices) in comparison to 28.3 per cent (at 1993-94 prices) of old methodology. By this excercise, poverty at all India level in 1993-94 was 50.1 per cent in rural areas, 31.8 per cent in urban areas and 45.3 per cent in the country as a whole as compared to the 1993-94 official estimates of 37.2 per cent rural, 32.6 per cent urban and 36.0 per cent combined. Expert group claims that, even though the suggested new methodology gives a higher estimate of rural headcount ratio at the all India level for 2004-05, the extent of poverty reduction in comparable percentage point decline between 1993-94 and 2004-05 is not different from that inferred using the old methodology (Table 5.8).

TABLE 5.8
Reduction in Poverty Incidence between 1993-94 to 2004-05

	Old Methodology			*New Methodology*		
	1993-94	*2004-05*	*Reduction*	*1993-94*	*2004-05*	*Reduction*
Rural	37.3	28.3	5.0	50.1	41.8	8.3
Urban	32.4	25.7	6.7	31.8	25.7	6.1
Combined	26.0	27.5	8.5	45.3	37.2	8.1

Source : Planning Commission, GOI, New Delhi.

As per the estimates of new methodology the reduction in poverty incidence in rural areas is 8.3 percentage point as compared to 5.0 percentage point according to old methodology. But the reduction levels in urban areas and country as a whole are almost the same in both the methodology. But the reduction levels in poverty incidence in different states is highly skewed (Table 5.9).

TABLE 5.9
Reduction in Poverty Incidence in Selected States between 1993-94 and 2004-05 as per New Methodology

(Percentage point decline)

State	*Rural*			*Urban*			*Combind*		
	1993-94	*2004-05*	*Poverty reduction*	*1993-94*	*2004-05*	*Poverty reduction*	*1993-94*	*2004-05*	*Poverty reduction*
(1)	*(2)*	*(3)*	*(4)*	*(5)*	*(6)*	*(7)*	*(8)*	*(9)*	*(10)*
Andhra Pradesh	48.1	32.3	15.8	35.2	23.4	11.8	44.6	29.9	14.7
Assam	54.9	36.4	18.5	27.7	21.8	5.9	51.8	34.4	17.4
Bihar	62.3	55.7	6.6	44.7	43.7	1.0	60.5	54.4	6.1
Gujarat	43.1	39.1	4.0	28.0	20.1	7.9	37.8	31.8	6.0
Haryana	40.0	24.8	15.2	24.2	22.4	1.8	35.9	24.1	11.8
Himachal Pradesh	36.7	25.0	11.7	13.6	4.6	9.0	34.6	22.9	11.7
J&K	32.5	14.1	18.4	6.9	10.4	-3.5	26.3	13.2	13.1
Karnataka	56.6	37.5	19.1	34.2	25.9	8.3	49.5	33.4	16.1
Kerela	33.9	20.2	13.7	23.9	18.4	5.5	31.3	19.7	11.6
Madhya Pradesh	49.0	53.6	-4.6	31.8	35.1	-3.3	44.6	48.6	-4.0

Maharashtra	59.3	47.9	11.4	30.3	25.6	4.7	47.8	38.1	9.7
Orissa	63.0	60.8	2.2	34.5	37.6	-3.1	59.1	57.2	1.9
Punjab	20.3	22.1	-1.8	27.2	18.7	8.5	22.4	20.9	1.5
Rajasthan	40.8	35.8	5.0	29.9	29.7	0.2	38.3	34.4	3.9
Tamil Nadu	51.0	37.5	13.5	33.7	19.7	14.0	44.6	28.9	15.7
Uttar Pradesh	50.9	42.7	8.2	38.3	34.1	4.2	48.4	40.9	7.5
West Bengal	42.5	38.2	4.3	31.2	24.4	6.8	39.4	34.3	5.1

Note : Negative sign in poverty reduction columns shows that poverty incidence in these states increased during 2004-05 in comparison to 1993-94.

Source : Planning Commission (2009) as per report of Expert Group to Review the Methodology for estimation of poverty.

CHART 5.14
Percentage Point Reduction in Poverty HCR between 1993-94 to 2004-05

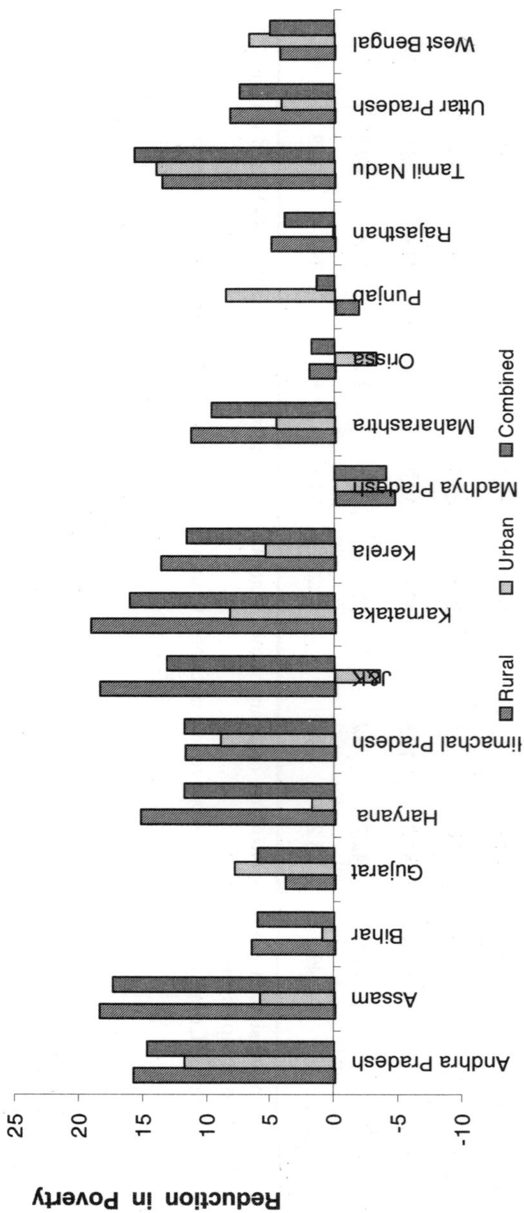

Another Expert group under the Chairmanship of N.C. Saxena (Ministry of Rural Development, GOI) has pegged up poverty line to 50 per cent for the purpose of Below Poverty Line Census 2009. World Bank's recent estimates states that 42 per cent of Indian population is living below new poverty line of US $ 1.25 per day income. Thus, there is no dearth of data on poverty and income levels of Indian households.

Yet there is a raging controversy about whether poverty levels in India have increased in the 1990s and post 1990s, a period coincident with the ushering in of macro-economic reforms. India, containing the largest number of poor in the world, is an obvious test case for whether economic liberalisation work, whether economic reforms have a human face etc.

Prof. Surjit S. Bhalla, came across a bizarre situation presented by NSS data. As per Planning Commission's estimates, based on NSS data, absolute poverty in India declined from 54 per cent in 1973-74 to 43 per cent in 1983-84 and further declined to 36 per cent in 1993-94. However, for 1998, poverty was reported to have increased by about 6 percentage points to around 42 per cent inspite of per capita consumption and income having grown by about 4.5 per cent per annum or about 20 per cent during the 4-year intervening period.

Prof. Bhalla questioned the 'findings' of NSS on the ground of spurt in growth during 1980s and onward. Indian economy grew by an average rate of 5.5 per cent during 1980s, 6 per cent during 1990s and 7.56 per cent during post 1990s. What is more relevant for the measurement of poverty point is the growth in per capita income (and/or consumption). Per capita income growth has gone up from 3.6 per cent in 1980s to 4.2 per cent in the 1990s and further to 5.5 per cent in post-1990s years. Thus, collecting the NSS data and National Account statistics, one is confronted with a bizarre situation of accelerated growth, higher per capita income and an increase in absolute poverty to levels observed in the early 1980s.[18]

Datta (1999), Dubey and Gangopadhyay (1998), Deaton and Tarozzi (1999) also did not indicate a wide acceptane of NSS data and the whole process of estimation of poverty incidence in India. Moreover, different set of estimation of poverty line and number of poverty headcount has made the whole issue more complex and complicated.

REGIONAL DIMENSIONS OF GROWTH, POVERTY AND INEQUALITY IN INDIA

Although the Indian economy have experienced higher order of growth since 1980-81, regional dimensions in GDP and per capita income are highly skewed. Disparity in regional economic growth, incidence of poverty and inequality are important issues for debate and analysis across the states.

Inter-regional disparities in India is a common phenomenon ever since India achieved independence. The draft plan of Eleventh Five Year Plan states "a widespread perception all over the country is that disparities among states, and regions within the states, between urban and rural areas, and between various sections of the community, have been steadily increasing in the past few years and that the gains of rapid growth witnessed in this period have not reached all parts of the country and all sections of the people in an equitable manner."[19] Thus, it is a proven fact that the forces of divergence have increased the inter-state as well as intra-state disparities even in a better growth environment in the Indian Economy. The Eleventh Plan document further states that "there is some evidence to indicate a movement towards convergence on human development indicators across the states, one of the reasons for this convergence could also be that most of the human development indicators have a value cap.[20] Process of economic liberalisation has resulted into higher growth of the economy, but the pattern of growth is not evenly distributed. Ahluwalia (2000)[21] and Rao *et. al.* (1999)[22] established in their studies that the divergence in growth performances across the states has increased, especially since 1991, during the era of market oriented policies. Mehta and Kumar (2009) have shown in their studies that there is a tendency of showing an increase in the dispersion of per capita NSDP across the states in the reform period.[23]

Present analysis of inter-regional disparities data presented by CSO for various periods have been used. The sub-periods are divided as under:

(i) 1960-61 to 1970-71
(ii) 1970-71 to 1979-80
(iii) 1980-81 to 1990-91
(iv) 1993-94 to 1998-99
(v) 1992-93 to 2005-06

(i) 1960-61 to 1970-71

Table 5.10 reveals that in terms of figures Orissa was the highest growing state with 9.7 per cent growth rate of NSDP at current prices during 1960s (Later on CSO explained that figure for Orissa was inflated because of the discrepencies in the use of deflator). Among the rest of the states Punjab (5.6%), Haryana (5.5%) and Himachal Pradesh achieved higher growth rates, thanks to green revolution.

Bihar was the slowest growing state with 0.7 per cent growth rate; Madhya Pradesh (1.5%), Rajasthan (1.3%), Uttar Pradesh (1.6%) and Andhra Pradesh (1.5%) were other major states lagging behind in growth process. These states recorded a negative growth rate in per capita Net State Domestic Product (NSDP) during the same period

(ii) 1970-71 to 1979-80

In the seventies, the pattern of growth changed slightly. Goa emerged as highest growing state with 6.1 per cent growth rate followed by Maharashtra (5.7%), Punjab (5.4%) and Haryana (4.8%). State likes Rajasthan (3.0%), Bihar (2.8%) and Andhra Pradesh (3.2%) did little better and got momentum. But Madhya Pradesh recorded lowest growth rate (1.3%) in NSDP, Kerala (–0.2%) and Madhya Pradesh (-1.0%) were the two states that recorded negative growth rate in per capita NSDP terms, while the growth rate in real per capita income in Assam, West Bengal, Bihar, Uttar Pradesh, Orissa, Rajasthan and Himachal Pradesh was less than 1.0 per cent.

(iii) 1980-81 to 1990-91

The growth momentum accelerated during 1980s with an average growth rate of 5.6 per cent for the whole country and thus, the country jumped out of 'Hindu Growth Rate' of 2-4 per cent to a 'Secular Growth Rate' of more than 5.0 per cent. Individual states showed the greatest consistency in the

TABLE 5.10
Growth Rates of Net State Domestic Product and Per Capita Net State Domestic Product at Current Prices for Selected States during Sixties and Seventies

(*Per cent*)

States	*Net State Domestic Product (NSDP)*		*Net State Domestic Product (NSDP) per capita*	
	1960-61 to 1969-70	*1970-71 to 1979-80*	*1960-61 to 1969-70*	*1970-71 to 1979-80*
Goa	NA	6.1	NA	3.6
Maharashtra	2.9	5.7	0.04	3.3
Punjab	5.6	5.4	3.5	3.2
Haryana	5.5	4.8	2.6	2.2
Gujarat	2.7	4.5	0.1	2.0
Karnataka	3.4	4.3	1.2	1.8
Delhi	5.1	6.2	0.7	1.7
Jammu & Kashmir	3.2	4.4	0.5	1.6
Tamil Nadu	2.1	3.4	0.1	1.6
All India	3.0	3.6	0.8	1.2
Andhra Pradesh	1.5	3.2	-0.4	1.1
Assam	4.0	3.0	0.9	0.8
West Bengal	2.5	2.9	0.02	0.7
Bihar	0.7	2.8	-1.3	0.6
Uttar Pradesh	1.6	2.6	-0.2	0.4
Orissa	9.7	2.3	7.3	0.3
Rajasthan	1.3	3.0	-1.1	0.2
Himachal Pradesh	5.6	2.4	3.4	0.2
Kerala	3.8	1.7	1.4	-0.2
Madhya Pradesh	1.5	1.3	-1.1	-1.0

Note : Deflators used in estimation of NSDP for Orissa in this period have discrepancies, as a result of which the State's growth rates are non-comparable.

Source : Central Statistical Organisation.

growth record during this decade as reflected in the decrease of measure of inter-state disparities from 2.22 to 1.71 (Table 5.12). The pattern of growth during this decade is a bit convergent. Haryana (6.3%), Maharashtra (6.0%), Rajasthan (5.9%), Goa (5.5%), Tamil Nadu (5.4%) and Punjab (5.4%) were the most rapidly growing states. Jammu and Kashmir was the lowest (2.2%). The three poor big brothers, i.e. Uttar Pradesh (4.9%), Madhya Pradesh (4.0%) and Bihar (4.7%) along with Orissa (5.0%) fared well during eighties (Table 5.11).

(iv) 1993-94 to 1998-99

A new series of GSDP data was released by CSO in the year 2000 and subsequently updated in November 2001. On the basis of new data, the growth rate of GSDP has been calculated for 1993-94 to 1998-1999 and presented in Table 5.11. The growth record shows an increase in the divergence of individual states. Standard deviation increased from 1.19 in the 1980s to 1.60 in the 90's in terms of GSDP broadly along the pattern that had come to be established during the decade of the seventies with some notable differences. However, the difference between the highest and the lowest value for GSDP growth rate across states in the seventies was 4.8 percentage point which increased to 5.5 percentage point during nineties, indicating widening of the spread over the preceding decade (Difference between the highest and lowest growth rates during eighties was only 1.8 percentage points). Another notable point during 90s was that Punjab and Haryana which were recording consistently higher growth rate since 1960s recorded a lower growth rate as compared to the national average. In contrast to this Karnataka, Gujarat, Maharashtra, Rajasthan, West Bengal and Tamil Nadu recorded much higher growth rates.

Thus, the overall disparity in inter-state growth of NSDP and per capita NSDP of states increased considerably during the nineties, as compared to the eighties and seventies.

(v) 1992-93 to 2005-06 (Era of Economic Reforms)

The process of economic reforms, started in 1991-92, got further momentum in subsequent years. All the sectors of the economy were liberated to make the economy market-based.

TABLE 5.11
Growth Rates of GSDP and Per Capita GSDP at Current Prices during Eighties and Nineties for Selected States

(Per cent)

States	*Gross States Domestic Product*		*Gross States Domestic Product per capita*	
	1980-81 to 1990-91	*1993-94 to 1998-99*	*1980-81 to 1990-91*	*1993-94 to 1998-99*
Karnataka	5.4	8.2	3.3	6.4
Gujarat	5.1	8.0	3.0	6.2
Tamil Nadu	5.4	6.8	3.9	5.8
Maharashtra	6.0	7.1	3.6	5.4
Rajasthan	5.9	7.7	3.8	5.3
West Bengal	4.8	6.8	2.6	5.0
All India	5.9	6.8	3.3	4.8
Goa	5.5	8.3	3.9	4.5
Kerala	3.2	5.5	1.7	4.2
Himachal Pradesh	5.0	6.7	3.1	3.9
Haryana	6.2	5.8	3.9	3.6
Andhra Pradesh	4.3	4.9	2.1	3.5
Punjab	5.4	5.0	3.5	3.0
Orissa	5.0	4.3	3.1	2.9
Bihar	4.7	4.2	2.5	2.6
Madhya Pradesh	4.0	4.4	2.1	2.3
Uttar Pradesh	4.9	4.5	2.5	2.3
Jammu & Kashmir	2.2	4.7	-0.4	1.6
Delhi	7.6	6.7	3.2	1.6
Assam	3.6	2.7	1.4	1.0

Note : Name of States is arranged in order of rank in rates of growth of per capita GSDP in 1993-94 to 1998-99.

Source : Central Statistical Organisation.

TABLE 5.12
Disparity in Growth Amongst States/UTs of India

Period	*Measure of Disparity (Standard Deviation)*		*Relative Measure of Disparity in growth between NSDP and per capita*
	NSDP	*Per capita*	
1960-61 to 1969-70	2.14	2.05	4.01
1970-71 to 1979-80	2.22	1.81	3.67
1980-81 to 1990-91	1.71	1.02	0.71
1993-94 to 1998-99	3.13	2.40	5.29
1999-00 to 2004-05	2.82	2.43	3.97

Source : GOI (2002); Tenth Five Year Plan, Vol. III, Planning Commission, p. 37 and Economic Survey, 2007-08.

Directional planning was substituted by indicative planning. Eighth Plan (1992-97) recorded a growth rate of 6.8 per cent, which was higher by 1.2 percentage point than its targeted growth rate of 5.6 per cent. However, the Ninth Five Year Plan could not perform in accordance with its predecessor and growth rate declined to 5.3 per cent against the targeted rate of 6.5 per cent. Net decline of 1.5 percentage points between Ninth and Eighth Five Year Plans was because of sharp decline in the growth rate of fastest growing states during Eighth Plan. Growth rate of Gujarat declined from 12.4 per cent during Eighth Plan to 4 per cent in Ninth Plan. Likewise, the growth rate of Maharashtra came down to 4.7 per cent from 8.5 per cent and that of Rajasthan declined to 3.5 per cent from 7.5 per cent. The growth rate of Tamil Nadu, Uttar Pradesh, Madhya Pradesh, Haryana also declined. Karnataka, Orissa, Manipur and Meghalaya were the only states, whose growth rate showed an increase in the Ninth Plan compared to the Eighth Plan (Table 5.13).

The pattern of growth across the states changed significantly during the Tenth Five Year Plan which recorded ever highest growth rate of 7.8 per cent, although wide variation in the growth rates are seen from the Table 5.13. The difference between the highest and lowest growth rates in

TABLE 5.13
Growth Rates of State Domestic Products in Various States

(% per annum)

Sl. No.	State/UTs	VIII Plan 1992-97	IX Plan 1997-2002	X Plan 2002-07	Eleventh Plan target
1.	Andhra Pradesh	5.4	4.6	6.7	9.5
2.	Bihar	2.2	4.0	4.7	7.6
3.	Goa	8.9	5.5	7.8	12.1
4.	Gujarat	12.4	4.0	10.6	12.2
5.	Haryana	5.2	4.1	7.6	11.0
6.	Karnataka	6.2	7.2	7.0	11.2
7.	Kerala	6.5	5.7	7.2	9.5
8.	Madhya Pradesh	6.3	4.0	4.3	6.1
9.	Maharashtra	8.9	4.7	7.9	9.1
10.	Orissa	2.1	5.1	9.1	8.8
11.	Punjab	4.7	4.4	4.5	5.9
12.	Rajasthan	7.5	3.5	5.0	7.4
13.	Tamil Nadu	7.0	6.3	6.6	8.5
14.	Uttar Pradesh	4.9	4.0	4.6	6.1
15.	West Bengal	6.3	6.9	6.1	9.7
16.	Chhattisgarh	NA	NA	9.2	8.6
17.	Jharkhand	NA	NA	11.1	9.8
Special Category States					
18.	Arunachal Pradesh	5.1	4.4	5.8	6.4
19.	Assam	2.8	2.1	6.1	6.5
20.	Himachal Pradesh	6.5	5.9	7.3	9.5
21.	Jammu & Kashmir	5.0	5.2	5.2	6.4
22.	Manipur	4.6	6.4	11.6	5.9
23.	Meghalaya	3.8	6.2	5.6	7.3
24.	Mizoram	NA	NA	5.9	7.1
25.	Nagaland	8.9	2.6	8.3	9.3
26.	Sikkim	5.3	8.3	7.7	6.7
27.	Tripura	6.6	7.4	8.7	6.9
28.	Uttranchal	NA	NA	8.8	9.9
	All India	6.8	5.3	7.8	9.0

Note : Average of 2002-03 to 2005-06 for all states except J & K, Mizoram, Nagaland (2003-03 to 2004-05) and Tripura (2002-03 to 2003-04).

Source : CSO (base 1999-2000 constant price) on 31.8.2007.

GSDP during the Tenth Plan is 7.3 percentage points which is ever highest (Table 5.13). Manipur, Jharkhand and Gujarat recorded a growth rate of above 10 per cent, while the growth rate of Punjab was well below the growth rate of Bihar. The story of Uttar Pradesh, Madhya Pradesh, Rajasthan remained almost the same in the Tenth Plan as compared to the Ninth Plan. These states could not improve their pace of growth even in the era of liberalisation of the economy. The newly created states—Jharkhand, Chhattisgarh and Uttaranchal have, however, fared well and registered higher growth rate than the national average. If one goes to measure the disparity in terms of standard deviation in GSDP amongst states, then one finds that overall inter-state disparity increased during Eighth and Ninth Five Year Plans but decreased slightly during the Tenth Plan.

Table 5.14 presents summary indicators of disparity in per capita income across states in India. It does not consider the

TABLE 5.14
Disparities in Per Capita GSDP

Year	*State with lowest per capita GSDP*	*State with highest per capita GSDP*	*Ratio of minimum to maxi-mum PCGSDP*	*Coefficient of variation*	*Gini coefficient*
1993-94	Bihar	Punjab	30.527	34.539	0.1917
1996-97	Bihar	Maharashtra	37.586	36.781	0.2071
1999-2000	Bihar	Maharasthra	28.899	37.417	0.2173
2001-02	Bihar	Punjab	21.556	35.610	0.2078
2002-03	Bihar	Punjab	21.608	36.686	0.2771
2003-04	Bihar	Punjab	22.705	36.230	0.2290
2004-05	Bihar	Maharashtra	20.105	38.440	0.2409

* 1993-94, 1996-97 and 1999-2000 as per TFC Report based on 1993-94 prices; 2001-02 and onward with base year 1999-2000 current price (excluding Goa); weighted by population, 1993-94, 1996-97 and 1999-2000 relates to 14 states and 2001-02 to 2004-05 relates to 27 states (excluding Goa).

Source : (i) Twelfth Finance Commission for 1993-04, 1996-97 and 1999-2000.
(ii) CSO for 2001-02, 2002-03, 2003-04, 2004-05.

inter-state distribution of income. The ratio of minimum to maximum per capita GSDP increased for three years from 21.56 per cent in 2001-02 to 21.61 per cent in 2002-03 to 22.71 per cent in 2003-04. The weighted coefficient of variation also shows an increase over the years. The Ginni coefficient indicated in column 6 reflects the income inequality across the states which increased from 0.2078 in 2001-02 to 0.2409 in 2004-05. In other words, the income inequality across states is worsening.

The differential performance across states has begun to raise important policy questions within India. To what extent are the differences a manifestation of global economic forces acting upon Indian economy, especially during the period of economic reforms and liberalisation of economy and to what extent do they reflect differences in economic policies at the state level.

As regards to the impact of growth on poverty incidence in individual states, normally, higher growth must result into higher decline in poverty HCR and thus, a lower poverty incidence. But it did not happen during the era of economic reforms Inter-state disparities in poverty reduction have increased between 1993-94 to 2004-05 (Table 5.16).

A low level of standard deviation in inter-state annual growth rates of NSDP and per capita NSDP at constant prices shows convergence in growth rate. But, the higher standard deviations in poverty HCR for rural, urban and combined show that wide variations exist among the states in the matter of poverty incidence. Not even this, the variations in the poverty incidence increased in 2004-05 as compared to 1993-94. The decline in poverty incidence is full of variations in different states (Table 5.15). If we correlate the growth rate with the poverty HCR and percentage point decline in poverty incidence between 1993-94, the results are disappointing in the sense that the correlation coefficients between annual average growth rate of NSDP and per capita NSDP with poverty HCR in rural areas are –0.1883 and –0.2156 respectively for urban areas –0.1470 and –0.3361 respectively, and for combined –0.2133 and 0.2737 respectively. A very weak negative correlation coefficients shows that higher growth has not translated into higher decline in poverty incidence (Table 5.16).

TABLE 5.15
Annual Average Growth Rates of NSDP and Per Capita NSDP at Constant Prices (at 1993-94 Prices)

State	*Annual Average NSDP*		*Growth rate Per capita NSDP*		*Poverty Incidence*		
	1993-94	*2004-05*	*1993-94*	*2004-05*	*1993-94*	*2004-05*	*Decline*
(1)	*(2)*	*(3)*	*(4)*	*(5)*	*(6)*	*(7)*	*(8)*
Andhra Pradesh	2.58	5.86	0.46	4.18	44.6	29.9	14.7
Assam	3.22	2.94	0.88	1.13	51.8	34.4	7.4
Bihar	-0.67	4.49	-2.79	2.01	60.5	54.4	6.1
Gujarat	7.54	5.76	6.62	3.66	37.8	31.8	6.0
Haryana	4.16	6.82	1.77	3.56	35.9	24.1	11.8
Himachal Pradesh	2.53	5.23	0.26	4.71	34.6	22.9	11.7
Jammu & Kashmir	4.17	3.98	1.64	1.87	26.3	13.2	13.1
Karnataka	5.25	5.01	3.62	5.33	49.5	33.4	16.1
Kerala	5.58	5.23	4.28	4.29	31.3	19.7	11.6
Madhya Pradesh	4.78	3.98	2.41	1.81	44.6	48.6	2.0
Maharashtra	6.44	5.01	4.16	3.15	47.8	38.1	9.7

(*Contd.*)

Table 5.15 (Contd.)

(1)	(2)	(3)	(4)	(5)	(6)	(7)	(8)
Orissa	-1.99	4.39	-3.83	3.00	59.1	57.2	1.9
Punjab	3.71	4.29	1.77	2.53	22.4	20.9	1.5
Rajasthan	7.67	5.76	5.35	3.25	38.3	28.9	9.4
Tamilnadu	5.38	4.60	4.13	3.66	44.6	40.9	3.7
Uttar Pradesh	2.48	3.76	0.48	1.41	48.4	34.3	14.1
West Bengal	5.35	7.17	3.26	5.55	39.4	37.2	2.2

Note : For 1993-94: Average of annual growth rates of 1991-92, 1992-93, 1993-94.
For 2004-05 : Average of annual growth rates of 2002-03, 2003-04, 2004-05.
For Poverty Incidence : Expert Group (2009) Methodology.

Source : (i) GOI (2001) : Indian Public FInance Statisitcs, 2003-04, Ministry of Finance, New Delhi.
(ii) GOI (2007) : Indian Public Finance Statistics, 2006-07, Ministry of Finance, New Delhi.
(iii) GOI (2009) : Report of Expert Group to Review Methodology of Poverty Estimation, Planning Commission.

CHART 5.15
Inter-state Disparities in Poverty Reduction between 1993-94 and 2004-05

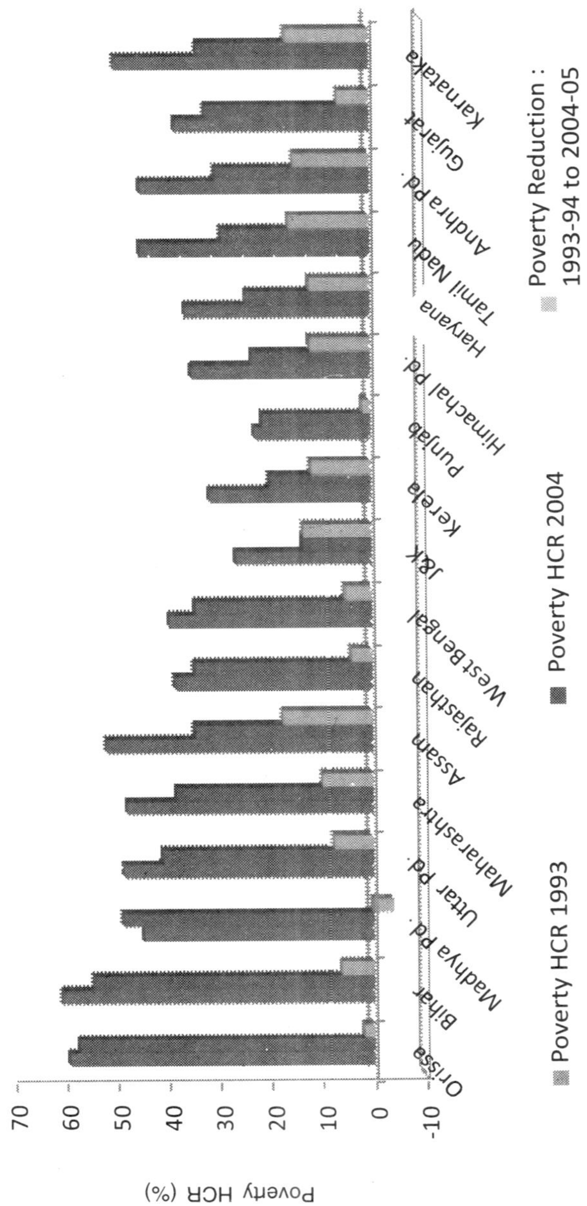

CHART 5.16
Inter-state Disparities in Per Capita NSDP and Poverty Incidence (2004-05)

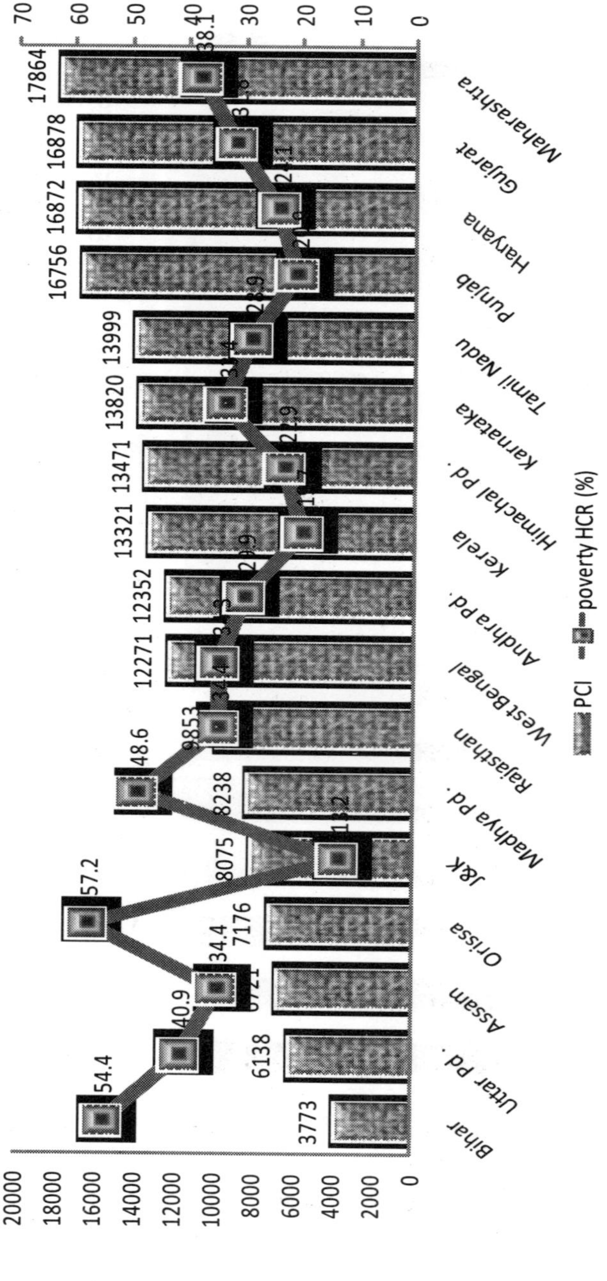

TABLE 5.16
Inter-state Variation in NSDP, Per Capita NSDP at Constant Prices and Poverty Incidence

	Standard deviation	*Coefficient of correlation*	
		With NSDP growth rate	*With per capita NSDP*
1. Annual Average growth rate of NSDP at constant price (at 1993-94 prices) – 2004-05	1.09	—	—
2. Annual Average growth rate of per capita NSDP at constant price (at 1993-94 prices) – 2004-05	1.32	—	—
3. Poverty HCR – Rural 1993-94	11.57	—	—
4. Poverty HCR – Rural 2004-05	13.35	–0.1883	–0.2156
5. Decline in poverty HCR – Rural (between 1993-94 to 2004-05)	7.26	–0.0062	0.1782
6. Poverty HCR – Urban 1993-94	8.97	—	—
7. Poverty HCR – Urban 2004-05	9.98	–0.1470	–0.3361
8. Decline in Poverty HCR–Urban (between 1993-94 to 2004-05)	5.03	0.4495	0.5002
9. Poverty HCR – Combined 1993-94	10.80	—	—
10. Poverty HCR – Combined 2004-05	12.35	–0.2133	–0.2737
11. Decline in Poverty HCR – Combined (between 1993-94 to 2004-05)	5.98	–0.0130	0.2269

Source : Compiled from (i) GOI (2006); Indian Public Finance Statistics, 2006-07, Ministry of Finance, and (ii) Report of Expert Group to Review the Methodology for Estimation of Poverty, 2009.

Bi-variate analysis presented in Table 5.16, suggests that neither the growth in NSDP nor the growth in per capita NSDP has a significant impact on the reduction in poverty across the states (a low negative coefficient of correlation

TABLE 5.17
Bi-variate Analysis of NSDP and Per Capita NSDP and Poverty Incidence

(at 1993-94 prices)

	Coefficient of Correlation with Poverty HCR (%)					
	1993-94			2004-05		
	Rural	*Urban*	*Combined*	*Rural*	*Urban*	*Combined*
(1)	(2)	(3)	(4)	(5)	(6)	(7)
(i) Average NSDP at constant price (1989-90 to 2002-03)	0.3866	0.5362	–0.3340	—	—	—
(ii) Annual average growth rate of NSDP at constant price (1989-90 to 2002-03)	–0.3699	–0.2665	–0.1182	—	—	—
(iii) Average per capita NSDP at constant price (1989-90 to 2002-03)	–0.4226	–0.2340	–0.2182	—	—	—
(iv) Annual average growth rate of per capita NSDP at constant price (1989-90 to 2002-03)	–0.3479	–0.2126	–0.1303	—	—	—

(v)	Average NSDP at constant price (2001-02 to 2004-05)	—	—	—	0.3019	0.2049	–0.1269
(vi)	Annual average growth rate of NSDP at constant price (1993-94 to 2004-05)	—	—	—	–0.1883	–0.1470	0.0241
(vii)	Average per capita NSDP at constant price (2001-02 to 2004-05)	—	—	—	–0.4217	–0.5400	–0.2339
(viii)	Annual average growth rate of per capita NSDP at constant price (1993-94 to 2004-05)	—	—	—	–0.2157	–0.3361	0.0941

Source : (i) GOI, India Public Finance Statistics, 2001-02 and 2006-07, Ministry of Finance.
(ii) Planning Commission (2009), Report of Expert Group to Review the Methodology for the Estimation of Poverty.

between growth rate of NSDP and poverty HCR and between growth rate of per capita NSDP and poverty HCR).

CHANGING FACE OF POVERTY IN INDIA

Period-wise break-up of growth trend and decline in show that higher growth does not mean the higher decline in poverty (Table 5.18).

TABLE 5.18
Poverty Reduction in Relation to GNP Growth Rates

Period	*Average annual growth rate of GNP*	*Average annual decline in the incidence of poverty*
1973-74 to 1977-78	4.60	0.72%
1977-78 to 1983-84	4.00	1.36%
1983-84 to 1987-88	4.00	1.12%
1987-88 to 1993-94	5.60	0.58%
1993-94 to 1999-2000	6.66	0.96%
1999-2000 to 2004-05	5.60	0.86%

Source : Compiled from Economic Surveys of various years and Draft Five Year Plans.

The Table 5.18 reveals that the average annual decline in the incidence of poverty in India was highest (1.36% per annum) during 1977-78 to 1983-84 despite a low average annual growth rate of GNP (2.89%) during the same period. The next highest decline in the poverty was during 1983-84 to 1987-88 (1.12% per annum) and the growth rate of GNP during this period was 4.61 per cent. Period from 1993-94 to 2004-05 saw ever highest growth rate of GNP in India but the decline in the incidence of poverty had remained in the order of 0.86 to 0.96 per cent. It shows that high growth rate of Gross National Product could not produce desired result on the reduction of poverty in India.

In 1977-78 more than 328 million people of India were living below the official poverty line, this figure came down to

238 million in 2004-05 (Estimates based on Expert Group 1993 methodology). But the face of poverty is constantly changing, compared with 1977-78. Process of globalisation and functioning of Indian economy as market economy did not help much the poor people despite a surge in the growth rate. Due to higher rates of 'agflation' poor persons today are more vulnerable to the risks associated with life. Poverty has changed its face over the time in India. Marginalized people (scheduled castes, scheduled tribes, OBCs, female headed households, women, children, slum-dwellers, marginal farmers and agricultural labourers) are at greater risk today.

Trend analysis of income poverty prompt some questions about the overall situation :

- How big is the poverty problem today?
- Where is poverty most pervasive?
- Where are the poor?

A comparison of the profile of people in income poverty in the 1970s with that in 2000s shows that income poverty is concentrated in rural areas of BIMARU states (including newly created states—Jharkhand, Chhattisgarh) along with Orissa, Andhra Pradesh, Maharashtra and West Bengal. Uttar Pradesh is the home of largest number of urban poor followed by Bihar, Maharashtra, Madhya Pradesh and West Bengal. But the face of income poverty is rapidly changing (Table 5.19). Today a poor person is more likely to be Biharee Bhaiya, Chhattisgarhia, Jharkhandi or Adivasi, a child, a woman, an elderly person in a urban area, a slum-dweller, landless labourer living in an environmentally fragile area or a refugee or a displaced person.

Urbanisation of Poverty

Urban poverty is much crueler than rural poverty since it exists in the midst of opulent wealth and its vulgar display. It is interesting to note that the ratio of urban poverty in some of the largest states (Andhra Pradesh, Chhattisgarh, Goa, Haryana, Karnataka, Madhya Pradesh, Maharashtra,

TABLE 5.19
The Changing Face of Income Poverty

Less likely to be affected	*More likely to be affected*	*And likely to be poor as a result*
Residents of Punjab, Haryana, J&K, Gujarat, Goa, Himachal Pradesh, Delhi, etc.	Residents of BIMARU Sates, Jharkhand, Chhattisgarh and Orissa	• Economic stagnation and slow employment growth • Increasing disparity • Lack of pro-poor growth • Increased marginalization from global trade and financial flows • Higher fertility and the spread of HIV/AIDS • Accelerated degradation of natural resoruces • Increased displacement from home and the state.
An adult male	A child, a woman or an elderly (in family some states)	• Increased cuts in social welfare • Greater disintegration of the • Higher unemployment, particularly chronic Unemployment and involuntary part time work. • High costs of social and economic transition • Increased time burdens.
A small farmer	A marginal farmer and an unskilled low wage worker.	• Continuing globalization and trade liberalization • Increased liberalization of labour markets
Rural	Urban	• Rapid demographic change and migration to urban areas • Growth of the low-productivity informal sector • Worsening access to productive resources • Inadequate development of urban housing and physical infrastructure
Settled	A refugee or internally displaced	• Increasing insurgency and conflicts • Deepening economic and environmental crises

Source : Compiled on the basis of Lipton and Maxwell (1992) : UNDP, Human Development Report, 1992.

Rajasthan*) is higher than that of rural poverty leading to the phenomenon of 'Urbanisation of Poverty'. Urban poverty poses the problems of housing and shelter, water, sanitation, health, education, social security and livelihoods along with special needs of vulnerable groups like women, children and aged people. Poor people in cities live in slums which are overcrowded, often polluted and lack basic civic amenities like clean and safe drinking water, sanitation and health facilities. Most of them are involved in informal sector activities where there is a constant threat of eviction, removal, confiscation of goods and almost non-existent social security cover. The 'India : Urban Poverty Report, 2009' prepared with the support of the UNDP has certain revealing facts. According to the study, an estimated 23.7 per cent of urban population was living in slums amid squalor, crime, disease and tension. The key finding of this report is that poverty in Indian cities is not an overflow of the poverty in villages but has happened because of the faulty nature of urbanisation. This is mainly due to poor city planning, urban land management and legislation. The distinct character of urban poverty is that it was not about only nutritional deficiency (a key parameter of estimation of poverty) but deficiencies in the basic human needs of housing, water, sanitation, medical care, education, and opportunity for income generation. The report finds that urban workers were being increasingly pushed into the informal sector, even as the space for informal economic activities was gradually sinking. Also within the informal sector, the profile of the work in urban areas has moved from wage-employment to self-employment, which carries its own uncertainties.[24]

So the urban poor is increasingly a street vendor, a rickshaw puller, a rag picker, a sweeper, washerman, a load carrier or a domestic servant. Beggers is another class of poor that has large concentration in urban areas. So is the case with the construction workers migrated from far-flung areas of

* As per estimates of Planning Commission for 2004-05 based on the methodology of Expert Group (1993's) recommendations. However, this phenomenon did not appear in the poverty estimates based on the methodology recommended by Expert Group (2009). But certainly states like Bihar, Karnataka, Madhya Pradesh, Manipur, Orissa, Rajasthan, Uttar Pradesh have higher urban poverty HCR than national average.

Bihar, Jharkhand, Chhattisgarh, Orissa, Bundelkhand, etc. No doubt these workers have contributed to the growth and development of cities, nevertheless no care has been taken to uplift them from the poverty. There is a growing trend to push them to the urban periphery, as they are increasingly seen as threat to the 'Globalcity' dreams. In that event, though the share of poor in urban population has fallen and is much less than in rural population, the absolute number of urban poor has increased. As many as 81 million or 25.7 per cent people (2004-05) subsist in urban areas on incomes that are below the poverty line. Eighty per cent of their meager income goes towards paying for goods and energy, leaving very little for meeting the cost of living in an increasingly monetised society.

Gender Dimensions of Poverty

There are many dimensions of poverty that affect the women. Women constitute a large set with their own characteristics that require further explorations. However, it is beyond doubt that the single women, unmarried, divorces/ separated and widowed are more vulnerable among the Female Headed Households (FHHs).

The incidence of income poverty among females tended to be marginally higher in both rural and urban areas. The percentage of female persons living in poor households was 28 per cent in rural and 26 per cent in urban areas in 1993-94 and 29 and 23 respectively in 2004-05. In contrast, the percentage of male persons living in poverty was 27 in rural and 26 in urban areas in 1993-94 and 27 and 23 in 2004-05*. The lower percentage of female persons among the poor despite higher female poverty ratio was due to an adverse sex ratio—which itself is a reflection of the discrimination that women and girls face over their life-cycle. It should be noted that the above measure of gender poverty ignores intra household inequalities in consumption. There are other dimensions of poverty such as food insecurity, malnutrition and illness associated more with female members.[25]

* Planning Commission's estimates based on Expert Group's (1993) methodology.

The women are much worse-off in terms of most social indicators is quite well known, SC and ST girls are the worse off in terms of most educational outcome indicators. For instance, in the critical age group of 15–49 years, when women are in their reproductive and most productive years, it is remarkable that 73 per cent of SC women, 79 per cent of ST women, and 61 per cent of OBC women are illiterate. 61 per cent of Muslim women were also illiterate, this percentage is relatively low, only because the rate of urbanisation among Muslims is higher than for other social groups. Gross enrolment ratios and dropout ratios for SCs and STs girls are much higher than the boys of their own class as well as their counterparts in non-SCs/STs girl (Table 5.20).

TABLE 5.20
Gross Enrolment, Dropout at Primary Stage (I–V) by Social Groups, 2004-05

	Gross Enrolment Ratio			*Dropout Rate*		
	Schedule Caste	*Schedule Tribe*	*Total*	*Schedule Caste*	*Schedule Tirbe*	*Total*
Boys	123.33	128.06	110.70	32.73	42.55	31.81
Girls	106.62	115.49	104.70	36.14	42.04	25.42
Total	115.30	121.91	107.80	34.21	42.32	29.00

Source : Selected Educational Statistics, Ministry of Human Resource Development (MHRD), GOI, 2007.

The nutrition status of SC and ST women remains a source of worry as well. A good 42 per ent of SC women and 46 per cent of ST women had a BMI less than 18.5, which is seen as the cut-off for malnutrition. The fact that as much as 30 per cent of the 'Other' women were also malnourished clearly indicates that there is a serious problem of under nutrition among most segments of the population, not just SCs and STs.[26] (Table 5.21).

Large scale migration of rural male workers to cities and other developed regions, has resulted into 'Feminization of

TABLE 5.21
Health and Nutrition Indicators by Social Group in 2005-06 (NFHS-3)

	Infant Mortality Rate			*Under Five Mortality Rate*		
	Rural	*Urban*	*Total*	*Rural*	*Urban*	*Total*
SC	71.0	50.7	66.4	94.7	65.4	88.1
ST	63.9	43.8	62.1	99.8	53.8	95.7
OBC	61.1	42.2	56.6	78.7	54.5	72.8
Others	55.7	36.1	48.9	68.2	42.1	59.2

Source : National Family Health Survey (NFHS-3), 2005-06, International Institute for Population Sciences, Mumbai.

Poverty' in Rural Areas.[27] In the absence of male bread earner of the family, the onus of family expenses lies with the women. Given the lower levels of support structures in urban locations for most poor households, the excessive monetisation in urban areas as opposed to rural areas, implications for poor households food security, access to health care, especially child care, and creditworthiness or asset ownership all get linked to the extent of women's earning capacities and productivity as well in urban areas.[28]

Poverty Among Children

Child poverty is widespread in India both in rural and urban areas. The percentage of children below 15 years living in below poverty line (BPL) households constituted 39 in rural and 41 in urban areas in 1993-94 and 44 in rural and 32 in urban areas in 2004-05. Among the poor population, the percentage of children increased from 44 in rural and 39 in urban areas in 1993-94, to 46 and 42 respectively in 1999-2000. This rising tendency in the proportion of children among the poor contrasts with the proportion of children in the population which was a constant 44 per cent in rural areas in 1993-94 as well as in 2004-05 and a marginal decline from 39 to 32 per cent in urban areas during the same period. The high and rising level of child poverty is not only linked to a high incidence of child malnutrition, but also undermines their future capabilities and adversely affects equality of opportunity.[29]

Class and Caste-based Dimensions of Poverty

The composition of the poor has been changing and rural poverty is getting concentrated in agricultural labour and artisanal households and urban poverty in casual labour households. Agricultural labour households accounted for 41 per cent of rural poor in 1993-94 as well as in 2004-05. The share of self-employed in agriculture among the rural poor had fallen from 32 to 21.6 per cent. Casual labour households accounted for 62.6 per cent tin 1993-94 in urban areas and 56.5 per cent in 2004-05.[30]

The occupational composition of rural poor varied across the states. In general, in developed States poverty was highly concentrated among agricultural labour households, and in contrast in backward States poverty extended to other occupational groups including self-employed in agriculture.

Among social groups, SCs, STs and backward castes accounted for 80 per cent of the rural poor in 2004-05, considerably more than their share in the rural population (Working Group on Poverty, Planning Commission, 2006). In 2004-05, while the HCR of the poor in the total rural population was 28.3 per cent, among the SCs it was 36.8 per cent. In urban areas, the HCR overall was 25.7 per cent, but among SCs it was even higher than in rural areas at nearly 40 per cent.[31]

The proportion of STs population among the rural population living in poverty is high. It is about 15 per cent in 2004-05—double that of their share in the total population of India. For rural population, the incidence of poverty among STs had fallen from 51.94 per cent in 1993-94 to 47.3 per cent in 2004-05 whereas it had fallen from 37.3 to 27.5 per cent in the total population. In 2004-05, the incidence of poverty among the STs had barely fallen compared to a decade earlier and it was a good 20 percentage points higher for the STs than for the rest of the population.[32]

The share of poor in the total urban population in 2004-05 was 25.7 per cent but 33.3 per cent of the STs in urban areas were poor. The HCR of the STs (47.3%) is higher than that of

SCs (36.8%) in rural areas, but the situation is the other way around in urban areas, i.e., of all STs living in rural areas a higher proportion is poorer than all SCs living in rural areas. On the other hand, of all SCs living in urban areas, more SCs are poor than all STs. In rural areas SCs don't have access to land and therefore are forced to migrate to urban areas more often. On the other hand, STs (unlike SCs) in rural areas have much better access to land, especially in the forested areas, but the quality of that land, and its productivity is low, and yields low incomes.

Concludingly, poverty in India is more pervasive in rural areas and certain pockets of urban areas such as slums. Rural economy is primarily agrarian economy that had highly skewed and comparatively low growth rates during the plans. Share of agricultural and allied activity sector in the Gross Domestic Product at Factor Cost has declined over the time. It is around 17.5 per cent in 2009-10. On the contrary, more than two third of country's population depends on agricultural sector. Thus, roughly 70 crore people survive on 17.5 per cent national income. So, the slow growth in agricultural and allied activities sector would certainly has little or no impact on the reduction of poverty on the reduction of poverty incidence in rural areas. Expansion of slums is the outcome of high levels of migration of poor people from rural areas. These slums are the homes of thousands of urban poor.

Higher levels of growth in aggregate form might have shown some impact on the reduction to poverty, but at disaggregate level, i.e. inter-state or intra-state level, prosperity of economy does not reflect on the poor. Inter-state and intra-state disparities in growth and poverty reduction leave the message that some specific measures, such as area specific approach of growth, development and poverty alleviation, are required to attain the goal of 'inclusive growth'.

NOTES AND REFERENCES

1. Government of India (1998): Nineth Five Year Plan, 1997-98 to 2001-02; Planning Commission, New Delhi, p. 3.
2. Bhagwati, Jagdish (1998): "The design of Indian Development", In Isher, J. Ahluwalia and IMD Little (eds.), *India's Economic Reforms and Development*, Oxford, pp. 24-25.

3. *Ibid.*, pp. 34-35.
4. Ferro, Manuela, David Rosenblatt and Niolas Stern (2002): Policies for Pro-poor Growth in India, Cornell University, p. 1.
5. Ravallian, Martin and Datta, Gaurav (2002): "Growth and Poverty in India : What we have learnt from the NSS", India Workshop on Poverty Measurement, *Monitoring and Evaluation*, January 11-12, 2002.
6. Ravallion (2001): "Growth, Inequality and Poverty", Looking Beyond Averages in World Bank; *World Development Report*, Vol. 29, No. 11,
7. Ravallion and Datta (2002), *op. cit.*, p. 3.
8. Datta, Gaurav and Martin, Ravallion (1998): "From Productivity and Rural Poverty in India", *Journal of Development Studies*, Number 34, April.
9. Ravallion (2001); *op. cit.*
10. Ferro, Manuela *et. al. op. cit.*, p. 5.
11. RBI (2008); Report of Currency and Finance 2008-09, Vol. I, pp. 27-29.
12. Government of India (2009); Economic Survey, 2008-09, Ministry of Finance, New Delhi, pp. 63-64.
13. Frankel, Jeffery and David, Romer (1999); "Does Trade Cause Growth", *The American Economic Review*, Vol. 39, No. 3.
14. Dollar David and Aart Kraay (2001); "Growth is good for Poor", World Bank Policy Research Working Paper, 2587, April.
15. World Bank (2002); "Globalization, Growth and Poverty Building on Inclusive World Economy", A Policy Research Report.
16. Govt. of India (2009); *Economic Survey*, 2008-09, Ministry of Finance, p. 129.
17. Ravallion and Datta (2001), *op. cit.*
18. Bhalla, Surjit, S. (2002): "Growth and Poverty in India : Myth and Reality" in M. Govind Raw (ed.), *Development, Poverty and Fiscal Policy*, Oxford University Press, New Delhi, pp. 16-19.
19. Government of India (2008): Eleventh Five Year Plan (2007-12), Planning Commission, New Delhi, Vol. I.
20. *Ibid.*, p. 137.
21. Ahluwalia, Montek Singh (2000): "Economic Peformance of States in Post-Reforms Period", *Economic and Political Weekly*, May 6, pp. 1637-48.
22. Rao, M. Govinda, K.P. Kaliranjan and Ricshand (1999): "Convergence of Incomes in Indian States—A Divergent View", *Economic and Political Weekly*, March 27, April 2, pp. 769-78.
23. Mehta, Rekha and Rakesh Kumar (2009): Regional Divergence in Per capita income Across Indian States : An Analysis Based on New Series 1999-2000 in Anil Kumar Thakur and Shyam Sunder Singh

Chauahan (eds.), *Inter Regional Disparities in India*, Deep and Deep, New Delhi, pp. 1-19.

24. Government of India (2009): India : Urban Poverty Report 2009, Ministry of Housing and Urban Poverty Alleviation, Oxford University Press, New Delhi.
25. Government of India (2008): Eleventh Five Year Plan (2007-12): Planning Commission, New Delhi, Vol. II, p. 83.
26. *Ibid.*, pp. 83-84.
27. Chauhan, Shyam Sunder Singh (1993), *Nirdhanta ka Narikaran*, Samaj Kalyan, Central Social Welfare Board, New Delhi.
28. Rustagi, Preeti, Sandeep Sarkar, Pinaki Joddar (2009): "Gender Dimensions of Urban Poverty", In *India : Urban Poverty Report 2009*, UNDP—Ministry of Housing and Urban Poverty Alleviation, New Delhi, Oxford University Press, p. 47.
29. Government of India (2008) : *op. cit.*, p. 89.
30. *Ibid.*, p. 90.
31. *Ibid.*, pp. 90-91.
32. *Ibid.*

CHAPTER

6

Policy Initiatives for Poverty Alleviation in India

- High Growth Rate : Low Poverty Incidence—'Growth Mediated' Approach
- Primacy of Investing in Human Development—'Capability Approach'
- Approach of State-Intervention through Income—Employment Generation Programmes—'Safety—Net and Supported Security' Approach
- Economic Reforms and Poverty Reduction—'Inclusive Growth' Approach

CHAPTER

6

Policy Initiatives for Poverty Alleviation in India

Government of India have relied on the following four approaches to reduce poverty since Independence :

(i) The effects of aggregate growth would spread to all groups in society such that poverty reduction is achieved side by side with increase in economic growth. This approach is termed as 'Growth Mediated Approach'.

(ii) Enhancement in capacities in terms of better health, education and skill would ultimately help people to uplift themselves out of poverty's vicious circle. Thus, the approach termed as 'Capacity Improving' (Capability Approach—as enunciated by Prof. Amartya Sen) was adopted and relied upon the core issue of human development through greater emphasis on elementary education and primary health care.

(iii) 'Interventionist Approach' during 1970s and continued till today, State has acted in this approach as an active player as well as a catalyst for the poverty reduction.

(iv) Finally, the concept of 'Inclusive Growth', as emerged during the preparation of Eleventh Five Year Plan.

The reliance placed on each of these approaches has varied over time. Overall, the slow reduction in poverty during the 1950s and 1960s in particular and the entire planning period in general, reinforced skepticism regarding the strength of any 'trickle-down' effect. Since the mid 1970s, however, the faster poverty reduction along with a higher economic growth has led to a greater appreciation of the contribution of growth to lasting poverty reduction and equally important—reinforced the need for investing more in human resource development since these investments not only contribute to faster long term growth, but also increase the capacity and ability to fight against poverty. Accordingly, the government's strategy over the past is based upon a mix of greater emphasis for accelerated and sustained labour–intensive growth, while expanding investment in human capital development. Side-by-side the government took specific initiatives for poverty alleviation through employment and income generation programmes.

HIGH GROWTH RATE : LOW POVERTY INCIDENCE—'GROWTH MEDIATED' APPROACH

The relationship between growth and poverty lies at the heart of development economics. While, many see aggregate growth as both necessary and sufficient for reducing poverty, and consequently focus their efforts on achieving the desired macro-economic outcomes, other's stress that the benefits from growth may not be evenly spread. In fact, critics of globalization often point out that growth of the macro-economy may well have an adverse effect on the most vulnerable members of society. Thus, the distributional impact of growth, as well as, its level, needs to be taken into account when considering the consequences for poverty, while poverty reduction has become the main goal of development efforts, there is an on-going and sometimes heated debate about the elements that should be at the center of any sensible poverty reducing strategy. By definition, poverty reduction in a given country is a function of the changes in average income and changes in income inequality. But this simple identity raises some obvious questions on what should be the right trade-off between pro-growth and pro-distribution interventions in a poverty strategy :

(1) Should a poverty strategy have a growth blast or instead mainly concentrate on empowering the poor to benefit from growth?
(2) Is inequality affected as a general rule by growth?
(3) Does lowering inequality promote or hinder economic growth?
(4) And how does the level of initial inequality affect the impact of growth on poverty reduction?

These questions have been examined in brief, drawing on a survey of recent literature on the relationship between growth, poverty and inequality.[1] The issue is relevant because even if poverty responds to both factors, gaining knowledge about their relative importance may be helpful when trying to strike the right balance between pro-poor and pro-growth interventions. Some analysis focuses on the growth-inequality relationship, with some paying attention to the potential impact that the growth process has on inequality and others stressing the potential effect of inequality on growth. These experts have largely focused on whether countries will have to face trade-offs between reducing inequality and improving growth performance, or instead whether there exists a virtuous circle in which growth leads to lower inequality, with lower inequality in turn leading to faster growth.

There is plenty of evidence suggesting that growth is important for poverty reduction (Deininger-Squire[2], Foster and Szekely[3], Dollar and Kraay[4], Bourguignon[5]). Kraay[6] disentangles the impact of growth on poverty reduction by identifying three potential sources of pro-poor growth (understood as growth that leads to a fall in a given poverty measure). These are: (i) a high growth rate; (ii) a high sensitivity of poverty to growth; and (iii) a poverty reducing pattern of growth. His results suggest that roughly 70 per cent of the variable in short-run changes in poverty can be explained by growth in average incomes. In the medium to long-run, growth would account for an impressive 97 per cent of the changes in (headcount) poverty. Virtually all of the remainder of the variance would be due to changes in relative incomes, with the cross country sensitivity of poverty to growth accounting for little of the variation. He also finds that the relevance of growth for poverty reduction declines as one move from headcount poverty to the squared poverty gap. He explains this finding by noting that more bottom sensitive poverty measures place more weight on changes in the distribution of income than on growth.

Other studies state the case for looking also at distribution. Focusing on the expected change in poverty (rather than on the share of variance explained) that would be associated with a one per cent growth rate (i.e. the growth elasticity of poverty), and how this impact is affected by inequality. Ravallion[7] presents a parsimonious empirical model of the relationship between poverty and growth where the rate of poverty reduction associated with a given growth rate depends on a distributional correction (one minus the initial gini index). Against this background, Ravallion concludes that "growth will be quite a blunt instrument against poverty unless that growth comes with falling inequality".[8]

Bourguignon concludes that at least for poverty HCR, assuming that income follows a log normal distribution may prove satisfactory. He finds that distributional changes is as much responsible for variation in poverty reduction across spells as the heterogeneity in growth rates itself. Bourguignon pinpoints two channels as to how redistribution affects growth: a permanent redistribution of income reduces poverty instantaneously through what was identified as the distribution effect, but also redistribution contributes to a permanent increase in the growth elasticity of poverty reduction—therefore accelerating the rate of poverty reduction for a given rate of growth.[9]

A growth strategy may be defined as a set of policies designed to promote economic growth by allocating resources, either indirectly by moulding the structure of incentives, or directly by redistributing resources between different sectors of production as well as between different owners of factors of production. Depending on the allocation of resources induced, any given growth strategy will lead to a certain rate of growth and a certain distribution of income among individuals. These effects on the rate of growth and the distribution of income, which together can be described as the pattern of growth, induced by a growth strategy will determine the impact the strategy will have on the rate of poverty reduction. Different growth strategies will differ in their impact on poverty because they will include different patterns of growth defined as above. The strategy of maximizing the rate of growth will not always induce the most pro-poor pattern of growth. Pro-poor growth has been broadly defined by a number of international organizations as growth that leads to significant reductions in poverty. But what is a significant reduction in poverty? How much must the poor benefit for growth to be considered pro-poor? In attempting to give analytical and operational content to the concept two broad definitions of pro-poor growth have emerged.

Some sets of theories are based on the premise that the income share of the poor population increases for a growth pattern to be regarded as pro-poor. The simpler version of these concepts are based on a relative concept of inequality and would simply state that the growth rate of the income of the poor is greater than the average growth rate (White and Anderson[10]). Thus (relative) inequality would fall with growth whenever growth is pro-poor. A more radical criterion (also proposed by White and Anderson) would require that the share of the poor in the income increase is at least as large as their population share. This version is much more difficult to meet in practice, and would require that (absolute) inequality declines. Third version of this concept is proposed by Kakwani and Pernia[11] and it is based on the comparison of the changes in poverty due to growth alone (i.e. holding inequality constant) and changes in poverty that take into account the actual changes in inequality.

Although intuitively appealing, this concept of pro-poor growth presents some limitations, particularly when applied in an operational context. First, pro-poor growth under this concept would be equated with inequality reducing growth. However, by focusing so heavily on inequality a policy package seeking an outcome that is consistent with this concept could lead to sub-optimal outcomes for both poor and non-poor households. For example, a society attempting to achieve pro-poor growth under this definition would favour an outcome characterized by average low income growth with a comparatively higher growth of income of poor households, over and outcome where the average income of the country is higher than the growth of income of poor households (even higher than the growth of income of poor households in first case). While the distributional pattern of growth favours poor households in the first scenario, both poor and non-poor households are better-off in the second scenario. Second, this definition might favour public sector interventions that reduce inequality regardless of their impact on growth. While in principle reductions in inequality may be welcomed and even become a policy objective, it is clear that a disregard for the impact of such actions on growth is likely to be of limited operational use.

It emerges from the above discussion, that growth is essential for the reduction of poverty irrespective of magnitude of its impact on the overall well-being of the people. Keeping in mind the above view, policy planners in India, during 1950s, 1960s and 1970s, relied heavily on the premises that higher growth would automatically reduce the poverty. Results from a World Bank research project using household surveys spanning forty years demonstrates that overall growth accounted for the lion's share of poverty reduction; 80 per cent of the reduction in the percentage of households below the poverty line between 1951 and 1970 and almost 100 per cent since 1970. Improvements in distribution (which occurred independently or as a result of deliberate government policies) achieved their greatest impact by the mid-1960s specially on reducing the intensity or severity of poverty, but with little impact on the incidence of poverty.[12]

The findings of World Bank clearly refute any presumption of "immiserising growth"—that is growth that tends to marginalise or impoverish significant segments of the population—in India over this forty year period. Growth and its distribution pattern during the first three decades of economic planning in India is characterised by following messages :

(i) India's development strategy during 1950s and 1960s, focussed heavily on capital intensive industralisation behind high tariff barriers, brought negligible gains to the vast number of rural poor. The jobs created during that period required higher level of skills and thus, were out of the reach of rural mass. Mahalanobis model's assumptions that higher growth would create a large number of jobs that would by supplied from rural sector had failed.

(ii) Investment in agriculture, especially during the era of green revolution, had not only raised the average living standards in rural India but had done so without accentuating inequalities. Green Revolution technology, initially suspected of conferring systematic advantages to large landlords, had generally proven scale neutral.[13]

(iii) Performance of individual states on the front of growth and poverty reduction varied in scale and magnitude between 1950-51 and 1993-94. Some states reduced poverty much faster than others. In addition to variations in growth, differences in initial endowments of human capital and physical infrastructure and in subsequent efforts at developing these resources appear to have been an important factor in the differences in long-term rates of poverty reduction. Unfortunately, no state effectively combined both policies to encourage growth and development of human resources and physical infrastructure.

(iv) Investment in education and health have been below those necessary to accelerate growth prospects and poverty reduction. Nationally, real outlays on education as a share of GDP have been falling. On an average total expenditure of centre and states on education has remained between 3.00–4.00 per cent of GDP. Public expenditure on health shows a more dismal picture with just 1.17 per cent of GDP spending on this vital sector of human capital formation. It is the irony of planning that investment on education and health, as per cent of total plan expenditure, during the entire period of planning has declined considerably. Plan outlay on education declined to 5.3 per cent of total plan outlay during the Tenth Plan from 7.2 per cent in First Plan. Public sector investment on health declined to 1.03 per cent of total investment during Tenth Plan from 3.33 per cent during the First Plan.

(v) From the time of the independence in 1947 to mid 1970s, when per capita income grew by a modest 1.7 per cent, the proportion of the population living in poverty declined at an annual rate of just 0.9 per cent. In the years of stronger per capita income growth—2.5 per cent between the mid-1970s and 1980s—the average reduction was almost three times as fast—2.4 per cent.[14]

(vi) The reduction in poverty incidence in various states is highly skewed. World Bank's analysis shows sharp disparities between development-oriented states and those lagging behind. Even within the states, different regions have achieved marked varied results.

Government of India's data about poverty reduction in relation to growth rates in GDP and per capita income give somewhat a different result. Table 6.1 reveals that Average annual decline in poverty HCR was highest between 1978-79 to 1983-84 (1.36 percentage point) and the growth of per capita income in this period was 4.18 per cent. Period from 1994-94 to 1999-2000 witnessed ever highest growth rate in GDP as well as per capita income, but the annual average decline in poverty HCR was 0.96 percentage point. The net conclusion of the findings of Table 6.1 is that higher per capita income does

TABLE 6.1
Poverty Reduction in Relation to Growth Rate of GDP and Per Capita Income at Factor Cost (at 1999-2000 Prices)

(*Per cent*)

Period	*Average Annual Growth Rate*		*Average Annual decline in the incidence of poverty*
	GDP	*Per capita Income*	
1973-74 to 1977-78	4.60	2.38	0.72
1978-79 to 1983-84	4.00	1.53	1.36
1984-85 to 1987-88	4.00	1.47	1.12
1988-89 to 1993-94	5.60	2.56	0.58
1994-95 to 1999-2000	6.66	4.50	0.96
1999-2000 to 2004-05	5.60	4.02	0.86

Source : Economic Survey, 2008-09 and Plan documents.

not mean higher reduction in poverty incidence. Coefficient of correlation between annual average growth rate of GDP and average annual reduction in poverty incidence is (–)0.4984, which establishes an inverse relationship between growth and poverty reduction—higher the growth, lower is the reduction in poverty incidence. This refutes the claim that higher growth rate will address the problem of poverty in more coherent manner. However, a (–)0.5387 correlation between annual average growth rate of PCI and reduction in poverty incidence shows a dismal result that higher is the PCI, lower is the reduction in poverty incidence.

What is more significant in India's case is a comparatively higher poverty HCR and a very low level of human development. Human Development Report 2009 indicates that India ranked 132 among 179 countries in Human Development Index (HDI). Indian Economy is now the 12th largest economy of the world (4th in terms of PPP—Purchasing Power Parity).[15] The annual growth rates in India have exceeded 8 per cent during 2004-08 period. Despite the sharp reduction in the number of Indians living in poverty, more than one in three people continue to live below the poverty line (37.2 per cent in

2004-05 as per Tendulkar Committee's estimates). Poverty varies from 9.00 per cent to 57.2 per cent and is concentrated amongst certain regions and social groups. Nearly half of the women are poor. More than 80 per cent of the rural poor in 2004-05 belong to SCs, STs and OBCs. More than 90 per cent workforce is employed in informal sector and abysmal working conditions with poor quality of employment. With jobs in formal and agricultural economy unable to keep pace with growth, the poor have no choice but to seek employment in informal sector, characterized by low wages, little social protection and exploitative contractual arrangements.

PRIMACY OF INVESTING IN HUMAN DEVELOPMENT—'CAPABILITY APPROACH'

Capability is a new approach towards poverty reduction. Poverty deprives a person to acquire capacity to work in more efficient manner and lead a decent life. The concept was pioneered by Nobel Laurate Prof. Amartya Sen as Capability Approach in the early 1980s. Professor Sen has developed, refined and defended a framework that is directly concerned with human capability and freedom.[16-18] From the outset Sen acknowledged strong connections with Adam Smith's analysis of 'necessities' and living conditions and Karl Marx's concern with human freedom and emancipation. Later Sen recognized that 'the most powerful conceptual connections', which he initially failed to appreciate, relate to Aristotle's theory of 'political distribution' and his analysis of *eudaimonia*—'human fluirishing'.[19-21]

While the roots of the 'Capability Approach' can be traced back to Aristotle, Classical Political Economy and Marx, it is possible to identify more recent links. For example, Sen often notes that Rawls's *Theory of Justice* (1971) and his emphasis on 'self-respect' and access to primary goods has 'deeply influenced' the Capability Approach.[22] Another connection, which is not really discussed, relates to Isaiah Berlin's classic essay 'Two Concepts of Liberty', which mounts a fierce attack on the positive concepts of freedom[23] that inspired Sen. Sen also takes the trouble to compare and contrast the Capability Approach with some close rivals, which concentrate on entitlements, the priority of liberty, human rights and human capital. In doing so he generally shows that each approach has something to offer, but only the Capability Approach can address all relevant concerns.[24]

The Capability Approach, however, probably has the most in common with the Basic Needs Approach (BNA) to development pioneered by Paul Streeten *et al.*[25] In an early paper entitled 'Goods and People', Sen tries to distinguish between the Capability Approach and Basic Needs Approach through a five-fold critique of the latter.[26] Conceptually Prof. Sen defined 'Capability Approach' in terms of expansion of human capabilities. According to him development should be seen as the expansion of human capabilities, not the maximisation of utility, or its proxy, money income.[27] Capability approach of poverty reduction rejects monetary income as its measure of well-being, and instead focuses on indicators of the freedom to lead a valued life. Thus, poverty is defined as deprivation in the space of capability approach, or failure to achieve certain minimal or basic capabilities, where 'basic capabilities' are the 'ability to satisfy certain crucially important functioning up to certain minimally adequate levels'.[28]

Sen's approach has following noteworthy characteristics :

(i) It is flexible and exhibits a considerable degree of internal pluralism which allows researchers to develop and apply it in many different ways;

(ii) It has no fixed or definitive list of capabilities. The reduction and weighing of capabilities depend on personal value judgements which are partly influenced by the nature and purpose of the evaluative exercise. Although, Sen did not provide an exhaustive list of capabilities that are regarded vital for poverty reduction, but he often provides examples of intrinsically valuable capabilities—such as being able to (a) live long, (b) escape avoidable morbidity, (c) be well nourished, (d) be able to read, write and communicate, and (e) take part in literary and scientific pursuits and so forth.[29]

(iii) The Capability Approach can be used to assess individual advantage in a range of different spaces. For example, the assessment of poverty might involve concentrating on a relatively small sub-set of basic capabilities. Evaluating well-being or human development on the other hand seems to require a much longer and more diverse list of capabilities. The focus of the Capability Approach can be broadened further to include 'agency', which recognises that individuals often have values and goals such as preserving the environment, purchasing free trade products or opposing injustice, tyranny and oppression that transcend and sometimes even conflict with personal well-being. The Capability Approach has also been adjusted to focus on inequality, social justice, living standards and rights and duties.

(iv) Sen recognises that the Capability Approach is not sufficient for all evaluative purposes. By itself the Capability Approach does not provide a complete theory of justice or development. We need to take note of other principles such as personal liberty, economic growth and efficiency.

Capability Approach has been further developed in more coherent, but different manner by Martha Nussbaum, a feminist philosopher.[30] She develops a definit list of 'Central Human Capabilities' with following indicators.

(a) Life : normal length of life,
(b) Health : good health, adequate nutrition and shelter,
(c) Bodily integrity : movement; choice in reproduction,
(d) Senses : imagination and thought, informed by education,
(e) Emotions : attachments,
(f) Practical reason : critical reflection and planning life,
(g) Affiliation : social interaction, protection against discrimination,
(h) Other species : respect for and living with other species, and

(i) Control over ones environment, politically (choice) and materially (prosperity).

Thus, capability approach of Prof. Amartya Sen and Central Human Capabilities of Nussbaum have more or less the same notion as that of 'Basic Human Need' approach of Streeten.[31]

Basic needs may be interpreted in terms of minimum specified quantities of such things as food, clothing, shelter, water and sanitation that are necessary to prevent ill health, undernourishment and the like[32] the Basic Human Needs approach reached the height of its popularity in the 1970s though it has made a come-back lately in the form of the Millennium Development Goals.

Capability approach, alongwith the concept of central human capabilities and basic human needs ultimately resulted into a major policy change in international development agencies and developing countries.

World Development Report 1990 heralded a major policy shift for the World Bank. Poverty reduction became the World Bank's overriding operational objective based on the dual strategy of labour-intensive growth and investment in human capital (health and education) with safety nets/transfers proposed for those excluded from growth. This position represented a widely held view of the main causal forces which would serve to reduce poverty in the years to come.

This strategy is based on a physiological model of deprivation and on human and economic capital-based conceptions of social change. It is an amalgam of three different approaches to poverty reduction, the direct transfer, human capital and production function approaches. The Human Capital approach to poverty reduction focuses on the links between investment in education, health and nutrition and the primary incomes of the poor. Emphasis is placed on the interrelationships between these variables as well as their relative importance in explaining changes in productivity. The human capital approach is the straightforward application of the analysis of human capital-based analysis of social change. This approach is closely related to the physiological deprivation model in so far as the primarily objective is to increase basic preference fulfillment by increasing primary incomes to increase basic needs satisfaction directly by social service provision.

Capability Approach in India

Countries that have been most successful in attacking poverty have encouraged a pattern of growth that makes efficient use of labour and have invested in the human capital of the poor. Both elements are essential. The first provides the poor with opportunities to use their most abundant asset-labour. The second improves their immediate well being and increase their capacity to take advantage of the newly created possibilities. Together, they can improve the lives of most of the world's poor.

India suffers severe deprivation in both the aspects of capability enhancement of human capital, education and health especially in BIMARU states of North and Orissa, Jharkhand and Chhattisgarh and a part of Andhra Pradesh and Maharashtra, where caste class and gender inequalities are significantly strong. In studies in Bihar and Uttar Pradesh poor women and men emphasized their extreme vulnerability and the ineffectiveness of state institutions, from schools to police. In the past, poverty reduction in many regions/states lagged behind that of certain development pockets of the country because of slower growth and significantly less progress in promoting mass education and basic health. More recently, however, growth has accelerated and poverty has decline, although the actual impact of growth on poverty reduction remains controversial because of measurement problem.

Inter-state and intra-state disparities in growth and development in India have further aggravated the problem. While the south, particularly the state of Kerala, having sharply better education and health, Kerala has life expectancies greater than those in Washington DC, despite vastly lower income levels. The effectiveness of public action in Kerala has been attributed to its strong tradition of political and social mobilisation. Success of Kerala model development lies in heavy investment in education and health. In areas with deep deprivation in health and education, the development of social infrastructure is critical. Higher spending will need to be matched by better service provision. This will require deep improvements in governance, often weakest in India's poorest regions. Also needed is more equitable service provision, which will require empowering women and *dalits*.

Much prior to the adoption of capability approach or the basic human need approach as the strategy of poverty reduction by the World Bank and other international agencies, policy planners in India realised the need and importance of specific policy measures that could give boost to alleviate the poverty and enhance the living standards of the people. Sixth Plan document specifically states, "A substantial increase in the overall rate of growth of the economy will no doubt create favourable conditions for a reduction in poverty and unemployment. However, in the light of past experience, it will not be realistic to rely solely on the growth process to find a solution to this problem. Specific policy measure will be needed not only to influence the composition of output in favour of mass consumption goods but also to ensure a more even, regional and class distribution of output, paying special attention to stimulating growth in more backward regions. In addition, the on-going poverty eradication programmes aimed at the specified target groups of population will also have to be improved and enlarged with regard to both contest and coverage. The objectives of these programmes will be to improve the productivity and therefore, income of the poor and also to ensure that employment opportunities are enlarged at a fast enough pace. Labour intensive village and small industries will need adequate encouragement to grow. Institutional reform designed to impart a greater redistributive bias to public policies in favour of the poorest sections will have to be pursued with greater vigour and effectiveness.[33]

Human resources development has been assigned a key role in development strategy in India so that trained and educated workforce can itself become an asset in accelerating economic growth and in ensuring social change in desirable direction. Education develops basic skills and abilities and fosters a value system conducive to, and in support of, national goals, both long-term and immediate. The resolution on the National Policy on Education, adopted in 1968, declared that the radical reconstruction of education as envisaged involved : (i) a transformation of the system to relate it more closely to the life of the people, (ii) a continuous effort to expand educational opportunity; (iii) a sustained and intensive effort to raise the quality of the education at all stages; (iv) an emphasis on the development of science and technology, and (v) the cultivation of moral and social values.[34]

The success of development process depends on the extent to which human resources are developed in terms of education, skills, health and well-being. India was a signatory to the Alma Ata Declaration (1978), whereby it was committed to achieve the goal "Health for All by 2000 AD". In accordance with these objectives several programmes were initiated during Fifth, Sixth and Seventh Five Year Plan for the development of education and health.

Minimum Needs Programme

Minimum Needs Programme, the most ambitious programme initiated for human resources development, introduced in the Fifth Five Year Plan. The concept of the MNP emerged and crystallised out of the experience of the previous plans that neither growth nor social consumption can be sustained, much less accelerated, without being mutually supportive. MNP programme was essentially an investment in HRD. The provision of free or subsidised services, through public agencies was expected to improve the consumption levels of those living BPL and thereby improve the productive efficiency of both the rural and urban workers. The integration of social consumption programmes with economic development programmes was necessary to accelerate growth and to ensure the achievements of plan objective. MNP had 8 components, namely : (i) Elementary Education, (ii) Rural Health, (iii) Rural Water Supply, (iv) Rural Roads, (v) Rural Electrification, (vi) Housing Assistance to Rural Landless Labourers, (vii) Environmental Improvement of Urban Slums, and (viii) Nutrition.

The overall performance of MNP indicated that the programme had brought about improvement to infrastructure and services available; however, the targets could not be achieved within the time framework. It was also a matter of concern that the performance under MNP was sub-optimal in states where the access to these services were poor prior to the initiation of the programme and over years the disparities in availability of services between states and between districts had widened.[35]

In view of sub-optimal performance of MNP, conference of Chief Ministers in 1996 resolved that the core of the social development plan for the seven Basic Minimum Services—(i) Primary Health Care, (ii) Provision of safe drinking water, (iii) Universalisation of primary education, (iv) Housing assistance to shelterless, (v) Nutrition support, (vi) Streamlining of PDS with a focus on the poor, and (vii) Connectivity of unconnected villages—should be initiated in a time bound fashion so as to increase the access of BMS to all people in rural and urban areas to enhance the quality of life of the citizen. Among these Primary Health Care, Elementary Education, and Provision of safe drinking water have been accorded higher priority, with a target of universal coverage by 2000 AD.[36] Thus, Basic Minimum Services Programme was a revised version of MNP.

Central government as well as state governments created massive infrastructure in rural and urban areas to make the primary health care accessible to all, especially the deprived class of the society (Table 6.2). Considerable achievements have been made over the last six decades to improve health

Table 6.2
Health Care Infrastructure in India

Items	*1951*	*1961*	*1971*	*1981*	*1991*	*2006*
Sub-Centres	0	0	28489	51406	130984	146000
Primary Health Centre	725	2565	5112	5740	20450	22669
Community Health Centre	0	0	0	217	2071	4045
Dispensaries	6515	9406	12128	16751	27431	NA
Hospitals	2694	3094	3862	6804	11174	NA
Hospital Beds	117198	230000	348655	569495	810545	NA

Source : GOI (1998); Ninth Five Year Plan (1997-2002), Planning Commission, Vol. I, p. 505.
GOI (2009); Economic Survey, 2009-10, Ministry of Finance.

standards such as life expectancy, child mortality, infant mortality, and maternal mortality (Table 6.3). Nevertheless, problems abound malnutrition affects a large proportion of children (Table 6.4). While poverty rates have decline significantly, malnutrition has remained stubbornly high. Malnutrition, as measured by underweight children below 3 years, constituting 45.9 per cent in children under 3 years of age as per the National Family Health Survey, 2005-06 (NFHS-III) has still remained much higher. What is more disturbing, malnutrition has not declined in a significant manner from its level of 47 per cent in NFHS-II (1988-89). Malnutrition reflects an imbalance of both macro and micro-nutrients that may be due to inappropriate intake and/or inefficient biological utilization due to the internal/external environment.

It may be observed that malnutrition cannot entirely be explained by poverty though it is an important determinant (Table 6.4). Even Punjab with poverty ratio of only 8.4 per cent has 27 per cent children below 3 years as underweight. Andhra Pradesh, Assam, Gujarat and Haryana are some other

TABLE 6.3
Selected Health Indicators of India

Items	*1951*	*1961*	*1971*	*1981*	*1991*	*Current level*
Crude Birth Rate	40.8	40.9	41.1	33.9	29.5	22.8(2008)
Crude Dealth Rate	27.4	22.8	18.9	12.5	9.8	7.4(2008)
Total Fertility Rate	NA	NA	18.9	4.5	3.6	2.7(2007)
Maternal Mortality Rate (per 1,00,000 live Births)	NA	NA	NA	NA	NA	254(04-06)
Infant Mortality Rate (per 1000 live Birth)	183	146	129	110	80	53(2003)
Child (0–4 yrs) Mortality rate per 1000 children	NA	NA	NA	41.2	26.5	16.0(2007)
Life Expectancy at Birth	1951-61	1961-71	1970 75	1981-85	1989-93	2002-06
Male	41.9	48.4	50.5	55.4	59.0	62.6
Female	40.6	44.7	49.0	55.7	59.7	64.2

Source : Economic Survey, 2008-09, p. 273.

TABLE 6.4
Incidence of Hunger, Poverty, Malnutrition and Availability of Public Health Facilities in Major States

State	*Inadequate food (%)*	*Poverty % of Population (URP)*	*Malnutrition under 3 yrs. underweight children (%)*	*Public health % of households drinking water facilities*	*Public health % of households access to toilet facility*
	2004-05	2004-05	2005-06	(2001)*	2005-06
(1)	(2)	(3)	(4)	(5)	(6)
Andhra Pradesh	0.5	15.8	36.5	80.1 (67.8)	42.4
Assam	5.0	19.7	40.4	58.8 (11.6)	76.4
Bihar	2.7	41.4	58.4	86.6 (4.2)	25.2
Gujarat	0.2	16.8	47.4	84.1(72.7)	54.6
Haryana	0.1	14.0	41.9	86.1 (61.1)	52.3
Himachal Pradesh	0.0	10.0	36.2	88.6 (65.1)	45.6
Karnataka	0.2	25.0	41.1	84.6 (57.4)	46.5
Kerala	2.3	15.0	28.8	23.4 (24.6)	96.0
Madhya Pradesh	1.6	38.3	60.3	68.4 (25.0)	27.0

(*Contd.*)

TABLE 6.4 (Contd.)

(1)	(2)	(3)	(4)	(5)	(6)
Maharashtra	0.8	30.7	39.7	79.8 (78.6)	53.0
Orissa	5.3	46.4	44.0	64.2 (10.2)	19.3
Punjab	0.7	8.4	27.0	97.6 (54.6)	70.8
Rajasthan	0.0	22.1	44.0	68.2 (45.4)	30.8
Tamilnadu	0.3	22.5	33.2	85.6 (84.2)	42.9
Uttar Pradesh	1.5	32.8	47.3	87.8 (10.3)	33.1
West Bengal	9.0	24.7	43.5	88.5 (27.9)	59.5
Chhattisgarh	2.2	40.9	52.1	70.5 (16.8)	18.7
Jharkhand	0.6	40.3	59.2	42.6 (11.3)	22.6
All India	1.9	27.5	45.9	77.9 (42.0)	44.5

Source : NFHS-3, NSSO, Planning Commission, O/O RGI.

* Figure in parenthesis give corresponding position regarding households using piped drinking water as per NFHS-3 (2005-06).

examples of high malnutrition among children with lower levels of poverty. The ICDS programme seems to have helped in providing public health education to mothers and thus contributed to the outcome in states like Tamilnadu and Himachal Pradesh. However, in order to have larger impact beyond nutrition to other health outcomes, a comprehensive programme for improving civic amenities of a public health nature to a defined standard is necessary to remove visible symbols of divide between rich and poor, that slums and other neighbourhoods with poor drainage and sewage create.

Improved health education and public health facilities are closely linked with nutrition outcomes. Improvement in income/consumption of poor has higher weightage in social welfare. In this regard access of poor to public goods, such as safe drinking water and sanitation has also a positive impact on the well-being of the poor. Literacy and public health are interrelated. Higher levels of literacy lead to quality public health which results into longevity and mortality reduction. BIMARU states alongwith Orissa and Chhattisgarh and Jharkhand have poor status of availability of safe drinking water supply and sanitary toilets. Unfortunately all these states have large number of poor in total population.

Government of India's investment on health and family welfare and AYUSH was Rs. 7494.2 crore, Rs. 6500.00 crore and Rs. 108.00 crore respectively during Eighth Plan. It increased to Rs. 31020.3 crore, Rs. 27125.0 crore and Rs. 775.0 crore respectively during Tenth Plan (Table 6.5).

Since 1995-96, household expenditure on health has been growing at the current rate of approximately 14 per cent overall. In 1995-96, households in India spent an estimated Rs. 33;253 crore at nominal prices which is estimated to have increased to Rs. 72,759 crore in 2001-02. With an overall growth rate of 14 per cent, household spending is likely to be close to Rs. 100,000 crore in nominal terms during 2003-04.[37]

Education

Education is a critical input in human resource development and is essential for the country's economic growth. Though the major socio-economic indicators—the growth rate of the economy, birth rate, death rate infant

Table 6.5
Allocation of Public Funds on Health and Family Welfare in India

(Rs. in Crore)

Period		Total Plan Investment Quality of Country	Health	Family Welfare	AYUSH*	Sub-total
(1)	(2)	(3)	(4)	(5)	(6)	(7)
First Plan	(Actuals)	1960.0	65.2	0.01	–	65.3
(1951-56)			(3.3)	(0.1)		(3.4)
Second Plan	(Actuals)	4672.0	140.8	5.0	–	145.8
(1956-61)			(3.0)	(0.1)		(3.1)
Third Plan	(Actuals)	8573.5	225.9	24.9	–	250.8
(1961-66)			(2.6)	(0.3)		(2.9)
Annual Plans (Actuals)		6625.4	140.2	70.4	–	210.6
(1966-69)			(2.1)	(1.1)		(3.2)
Fourth Plan	(Actuals)	15778.8	335.5	278.0	–	613.5
(1969-74)			(2.1)	(1.8)		(3.9)
Fifth Plan	(Actuals)	39426.2	760.8	491.8	–	1252.6
(1974-79)			(1.9)	(1.2)		(3.1)

Annual Plan	(Actuals)	12176.5	223.1	118.5	–	341.6
(1979-80)			(1.8)	(1.0)		(2.8)
Sixth Plan	(Actuals)	109291.7	2052.2	1387.0	–	3412.2
(1980-85)			(1.8)	(1.3)		(3.1)
Seventh Plan (Actuals)		218729.6	3688.6	3120.8	–	6809.4
(1985-90)			(1.7)	(1.4)		(3.1)
Annual Plan	(Actuals)	61518.1	960.9	784.9	–	1745.8
(1990-91)			(1.6)	(1.3)		(2.9)
Annual Plan	(Actuals)	65855.8	1042.2	856.6	–	1898.8
(1991-92)			(1.6)	(1.3)		(2.9)
Eighth Plan	(Outlays)	434100.0	7494.2	6500.0	108.0	14102.2
(1992-97)			(1.7)	(1.5)	(0.02)	(3.2)
Ninth Plan	(Outlays)	859200.0	19818.4	15120.2	266.35	35204.95
(1997-02)			(2.31)	(1.76)	(0.03)	(4.09)
Tenth Plan	(Outlays)	1484131.3	31020.3	27125.0	775.0	58920.3
(2002-07)			(2.09)	(1.83)	(0.05)	(3.97)
Eleventh Plan (Outlays)		2156571.0	136147.0**		3966.0	140135.0
(2007-12)			(6.3%)		(0.18%)	(6.5%)

* Deptt. ISM & H (now AYUSH) was created during 8th Plan period.

** Deptt. of Health and Family Welfare merged from 2005.

Figures in brackets indicate percentage to total plan investment outlay.

Source : National Health Profile 2007, p. 125.

mortality rate, maternal mortality rate and literacy rate, etc. are all inter-related, the literacy rate has been the major determinant of the increase or decrease in the other indicators, literacy rate, especially female literacy has a high positive correlation with birth rate and life expectancy, a high negative correlation with infant mortality rate and maternal mortality rate. Literacy is also a key determinant of empowerment of women.

Literacy and skill development are closely interlinked, and both are key factor of human resources development. Government was committed to provide free and compulsory education for all children under 14 years of age vide article 45 of the Constitution of India. However, the task of providing elementary education for all, with concrete plans of action, gained greater momentum only after the National Policy of Education, 1986 (revised in 1992).

India is a signatory of World Declaration on Education for All (EFA) adopted in Jomtein in 1990. India, alongwith the rest of the world took all possible steps for the improvement of basic education in all facets—Early Child Care Education, elementary education, education for adolescents, adult education, gender equality, and quality improvement.

Government of India took following measures for the enhancement of the level of literacy and skill development.

National Literacy Mission, 1988 : It was the first initiative to make the National Policy of Education, 1986, a good and solid start. The NLM had the following aims[38] :

- Increase motivation,
- Secure participation through mass mobilisation,
- Increase the involvement of voluntary agencies,
- Enhance the quality of existing programmes with improved techno-pedagogic inputs,
- Expansion of Mass Functional Literacy Programme,
- Ensure the availability of quality learning materials, and
- Universalisation of education.

Operation Black Board : In pursuance to National Literacy Mission, Operation Black Board was launched in 1987 as a centrally sponsored scheme. The scheme was intended to improve the school infrastructure in primary and upper primary school.

National Programme of Nutritional Support, 1995 : This programme was launched on 15th August 1995. Three kgs of foodgrains per month was provided to each primary school going child, under this programme. The programme had twin objectives of increasing attendance in the school and arresting the trend of dropout and improving the nutritional status of the children.

Mid-day Meal Scheme : With a view to enhancing enrolment, retention and attendance and simultaneously improving nutritional levels among children, the National Programme of Nutritional Support to Primary Education (Mid-Day Meal Scheme) was launched on 15th August 1995, initially in 2408 blocks in the country. By the year 1997-98 the MDM was introduced in all blocks of the country. Cooked mid-day meal with 300 calories and 8-12 grams of protein to all children studying in class I-V in Government and aided schools and EGS/AIE centres. In October 2007, the scheme has been extended to cover children in upper primary (classes VI to VIII) initially in 3479 educationally backwards blocks. The programme has been extended to all areas across the country from 2008-09. The caloric value of mid-day meal at upper primary stage is 700 calories and 20 grams of protein by providing 150 gms of foodgrains per child per school day.

Mid-day meal programme, the largest such programme in the world, has its origin in Tamilnadu where the scheme was started on a humble scale way back in 1925-26 by the Corporation of Madras. Subsequently, philanthropists and voluntary organisations were urged to start free school lunch centres in village and towns all over the states. In July 1956, the school lunch programme was launched as a 'peoples' movement' for organised charity as part of the School Improvement Efforts. Government of Tamilnadu took up the school lunch programme in 1957. Tamilnadu has a distinction of being the first state in the country to launch of Nutritious Meals Programme for school children in classes Ist to Xth.

Mid-day meal programme, provides nutritional support to school going children, in all government, aided schools and

EGS/AIE centres. Majority of students in these schools belong to weaker sections of the society. The rationale of the programme are : (i) Promoting school participation, (ii) Preventing classroom hunger, (iii) Facilitating the healthy growth of children, (iv) Intrinsic educational value, (v) Fostering social equality, (vi) Enhancing gender equity, and (vi) Help in addressing the problem of insecurity, anxiety and stress because of physiological deprivation. Thus, mid-day meal scheme is a drive towards poverty alleviation through nutritional support and creation of a base for human resources development.

Minimum Levels of Learning (MLL) : Merely the entry of a child into a school is not enough for the creation of solid base of HRD. Basically, it is the level of learning that prepare the children for further improvement of schooling and skill development. Keeping in view the need of enhancement of learning, the GOI has introduced the programme of Minimum Level of Learning with the objective of specifying competencies which all primary school students should attain at mastery level of Language, Mathematics and Environmental studies and to develop curricula and text-book in relation to those. The first phase was implemented through voluntary organisations, research institutions, SCERTSs and DIETs. Later on, the MLL approach has been introduced in schools in different states.

District Primary Education Programme : The programme, partially funded by a loan from World Bank, was initiated in November, 1994. The programme aims at operationalising strategies required for achieving the goal of universal elementary education through specific planning and target setting at the district level. The intervention was based on the concept of decentralised management, community mobilisation and contextual and research-based inputs.

Sarva Shiksha Abhiyan : The Sarva Shiksha Abhiyan (SSA) was launched into achieve the goal of Universalisation of Elementary Education (Universal Access, Universal Enrolment, Universal Retention, Universal Achievement, and Equity) through a time-bound integrated approach in partnership with states. SSA is the culmination of all previous endeavors and experiences in implementing various education programmes.

While each of these programmes and projects has a specific focus—operational blackboard on improving physical infrastructure; DPEP on primary education; Shiksha Karmi Project on Teacher's Absenteeism, and Lok Jumbish Projects on girls' education, SSA has been the single largest holistic programme, addressing all aspects of elementary education covering over one million elementary schools and Education Guarantee Centres/Alternative and Innovative Education Centres and about 20 crore children. SSA had the following objectives:[39]

- All children to be in schools by 2003,
- All children to complete five years of primary schooling by 2007,
- All children to complete eight years of schooling by 2010,
- Focus on elementary education of satisfactory quality with emphasis on education for life,
- Bridge all gender and social disparities at the primary stage by 2007 and the upper primary level by 2010, and
- Universal retention by 2010.

The achievements of SSA till September 2009 are opening of 2,88,155 new schools, construction of 2,40,888 school buildings, construction of 10,26,831 additional classrooms, 1,84,652 drinking water facilities, construction of 2,86,862 toilets, supply of free textbooks to 9.05 crore children, appointment of 10.11 lakh teachers and in-service training for 21.79 lakh teachers.[40] With the creation of these facilities access to primary education is nearly achieved. So far as the universal enrolment is concerned, total enrolment at elementary education level increased from 1.59 million in 2001-02 to 182 million in 2004-05. Gross Enrolment Ratio at primary level was 107.8 per cent in 2004-05 as compared to 96.3 per cent in 2001-02. Gross Enrolment Ratio at upper primary level was 69.9 per cent in 2004-05 as compared to 60.2 per cent in 2001-02.[41] However, social and gender disparities, existing at both primary and upper primary education levels, continue to be a important issue to be tackled, with more concerted and sustained efforts, especially in Bihar, Rajasthan, Jharkhand, Madhya Pradesh, Gujarat and Uttar Pradesh.[42]

SSA interventions have brought down the number of out-of-school children from 32 million in 2001-02 to 7.0 million in 2004-05. The social composition of out-of-school children indicates that 9.97 per cent of Muslim children, 9.54 per cent of scheduled tribes, 8.17 per cent of SCs, and 6.97 per cent of OBCs children were out of school and overwhelming majority (68.7%) was concentrated in five states, viz. Bihar (23.6%), UP (22.2%), West Bengal (9%), Madhya Pradesh (8%) and Rajasthan (5.9%).

Mahila Samakhya : Mahila Samakhya (MS), an externally aided project for women's empowerment by creating an environment for women to learn at their own place, set their own priorities, and seek knowledge and information to make informed choices. MS was started with Dutch assistance in 1989. Since 2005-06 it is being funded by GOI. The programme is implemented in 9 states, covering 83 districts, 339 blocks, including 233 educationally backward blocks and 20380 villages. It provides for vocational and skill development as well as educational development of adolescent girls and women in rural areas. The programme has a great success as it has strengthened women's abilities to effectively participate in village level education programmes.

National Programme for Education of Girls at Elementary Education: NPEGEL is being implemented in educationally backward blocks (EBBs) where the level of rural female literacy is less than the national average and the gender gap is more than the national average and blocks having at least 5 per cent SC/ST population with SC/ST female literacy below 10 per cent. It is also being implemented in select urban slums. About 3,286 educationally backward blocks are covered under the scheme in 25 states. Under NPEGEL, 39,852 model schools have been opened in addition to supporting 11,261 Early Childhood Care and Education (ECCE) centres. Besides, 27,282 additional classrooms have been constructed, and 2,11,215 teachers have been given training on gender sensitization. Remedial teaching has also been provided to 11,44,370 girls apart from holding bridge courses covering 89,462 girls and additional incentives like uniforms, etc. to about 1,60,73,048 girls (up to January 31, 2009).

Total Literacy Campaign (TLC) : In pursuance of National Policy on Education 1986 and Plan of Action 1992, Total Literacy Campaign was started in the country to energise adult education and non-formal education to eradicate illiteracy. The efforts made by TLCs and Post-Literacy Projects to eradicate illiteracy yielded commendable results that reflect in the rise in literacy from 52.2 per cent in 1991 to 64.8 per cent in 2001. The gap between urban-rural literacy has decreased during the last decade of twentieth century. The literacy rate for females increased at a faster rate than that of males. However, gender and regional disparities in literacy still continue to persist.

As a separate class Muslims are a deprived class so far as the literacy level is concerned. 59.1 per cent Muslims (67.6 per cent males and 50.1 per cent females) are literate as against 65.37 per cent literates in the country as a whole. Female literacy rates among Muslims are particularly low in Haryana (21.5%), Bihar (31.5%), Nagaland (33.3%) and Jammu & Kashmir (34.9%). Low level of literacy alongwith high levels of IMR and MMR among Muslims need specific efforts for their upliftment.

Besides the pro-active strategies for the development of elementary education, Government of India and the States as well adopted various measures for the improvement of Secondary and Higher Education in the country. But, the achievements so far are disappointing with 51.65 per cent GER for Secondary education and only 27.82 per cent for higher secondary education. The dropout rate at secondary level (Class I-X) is as high as 62 per cent. There are glaring inter-state and intra-state variations in enrolment, dropouts and access to secondary and higher secondary schools. At the national level, the average number of secondary/higher secondary schools per one lakh population is as low as 14 and it is lower than the national average in Bihar (4), UP (7), WB (10), Jharkhand (4) and Chhattisgarh (12). Consequently, the GER in these states is lower than the national average of 39.91 per cent.

Although, the growth of the higher education system in India, in terms of number, seems quite impressive with 378 universities, 18,064 colleges in 2007 as compared to 28 universities and 268 colleges in 1950. But this system lacks all the four aspects of higher education—access, equity, quality and relevance. Gross Enrolment Ratio in higher education is around 11 per cent which is very low compared to the world average of 23.2 per cent, 36.5 per cent for countries in transition, 54.6 per cent for the development countries and 22 per cent for Asian countries. Further, with high disparities, inclusive higher education has been an elusive target. 370 districts with GER less than the national average need enrolment drives and rapid expansion of higher education system.[43]

APPROACH OF STATE INTERVENTION THROUGH INCOME-EMPLOYMENT GENERATION—'SAFETY-NET AND SUPPORT SECURITY' APPROACH

The nature and extent of poverty in India is multi-dimensional. Hence, it is imperative that programmes of poverty alleviation rely on a multi-pronged approach. Data on poverty and its analysis has identified that there is a geography of poverty, with poverty being concentrated in the rural areas of certain States (mainly the BIMARU States alongwith Jharkhand, Chhattisgarh, Orissa, Maharashtra and Andhra Pradesh). It also pointed out that there is a sociology of poverty, with certain social groups increasingly concentrated among those who are identified as poor (specially the SCs, STs and OBCs, women of deprived classes, etc.). It is also noted that there are identifiable occupational features of the poor; they are concentrated in agricultural labour and artisanal households in rural areas, and among casual labourers in urban areas. Casual labourers in urban areas are essentially distress migrants from rural areas in States where agricultural land-man ratio is very adverse, and where agricultural incomes have not been growing—reinforcing the need for both land reforms as well as measures to increase productivity.

This diversified nature and its magnitude across the states forced the government to attack on poverty from all sides. Rapid growth in GDP and per capita income have been the driving forces of poverty reduction strategy. Side-by-side investment in education and health as a part of capacity improvement, has created a base for human resources development, but with sub-optimal performance. The another approach, that has been given priority for poverty reduction since Fifth Plan, is the 'Safety-Net and Supported Security' approach.

The problem of poverty could not be tackled through growth alone, which itself was slow over a long period of time. Hence, direct intervention through poverty alleviation programmes became necessary. Self-employment and wage-employment programmes were taken up in the Government component of the public sector plan. In view of this the Eighth Five Year Plan had focussed on "creation of a social security net through employment generation, improved health care and provision of extensive education facilities through out the country" and "creation of appropriate organisations and delivery systems to ensure that the benefits of investment in social sectors reach the intended beneficiaries."[44] Thus, employment generation, literacy, education, health, drinking water and provision of adequate food and basic infrastructure were listed as priorities in nineties. This approach aims to transfer cash or in-kind income to the poor by providing subsidised goods and services or employment guarantees. As such, its primary benefit is realised directly by the transfer and not mediated by the above forms of capital (although second-order effects may work through these forms of capital if say, nutrition subsidies build human capital which increases productivity, etc.). This approach is situated within the purview of the physiological deprivation model. The objective of increasing (or smoothing) income levels of the poor and/or supplying basic goods and services (health, nutrition, etc.) is intended to facilitate basic preference fulfilment and/or basic need satisfaction.

The three main categories of direct transfer (safety-net) interventions are: in-kind transfers, cash transfers and public employment schemes. In kind transfers are of four types—price subsidies, quantity rationing schemes, food stamps and nutrition interventions often targeted to the poor by food type (coarse grains, roots) or by characteristics of the recipient (geographic, gender, etc.). Cash transfer measures with a poverty focus include social assistance, such as old-age, widow or disability pension schemes, and family assistance programmes. Public works schemes serve the function of creating or maintaining basic infrastructure (roads, irrigation, health, education, etc.) by providing employment for those facing chronic or seasonal underemployment or unemployment.

Public Distribution System

The PDS is a major state intervention in the country aimed at ensuring food security to all the people, especially the poor. The PDS operates through a large distribution network of around 4.89 lakh fair price shops (FPS), and is supplemental in nature. Under the PDS, the Central Government is responsible for the procurement and transportation of foodgrains upto the principal distribution centres of the FCI while the State Governments are responsible for the identification of families living below the poverty line, the issue of ration cards, and the distribution of foodgrains to the vulnerable sections through FPSs. PDS seems to have failed in serving the second objective of making foodgrains available to the poor. If it had, the consumption levels of cereals should not have fallen on average—as it has consistently over the last two decades. Thus, PDS is being operated as direct intervention programme in the form of cash support (as subsidised supply of foodgrains, sugar, edible oils and kerosene).

With a view to improving its efficiency, the PDS was redesigned as Targeted Public Distribution System (TDPS) with effect from June 1997. The TPDS envisages identifying the poor households and giving them a fixed entitlement of foodgrains at subsidized prices. Under the TPDS, higher rates of subsidies are being given to the poor and the poorest among the poor. The APL families are also being given foodgrains under TPDS but with lower subsidy. The scale of issue under TDPS for Antyodaya cardholders began with 10 kg per family per month, which has been progressively increased to 35 kg per family per month with effect from April 2002.

Under the TPDS, the identification of BPL families was to be carried out by the State Governments based on criteria adopted by the Ministry of Rural Development (MORD). However, the total number of beneficiaries was to be limited to the State-wise poverty estimates (1993-94) of the Planning Commission projected to the population as on 1.03.2000. Against a total ceiling of 6.52 crore BPL households (as per the poverty estimates of the Planning Commission for 1993-94 and population projection of the Registrar General as on 01.03.2000), more than 8 crore BPL ration cards have been issued. Similarly against the figure of 18.03 crore households in the country (as per the population projections as on 1.03.2000 of the Registrar General of India), the total number of ration cards issued is around 22.32 crore. This does raise problems at the field level.

PDS works as shock absorber during the hyper inflation, particularly the 'agflation' under which the prices of essential commodities such as foodgrains rises exorbitantly. Thus, it saves people from decrease in their income in real sense (in terms of purchasing power). But, operationally, PDS is being regarded as the programme with highest possible leakages. As identified by various studies, the major deficiencies of the TPDS include: (i) high exclusion and inclusion errors, (ii) non-viability of FPSs, (iii) failure in fulfilling the price stabilization objectives, and (iv) leakages.

The Programme Evaluation Organization's (PEO's) study (2005) establishes large-scale exclusion and inclusion errors in most States. Following deficiencies have emerged in the functioning of PDS[45] :

- Only 22.7 per cent FPSs are viable in terms of earning a return of 12 per cent on capital.
- The offtake by APL cardholders was negligible except in Himachal Pradesh, Tamil Nadu and West Bengal.
- The offtake per BPL card was high in WB, Kerala, Himachal Pradesh and Tamilnadu.
- The offtake by the poor under TPDS was substantially higher than under universal PDS.
- There are large errors of exclusion and inclusion and ghost cards are common.

- High exclusion errors mean a low coverage of BPL households. The survey estimated that TPDS covers only 57 per cent BPL families.
- Errors of inclusion are high in Andhra Pradesh, Karnataka, and Tamil Nadu. This implies that the APL households receive an unacceptably large proportion of subsidized grains.
- Leakages vary enormously between States. In BIhar and Punjab, the total leakage exceeds 75 per cent while in Haryana and UP, it is between 50 and 75 per cent.
- Leakage and diversion imply a low share of the genuine BPL households of the distribution of the subsidized grains. During 2003-04, it is estimated that out of 14.1 million tonnes of BPL quota from the Central Pool only 6.1 million tonnes reached the BPL families and 8 million tonnes did not reach the target families.
- Leakage and diversion raised the cost of delivery. For every 1 kg. that was delivered to the poor, GOI had to issue 2.3 kg. from the Central Pool.
- During 2003-04, out of an estimated subsidy of Rs. 7258 crore under TPDS, Rs. 4123 crore did not reach BPL families. Moreover, Rs. 2579 crore did not reach any consumer but was shared by agencies involved in the supply chain.

Several alternatives have been suggested to plug the holes of PDS. Some of which are followings[46] :

Food Stamps

If markets are integrated, food stamps system may be introduced, which is supposed to be more effective than the present system. In the long-run, as markets get better integrated, the PDS function need not remain restricted to designated FPS and a food coupon system valid even outside PDS outlets may become possible. Food coupons may allow wider choice of consumers in terms of commodities and outlets. This is a course which should be followed with considerable caution in view of the experience of other countries, and the possibility of counterfeiting. However, the more important reason food stamps have not been successful elsewhere has been the erosion in the value of the coupons where it was fixed in nominal terms. If the coupon system is to succeed the PDS suggested above, the value of the coupon should be indexed to food inflation. The coupon system should not lead to a dilution of the Central Government commitment to food security. Cash for food subsidies (sometimes known as food stamps) eliminate the need for dual retail marketing mechanisms.

Multi-Application Smart Cards (MASCs)

MASCs is one of the technological break-throughs of recent times. MASCs facilitate simplification of procedures and enhancing the efficiency in administering various schemes. The National e-Governance Policy fully recognizes the significance of this technology revolution. On the spot availability of proof of identity, authentic transaction history, and entitlement details are required at the point of service delivery. It will also allow other innovations/experiments such as the division of the PDS food entitlement between the Head of household and his/her (non-earning) spouse or transfer of entire household entitlement to the housewife/mother. Similarly, different models can be used for kerosene supply and fertilizer supply to farmers. In other words, the precise model for delivery of the subsidy or income transfer to individuals/households can be decided separately and/or modified overtime.

Web-Enabled Systems

Many departments of the Central Government, notably the MORD, are in the process of developing web-enabled systems that provide information about government programmes to beneficiaries and also details of the benefits received by the targeted beneficiaries. Easy access to such information is the most effective means to empower the beneficiaries and their well-wishers/representatives. Such web-enabled systems can be created for the PDS.

Food Bank

Establishing Food Bank under the direct control of

Panchayati Raj Institutions (PRIs) is another innovative scheme to safeguard the interests of poor. These food banks will help in achieving nutrition security for all and insulating the economically and socially deprived sections of the community from seasonal food insecurity. Main feature of the proposed food bank are :

- One foodbank for every village or cluster of villages with population ranging from 2000 to 5000;
- Supervised by a society or council choosen by the Gram Sabha;
- Managed by a stakeholder council, with different operations assigned to different SHGs; and
- To be implemented with honesty, political neutrality, fairness, absence of discrimination based on religion, caste, class, gender and political belief.

A diagrammatic representation of the proposed Community Food Security System suggested by the M.S. Swaminathan, Research Foundation, Chennai is given in Chart 6.1.

Integrated Child Development Services (ICDS)

Integrated Child Development Services (ICDS) scheme was launched in 1975, with the following objectives :

- To improve the health and nutrition status of children 0–6 age group by providing supplementary food;
- To provide food supplements to pregnant and lactating women;
- To provide conditions necessary for pre-school children's psychological and social development through early stimulation and education; and
- To enhance the mothers ability to provide proper child care through health and nutrition education.

Initially the ICDS scheme focussed on drought prone areas and blocks with high proportion of scheduled caste and scheduled tribes. Over the years the ICDS coverage has

CHART 6.1

Community Food Security System

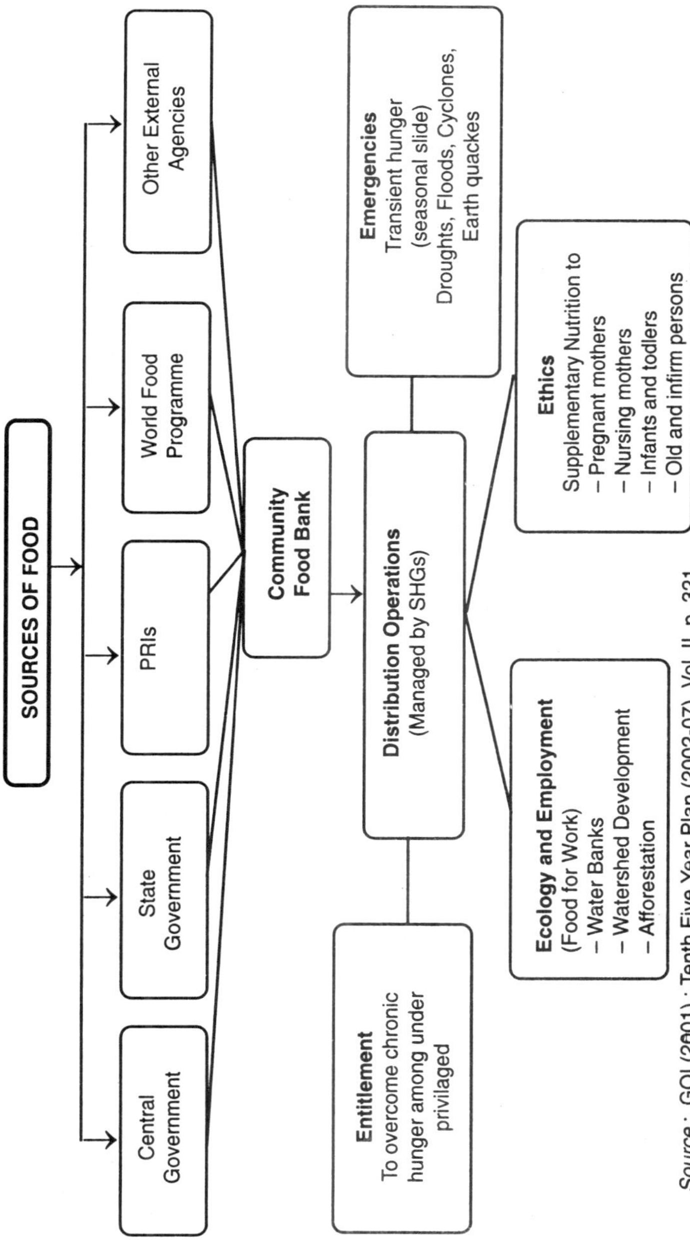

Source : GOI (2001) : Tenth Five Year Plan (2002-07), Vol. II, p. 321.

progressively increased. The ICDS programme is unique in the sense that apart from being a state sponsored programme, it has deep penetration in the community through 'Anganwadis' selected locally. These Anganwadis have developed a closed rapport among women of the community and emerged as 'opinion leaders'.

ICDS, which has been in existence for over three decades, is intended to address the problem of child and maternal malnutrition, but has clearly had limited impact. Child malnutrition has barely declined at all in a decade and half, anaemia among women and children has actually risen. Nearly one third adult women are undernourished in 2005-06 as they were at the end of 1990s.[47]

Cash Transfer Measures with a Poverty Focus

Sometimes cash assistance becomes necessary, especially to help those segments of the population that are unable or incapable to earn that much income which is essential to purchase goods and services essential for the very survival of mankind. Article 41 under the directive principles of state of the constitution of India puts the onus on the state to make effective provision for securing the right to work, to education and to public assistance in cases of unemployment, old age, sickness and disablement and in other cases of underserved want. Government of India initiated National Social Assistance Programme to fulfil the above obligation.

For the first time in India, the NSAP was launched on 15 August 1995. The basic aim of this programme is to provide social assistance benefit to the rural poor in case of old age, death of primary bread earner and for poor women during maternity. It aims at providing them with a modicum of dignity and support, thereby ensuring a minimum quality of care and attention from the community. It provides an opportunity for linking the social assistance package to schemes for poverty alleviation and provision of basic needs. This programme is implemented through a synergistic partnership with State Governments and under the direct supervision of DRDAs in close collaboration with the various PRIs. This programme included three schemes viz., National

Old Age Pension Scheme (NOAPS), National Family Benefit Scheme (NFBS), and National Maternity Benefit Scheme (NMBS).

- Under NOAPS, old age pension of Rs. 75 per month was provided to persons of 65 years and above who are destitute. This amount has since been enhanced to Rs. 200 per month from the year 2006-07. The response for this scheme has been overwhelming from the poor as well as the State Governments. Many States are matching these pension amounts equally and many more are extending the coverage of this scheme to all those identified from among BPL families. The scheme is redesignated as Indira Gandhi National Old Age Pension Scheme on 19th November, 2007. Originally all the 'destitutes' above the age of 65 years were eligible for pension. But, now all the old age people of 65 years and above living BPL are eligible for pension.
- The NFBS provides a lump sum family benefit of Rs. 10000 to the bereaved household in case of the death (natural or accidental) of the primary bread-earner (male or female) whose earnings contribute substantially to the total household income. This scheme is applicable to all the eligible persons in the age group 18 to 64. The bereaved household should belong to BPL families to qualify for this benefit.
- Under the NMBS there is a provision for payment of Rs. 500 per pregnancy to women belonging to poor households for pre-natal and post-natal maternity care upto the first two live births. This benefit is provided to eligible women of 19 years and above. The objective of the scheme is to extend financial assistance to pregnant women from BPL households, for the first two live births. To ensure better linkage with nutrition and national population control programmes, NMBS was transferred to Department of Family Welfare and is renamed as Janani Suraksha Yojana in 2001-02. It is now a part of the NRHM.

Poverty Alleviation Programmes

Direct attack on poverty came into prominence in 1971, when the then Prime Minister of India (late) Mrs. Indira Gandhi, floated the slogan, 'Garibee Hatao' and won the Lok Sabha election (1971) with thumping majority. Accordingly several programmes of employment generation and poverty alleviation were started during Fifth Plan and subsiquent Five Year Plans. Some of these programmes were as under.

Prime Minister's Crash Programme (PMCP)

Crash Programme was launched in 1971-72. It aimed at creating employment opportunities in rural areas for unskilled labourers during the lean season. Several projects of construction of rural roads, digging of ponds and drainage canals were taken up. It was implemented by Block Development officials. Despite its several weaknesses the programme had some positive impact on the generation of employment.

Marginal Farmers' and Agricultural Labours' Programme

It was the first programme, started on 2nd Oct. 1971, to assist the marginal farmers' and agricultural labourers' to increase their productivity and capabilities to generate higher level of income so as to overcome the poverty. This programme was conceived on the recommendations of All India Rural Credit Review Committee during the early period of Fourth Five Year Plan. The Programme aimed at :

- Production Oriented Programme to increase agricultural production, employing modern scientific methods of farming;
- Improved marketing facilities; and
- Employment creation.

Small Farmers Development Agencies (SFDA)

Small Farmers Development Agencies programme was launched in 1971. It aimed at the target group of small and marginal farmers and agricultural labourers. The objective of the programme was to assist persons specifically identified from the target group in raising their income level. This was to be achieved by helping them, on the one hand, to adopt improved agricultural technology and acquiring means of increasing agricultural production like minor irrigation sources, and on the other hand, to diversify their farm economy through subsidiary activities like animal husbandry, dairying, horticulture, etc. The agencies were to make particular efforts to ensure that the needed inputs and credit were made available to the targeted groups by respective credit agencies.[48] The actual impact of MFAL and SFDA on the income of the beneficiaries therefore varied a great deal. Where, however, assistance had been given for developing minor irrigation sources or for acquiring milch cattle, sheep, goats, poultry, etc., the impact had been significant.[49]

Antyodaya Programme

'Antyodaya' programme was conceived by Sri Bhairon Singh Shekhawat, Ex-Vice-president of India (the then Chief Minister of Rajasthan), during 1977-78 for the upliftment of rural destitutes. Basically the programme was launched in Rajasthan, but later on it was adopted by other states too. The Antyodaya was aimed to the most disadvantageous persons of the society. It helped target destitutes to acquire some income generating activity on sustainable basis. Despite its impressive impact on the generation of income and creation of employment, the 'Antyodaya' was discarded purely on political grounds by successive governments.

Integrated Rural Development Programme (IRDP)

IRDP, a 'flagship' programme of poverty alleviation had following five sub-components :

- IRDP—Integrated Rural Development Programme.
- TRYSEM—Training of Rural Youth for Self-Employment.
- DWCRA—Development of Women and Children in Rural Areas.
- SITRA—Supply of Improved Tool Kits to Rural Artisans.
- GKY—Ganga Kalyan Yojna.

The concept of an Integrated Rural Development Programme was first proposed in the Central budget of 1976-77, and a beginning was made. This programme was intended to assist the rural population to derive economic benefits from the developmental assets of each area. Besides the small and marginal farmers, this programme was more specific in regard to agricultural workers and landless labourers and additionally brought within its purview rural artisans too. The programme emphasised the family rather than individual approach in identification of beneficiaries. Though conceptually this programme was comprehensive in scope and sought to secure, through a process of block level planning, fuller exploitation of the local growth potential with a view to making an optimum impact on the local poverty situation, in point of fact it has also tended to operate on the same lines as the SFDA.

The IRDP has been successful in providing incremental income to the poor families, but in most cases the incremental income has not been adequate to enable the beneficiaries to cross the poverty line on a sustained basis mainly because of a low per family investment. The results of the Evaluation (September 1992-August 1993) revealed that of the total beneficiaries assisted under the programme, 15.96 per cent of the old beneficiary families could cross the revised poverty line of Rs. 11,000 (at 1991-92 prices), while 54.4 per cent of the families were able to cross the old poverty line of Rs. 6,400 per annum. But, the analysis by income group of families revealed that in case of those within initial income of Rs. 8,501–11,000, 48.22% of beneficiary families could cross the poverty line of Rs. 11,000 which was quite encouraging. The analysis of the family income of the beneficiaries reveals that a large percentage (57.34%) of the families had annual income from assets of more than Rs. 2,000. The annual income from the asset was more than Rs. 6,000 in 29% cases.[50]

The major constraint in the implementation of IRDP has been subcritical investments which have adversely affected the Incremental Capital Output Ratio (ICOR) levels and thereby undermined the viability of the projects. Though the average per family investment had been rising steadily in monetary terms, in real terms the increase had been inadequate and in some cases sub-critical due to the inflationary trends and the increase in the cost of assets.[51]

The overall experience of the working of the poverty alleviation programme is by no means uniform in the country. In general, the performance of IRDP has been better in the relatively developed regions which are well provided with infrastructure and where level of awareness among the beneficiaries was high. Even in the less developed areas, performance had been satisfactory wherever special provisions follow-up measures for greater involvement of people through their representatives were adopted.

Training of Rural Youth for Self-Employment (TRYSEM)

The Scheme of TRYSEM, a facilitating component of IRDP, aims at providing basic technical and entrepreneurial skills to the rural poor in the age group of 18 to 35 years to enable them to take up income generating activities was started on 15th August, 1979.

There has been a poor convergence of TRYSEM with IRDP which has also been reflected in the Fourth Round of the Concurrent Evaluation of IRDP (1992-93). Only 3.88 per cent of the IRDP beneficiaries had received training under TRYSEM. It was also observed that the rural youth trained under TRYSEM were only interested in the stipendiary benefits they received during the course of training and therefore, had not utilised the knowledge gained under the programme for furthering their self-employment prospects. In practice, therefore, such expenditure on training had become infractuous because of an absence of linkages between the employment opportunities available and training provided. Clearly, TRYSEM has been a weak link in the overall strategy for self-employment in rural areas.[52]

Development of Women and Children in Rural Areas (DWCRA)

The special scheme for Development of Women and Children in Rural Areas (DWCRA) aimed at strengthening the gender component of IRDP. It was started in 1982, on a pilot basis, in 50 districts and later on extended to all the districts of the country.

DWCRA was directed at improving the living conditions of women and, thereby, of children through the provision of opportunities for self employment and access to basic social services. The main strategy adopted under this scheme was to facilitate access for poor women to employment, skill upgradation, training, credit and other support services so that the women as a group could take up income generating activities for supplementing their incomes. It seeked to encourage collective action in the form of group activities which were known to work better and were more sustainable than the individual effort. It encouraged the habit of thrift and credit among poor rural women to make them self-reliant. The scheme also envisaged that this target group would be the focus for convergence of other services like family welfare, health care, nutrition, education, child care, safe drinking water, sanitation and shelter to improve the welfare and quality of life of the family and the community. In the implementation of DWCRA, some States like Andhra Pradesh, Kerala, Tripura and Gujarat have performed very well while in the other States, the performance and impact of DWCRA has been relatively poor.

Supply of Improved Toolkits to Rural Artisans (SITRA)

Launched in July 1992, as a sub-scheme of IRDP in selected districts, this scheme had since been extended to all the districts of the country. Under the scheme, a variety of crafts persons, except weavers, tailors, needle workers and beedi workers, were supplied with a kit of improved hand tools within a financial ceiling of Rs. 2,000, of which the artisans had to pay 10 per cent and the remaining 90 per cent was a subsidy from the Government of India. The supply of power driven tools, subject to a ceiling of Rs. 4,500, was also permitted under this scheme. Beyond this, any additional finance required by the artisans could be provided through loans under IRDP. The rural artisans were trained under TRYSEM for which an age relaxation has been provided to them.

Ganga Kalyan Yojna (GKY)

Ganga Kalyan Yojna, a sub-scheme of IRDP was launched

during 1996-97 with the objective of providing irrigation through exploitation of groundwater (basewells and tubewells) to individuals and groups of beneficiaries of small and marginal farmers belonging to the BPL. The individual/groups were assisted through subsidy by Government and term credit by financial institutions including SC/ST/OBC finance and development corporation. The beneficiaries under the scheme were small and marginal farmers living BPL, other than those who had already been assisted under any irrigation programme of State or Central Government.

Swarnajayanti Gram Swarozgar Yojna (SGSY)

The marginal impact of self-employment programmes led to the constitution of a committee by the Planning Commission in 1997 to review self-employment and wage-employment programmes. The committee recommended the merger of all self-employment programmes for the rural poor and a shift from the individual beneficiary approach to a group-based approach. It emphasised the identification of activity clusters in specific areas and strong training and marketing linkages. The committee's recommendations were accepted by the Government.[53] On 1 April 1999, the IRDP and allied programmes, TRYSEM, DWCRA, SITRA and GKY including the Million Wells Scheme (MWS), were merged into a single programme known as Swarnajayanti Gram Swarozgar Yojana (SGSY).

Antyodaya Anna Yojana (AAY)

AAY launched on December 25, 2000 provides foodgrains at a highly subsidized rate of Rs. 2.00 per kg for wheat and Rs. 3.00 per kg for rice to the poor families under the Targeted Public Distribution System (TPDS). The AAY has been further expanded by another 50 lakh BPL families from August 1, 2004 by including *inter alia*, all households at the risk of hunger. As announced in Union Budget 2005-06. The AAY was further expanded to cover another 50 lakh BPL households which extends its coverage to 2.5 crore households.

Urban Poverty Alleviation Programmes

So far as the poverty alleviation in urban areas is

concerned, the government gave serious thinking during Sixth Five Year Plan. Following specific programmes were launched to eradicate poverty in urban areas.

(i) Self-Employment to the Educated Unemployed Youth (SEEUY)

Self-Employment to the Educated Unemployed Youth programme was started by the Government of India during 1983-84. Under this scheme, such educated unemployed youth (Matric or above education) having age limit between 18-35 years and also having annual family income below rupees 10,000 were eligible for obtaining loan, including 25 per cent capital subsidy given by the Central Government. Since 1 April, 1994, this scheme has been merged with Prime Minister's Rozgar Yojana.

(ii) Self-Employment Programme for the Urban Poor (SEPUP)

The Government of India started this programme in the year 1986, with the aim to provide self-employment opportunities, with the assistance of subsidies and bank loans to the families living below the poverty line in the metropolitan, urban and semi-urban areas. This programme continued till 1991-92 but in 1992-93 this was combined with 'Scheme of Urban Micro Enterprise' of the Nehru Rozgar Yojana.

(iii) Prime Minister's Integrated Urban Poverty Eradication Programme (PMIUPEP)

The Prime Minister's Integrated Urban Poverty Eradication Programme (PMIUPEP) was launched on 18 November, 1995. The general objective of PMIUPEP was to attack the several root causes of urban poverty simultaneously. Besides the objectives of employment generation and skill development, the PMIUPEP also aimed at effective achievements of social sector goal, community empowerment, covergence through sustainable support system, environment improvement and shelter upgradation. Under this plan, efforts were being made to create new opportunities of employment.

The unemployed persons were trained in handicrafts and were encouraged to adopt self-employment ventures. Since December 1, 1997 this scheme has been replaced by Swarna Jayanti Shahri Rozgar Yojana (SJSRY).

(iv) Urban Basic Services for the Poor (UBSP)

The scheme named Urban Basic Services for the Poor was started during 1990-91. The objective of this scheme was to introduce absolute improvement in the lives of the people living in the slums. Since December 1, 1997 this plan has been merged with 'Swarnajayanti Shahri Rozgar Yojana'.

Wage Employment Programmes

Wage employment programmes, an important component of the anti-poverty strategy, have sought to achieve multiple objectives. They not only provide employment opportunities during lean agricultural seasons but also help rural poor during floods, droughts and other natural calamities. They create rural infrastructure which supports further economic activities. These programmes also put an upward pressure on market wage rates by attracting people to public works programmes, thereby reducing labour supply and pushing up demand for labour. While public works programmes to provide employment in times of distress have a long history, major thrust to wage employment programmes in the country was provided only after the attainment of self-sufficiency in food grains in the 1970s.

Some of the important wage employment programmes are given in the following Table 6.6.

It is argued that employment programmes help the poor in more concrete manner. The poverty alleviation programmes such as IRDP have in general two weaknesses which make them less effective.

(i) The household enterprises of the type visualized under various programmes were inherently uneconomic and were in any case handicapped for lack of necessary infrastructure.

(ii) Owing to the illiteracy and weak economic condition of the beneficiaries and the existence of a chain of

TABLE 6.6
Wage Employment Programmes in India

Sl. No.	Name of WEP	Year & Date of commencement	
For Rural Areas			
1.	Prime Minister's Crash Programme	1971-72	April 1, 1971
2.	Food for Work Programme	1977-78	April 1, 1977
3.	National Rural Employment Programme	1980-81	Dec., 2, 1980
4.	Rural Landless Employment Guarantee Programme	1983-84	Aug. 15, 1983
5.	Jawahar Rozgar Yojana	1989-90	April 1, 1989
6.	Employment Assurance Scheme	1993-94	Oct. 2, 1993
7.	Sampurna Gramin Rozgar Yojana	2001-02	Sept. 25, 2001
8.	Jai Prakash Narayan Rozgar Guarantee Yojana	2002-03	
9.	National Food for Work Programme	2004-05	Nov. 14, 2004
10.	National Rural Employment Guarantee Scheme	2005-06	Feb. 2, 2006
For Urban Areas			
1.	Self-Employment to the Educated Unemployment Youth	1983-84	
2.	Self-Employment Programme for the Urban Poor	1986-87	Sept. 1, 1986
3.	Nehru Rozgar Yojana	1989-90	April 1, 1989
4.	Scheme of Urban Wage Employment	1990-91	
5.	Swarnajayanti Shahri Rozgar Yojana	1997-98	Dec. 25, 1997

intermediaries only a small portion of the intended outlay reached the actual beneficiaries.

Employment programme, on the other hand can provide

secure wage-income to the poor, through the creation of durable community assets.

Mahatma Gandhi National Rural Employment Guarantee Programme (MGNREGA)

Chronic unemployment, particularly during lean seasons, has been a major cause of poverty in rural areas. The problem is more serious in areas that are more dependent on agriculture. Increasing dependence on casual employment made the situation worse as a large proportion of the chronic poor are wage labourers. There has been a steady increase in the share of rural population working as hired labour. Most of the casual hired labourers are SCs and STs. While male rural casual labourers have an option to work in non-farm activities, women casual labourers have no choice but to seek employment in farms. Growth in casual labour was strong among the landless and especially rapid after the 1987 drought. In the 1990s there was an explosion of self-employed people choosing to do subsidiary work as casual labourers. The incidence of poverty among rural casual workers is greatest among non-workers who do occasional casual work and especially among women. Most ST and 40 per cent of SC casual workers are poor, the landless casual workers being the poorest. On an average, women are poorer than men casual labourers.[54]

Workfare programmes have been important programme interventions in India and elsewhere in developing countries since long. These programmes typically provides short-term employment to unskilled workers on public works. They provides income transfers to poor households during periods when they suffer on account of absence of opportunities of employment. In areas with high unemployment rates and under employment, particularly seasonal unemployment, transfer benefits from workfare programmes can prevent poverty from worsening, especially during lean periods. Durable assets that these programmes create have the potential to generate second sound employment benefits as requisite infrastructure is developed.

India has a long history and experience in implementing wage employment programmes since 1971. However, beginning with Jawahar Rojagar Yojana in 1989, the outreach of these programmes increased significantly as in the period 1989 to 2006. These wage employment programmes implemented by State Government with Central assistance were self-targeting, and the objective was to provide enhanced livelihood security, especially of those dependent on casual manual labour.

Based on the experience of these programmes the National Rural Employment Guarantee Act (NREGA) was enacted in 2005 to reinforce the commitment towards livelihood security in rural areas. The Act was notified on 7 September 2005. The significance of NREGA lies in the fact that it creates a right-based framework for wage employment programmes and makes the government legally bound to provide employment to those who seek it. In this way the legislation goes beyond providing a social safety net, and towards guaranteeing the right to employment. The experience with NREGA so far been encouraging.

National Rural Employment Guarantee Programme was officially launched by Dr. Manmohan Singh, the Prime Minister of India, on 2nd February, 2006 in Ananthpur district of Andhra Pradesh. Starting with 200 districts across the country in Phase-I during 2006-07, NREGA was extended to additional 130 districts in Phase-II during 2007-08. From 1 April 2008 onwards the programme is extended to whole of rural India. Accordingly Sampoorna Grameen Rozgar Yojana (SGRY) is merged with the NREGA and therefore cease to exist with effect from 1 April 2008.

The objective of the NREGA is to enhance the livelihood security of the people in rural areas by guaranteeing 100 days of wage employment in a financial year to a rural household whose members volunteer to do unskilled manual work. The Act further aims at creating durable assets and strengthening the livelihood resource base of the rural poor. The choice of works suggested in the Act address causes of chronic poverty like drought, deforestation, soil erosion, etc. so that the process of employment generation is on a sustainable basis.

However, NREGA is not supply driven but demand driven. It makes NREGA different from earlier programmes of employment generation. Resource transfer under NREGA is

TABLE 6.7
Impact of MNREGA

Sl. No.	*Item on*	*Impact*	
		Result	*Details*
(1)	*(2)*	*(3)*	*(4)*
1.	Poverty	Increasing Employment Opportunities	During the first year of implementation (FY 2006-07) in 200 districts, 2.10 crore households were employed and 90.5 crore persondays were created. In 2007-08, 3.39 crore households were provided employment and 143.59 crore persondays were generated in 330 districts. In 2008-09, 4.49 crore households have been provided employment and 216.01 crore persondays have been generated across the country.
2.	Minimum Wages	Enhancing Wage Earnings	At the National Level, average wage paid under NREGA has increased from Rs. 65 (FY 2006-07) to Rs. 84 in FY 2008-09. The enhanced wage earnings have led to a strengthening of the livelihood resource base of the rural poor in India; in 2007-08, more than 68 per cent of funds utilised (Rs. 10,738.47 crore as wage expenditure) were in the form of wages paid to the labourers. In 2008-09, 67 per cent of the funds have been utilized in the form of wages (Rs. 18155.20 crore as wage expenditure in FY 2208-09).
3.	Promoting Equality	Higher Workforce Participation	The Programme had a high workforce participation of marginalized groups like SC/ST (57%) in FY 07-08. In FY 2008-09, the participation of SC/ST has been 55 per cent. Women workforce participation has also surpassed the statutory minimum requirement of one 48 per cent of

(*Contd.*)

TABLE 6.7 (Contd.)

(1)	(2)	(3)	(4)
			workers this year were women in FY 2007-08, women participation was 43 per cent, which has increased to 48 per cent in FY 2008-09.
4.	Financial Inclusion	Opening of Accounts in Banks/POs	The Central Government has been encouraging the state governments to make wage payment through bank and post office accounts of wage seekers. Thus, far in FY 2008-09, 6.85 crore NREGA bank and post office accounts have been opened to disburse wages.
5.	Insurance coverage	Insurance cover to workers	NREGA workers have been identified as a category for Jan·Shree Bima Yojna for insurance cover.
6.	Natural Resources	Protection of Natural Resources	Salutary effects have also been noted on natural resources through water conservation, land development and afforestation projects taken up in large measure under NREGA. In FY 06-07, 8.35 lakh works were undertaken with 54% water conservation. In FY 2007-08, 17.8 lakh works were undertaken, of which 49% constituted water conservation, 17% rural connectivity, 16% land development, and provision of irrigation facility to individual beneficiaries constituted arond 15% with remaining 3% work related to other activities. In FY 2008-09, 27.20 lakh works have been undertaken, of which 46% relate to water conservation, provision of irrigation facility to individual beneficiaries constituted around 20%, 18% rural connectivity, 15% land development and remaining 1% works related to other activities. Of these total 27.13 lakh work undertaken, around 12.00 lakhs work have been already complated.

Source : Annual Report, 2008-09, Ministry of Rural Development.

based on the demand for employment and this provides another critical incentive to States to leverage the Act to meet the employment needs of the poor.

Provisions regarding preparation of a labour budget, annual shelf of Projects and Perspective Plan have made the programme unique in letter and spirit. Likewise, provisions of Right to Information Act and Social Audit have made the government functionaries more accountable.

NREGA has acquired a great success in the empowerment of workers, particularly the women workers. Empowerment of workers and creation of durable assets depend to a great extent on the linkages between NREGA and other development programmes. Linkages with human development programmes much as National Rural Health Mission (NRHM), National Mission for Literacy and Elementary Education, and other livelihood and infrastructure initiatives that have been taken during the last decades will certainly help in mitigating the curse of poverty of millions of the people of India.

ECONOMIC REFORMS AND POVERTY REDUCTION— 'INCLUSIVE GROWTH' APPROACH

It is a well known fact that most of the employment growth in the 1990s and onward, has occurred in the unorganised sector, which is of low quality and characterised by vulnerabilities. Not surprisingly, the growth in employment over this period has not helped in alleviating poverty to the desired extent. The problem of hardcore poverty continues to remain formidable. This shows that the series of poverty alleviation programmes undertaken by the government between 1993-94 and 2004-05 have had only a limited impact in improving the situation. A major reason for this is the deceleration in the growth rate of agriculture and the big drop in the generation of new employment opportunities in this sector.

Economic reforms, started in early nineties have brought the Indian economy at the level of second fastest growing economy of the world, with the annual average growth rate in range of 8-9 per cent. Certain measures of economic reforms such as proportionate decrease in public investment in social sector during post-reforms era, especially education and health, and agriculture to curb the fiscal deficit resulted into poor performance of these sectors. Higher growth of manufacturing sector and external sector did not help the rural poor to overcome the curse of poverty. If economic reforms are to gain popular support, the benefits of growth have to reach poor and the marginalised. To tackle hardcore poverty, there is a strong case to foster the growth of rural enterprises by involving, among others, SHGs and micro-finance institutions on a much bigger scale, apart from stepping up public investment in education, health and agriculture on a big scale.

Despite six decades of planning and a number of government led anti-poverty programmes, the high rate of poverty still remains a challenge. Governance inefficiencies and low levels of transparency have been widely accepted as the dominant hurdle. Post-reforms, wealth has been accumulated by a small segment of the population. Income and wealth distribution is excessively skewed, leading to social unrest, conflict activism and dispute. It is from this perspective that a concept of 'Inclusive Growth' has emerged as an effective approach of poverty alleviation.

Inclusive growth means an emphasis towards more equitable distribution of income and building capabilities in terms of attainment of better health and education. The general notion about the success of inclusive growth is little apprehensive. The argument is although the poor are getting richer, the rich are getting richer faster than the poor. An indepth analysis of inclusion growth has been done in Chapter VII.

Nevertheless, it can be said that this strategy is based on sound macro-economic policies which establish the preconditions for rapid growth and support key drivers of this growth. It include sector specific policies which ensure that the structure of growth that is generated, and the institutional environment in which it occurs, achieves the objectives of inclusiveness in all its many dimensions.

Poverty in India is still a major obstacle in the development of the country, despite several efforts of the government—Central as well as States. Higher growth rates of the order of 7-9 per cent makes the Indian economy second fastest growing economy of the world, but its 128th rank in World Human Development Index puts her into the club of poor countries. High incidence of poverty, growing unemployment in rural areas, deterioration of quality of employment in urban areas, wide scale malnutrition among women and children, pathetic conditions of tribals higher levels of illiteracy and a low level of standard of living refute the claim of government that the country is moving fast to become a developed economy in near future. Large scale leakages in the flow of funds meant for the upliftment of poor and downtroden, resulted into performance much below the desired level. Poor governnance lack of accountability, political interference are the main causes of poor performance of poverty alleviation programmes.

Notes and References

1. Lopez, J. Humberto (2004); "Pro-poor Growth : A Review of What We Know (and What We don't); *The World Bank*, Washington DC.
2. Deinger, K. and L. Squire (1996); A New Data Set Measuring Income Inequality. *The World Bank Economic Review*, 10 : 565-571.
3. Foster James, E. and M. Szekely (2001); "Is Economic Growth Good for the Poor ? Tracking Low Incomes Using General Means", Paper Presented at the WIDER Conference on Growth and Poverty, Helsinki, May 25-26.
4. Dollar, David and Kraay, Aart (2002); Growth is Good for Poor, *Journal of Economic Growth*, Springer, Vol. 7(3), pp. 195-225.
5. Bourguignon, F. (2003); "Growth Elasticity of Poverty Reduction : Explaining Heterogeneity Across Countries and Time Periods" In, T. Eicher and S. Turnovsky (eds.), Inequality and Growth, Theory and Policy Implications.
6. Kraay, Aart (2005); "Aid, Growth and Poverty", World Bank, Washington D.C. (Paper presented at IMF Seminar on Foreign Aid and Macro Economic Management, Maputo, March 14-15, Kraay, Aart (2006), "When is Growth Pro-Poor", Cross-Country Evidence, *Journal of Development Economics*.
7. Ravallion Martin (1997); "Can Hingh Inequality Development Countries Escape Poverty", *Economics Leters*, 56 : 51-57.
8. Ravallian, Martin (2004); "Pro-poor Growth : A Primer." The World Bank, Policy Research Working Papers, No. 1, 3408.
9. Bourgnignon Francis (2003); "From Income to Endowments : The difficult task of expanding the income poverty paradigm", DELTA Working papers.

10. White, H. and A. Anderson (2000); "Growth *v.* Redistribution : Does the Pattern of Growth Matters?", DFIED White Paper on Eliminating World Poverty; Making Globalisation Work for Poor.
11. Kakwani, M. and E. Pernia (2000); What is pro-poor Growth? *Asian Development Reivew,* 18 : 1-16.
12. World Bank (1997); India : Achievements and Challenges in Reducing Poverty, Washington DC, p. XVI.
13. *Ibid.,* p. XVII.
14. *Ibid.,* p. 36.
15. UNDP (2009); Human Development Report, 2009, Oxford Univrsity Press, New Delhi.
16. Sen, A.K. (1977); "Rational Fools : A Critique of the Behavioural Foundations of Economic Theory", Reprinted in Choice, Welfare and Measurement, Oxford Blackwell, 1982.
17. Sen, Amartya K. (1980); "Equity of What", In Sterling M. McMurrin (ed.), *The Tanner Lectures on Human Value,* Salt Lake City; University of Utah Press, pp. 195-220.
18. Sen, Amartya K. (1983); "Development : Which Way Now?", *Economic Journal,* 93 : 745-62.
19. Sen, Amartya K. (1993); "Capability and well-being", In Martha C. Nussbaum and Amartya K. Sen (eds.), *The Quality of Life,* Oxford, Clarendon Press, pp. 30-53.
20. Nussbaum, Martha Craven (1988); .Nature, Function and Capability : Aristotle on Political Distribution. Oxford Studies on Ancient Philosophy, Supl., pp. 145-84.
21. Nussbaum, Martha Craven (1990); 'Aristotelian Social Democracy' in Bruce Douglas, Gerald Mara and Henry Richardson (eds.), *Liberalism and the Good,* New York, Routledge, pp. 2003-52.
22. Berlin, Isaiah (1958); "The Concepts of Liberty", Reprinted in Isaiah Berlin (1982); Four Essays on Liberty, Oxford University Press.
23. Sen, Amartya K. (1992); *Inequality Re-examined,* Oxford, Clarendon Press, pp. 30-57.
24. Clark, David A. (2006); "The Capability Approach : Its Development, Critiques and Recent Advances", Global Poverty Group, Institute for Development Policy and Management, University of Manchester, U.K., p. 3.
25. Streeten, P.P., S.J. Burki *et al.* (1981); First Things First, Meeting Basic Human Needs in Development Countries, New York.
26. Sen, Amartya K. (1984); *Resources, Values and Development,* Oxford, Basil Blackwekk, pp. 513-15.
27. ———, (1985); *Commodities and Capabilities,* Oxford, Elsevier Science Publishers.
28. ———, (1993); *op. cit.,* p. 41.
29. ———, (1984); *op. cit.,* p. 497.

30. Nussbaum, M. (2000); Women and Human Development : A Study in Human Capabilities, Cambridge, Cambridge University Press, pp. 11-15.
31. Streeten *et al.* (1981); *op. cit.*
32. *Ibid.*
33. Government of India (1982); Sixth Five Year Plan (1980-85), Planning Commission, p. 4.
34. Government of India (1986); Seventh Five Year Plan (1985-90), Planning Commission, Vol. II, p. 252.
35. Government of India (1998); Nineth Five Year Plan (1997-2002); Planning Commission, Vol. I, pp. 393-94.
36. *Ibid.*, p. 394.
37. Government of India (2007); National Health Profile, 2007, p. 127.
38. Government of India (2003); Tenth Five Year Plan, Planning Commission, Vol. II, p. 23.
39. *Ibid.*, p. 30.
40. Government of India (2010); Economic Survey (2009-10); p. 281.
41. Government of India (2008); Eleventh Five Year Plan (2007-12); p. 3, Vol. III.
42. *Ibid.*, p. 2.
43. Government of India (2008); Selected Educational Statistics, MHRD.
44. Government of India (1993); Eighth Five Year Plan (1992-97), Vol. II, p. 107.
45. Government of India (2008); *op. cit.*, Vol. III, p. 135.
46. *Ibid.*, p. 140.
47. Government of India (2008); *op. cit.*, Vol. III, p. 141.
48. Government of India (1980); Sixth Five Year Plan (1980-85), Planning Commission, pp. 174-75.
49. *Ibid.*, p. 87.
50. Government of India (1997); Ninth Five Year Plan (1997-2002); Planning Commission, Vol. I, p. 321.
51. *Ibid.*, pp. 321.
52. *Ibid.*, pp. 334-35.
53. Government of India (2008); *op. cit.*, Vol. I, p. 1.
54. Government of India (2008); *op. cit.*, Vol. III, pp. 87-88.

CHAPTER

7

Alternative Strategies for Poverty Reduction : An Area Specific Approach

- Inclusive Growth
- Improving the Quality of Life through Heavy Investments in Social Infrastructures—Health and Education
- Economic Empowerment of Poor—Especially Women, *Dalits* and Tribal People
- People's Participation in Decision-making
- Good Governance

CHAPTER

7

Alternative Strategies for Poverty Reduction

An Area Specific Approach

Traditional approaches that have been adopted in India for the reduction of poverty during the last 60 years of planning could not produce desired result. The magnitude and spread of poverty is still high in India in comparison to other developing countries. The main cause of poor performance on poverty reduction front is the unified and universal nature of policies of development adopted in a continental country like India that has vast differentials in regional endowments as well as geo-climatic conditions. Not even this, there are diversities in culture, religion, customs, rituals, fooding habits. Inter-state disparities in the availability of infra-structural facilities, natural resources and financial resources have reflected in growth pattern that produced highly skewed results in poverty reduction.

Poverty reduction programmes in India have been centrally sponsored, implemented by the state governments within the framework of elaborate guidelines and norms developed by the Central Government. Although each state has been encouraged to introduce innovative approaches within these parameters, in practice, the poverty reduction programmes in India have been macro in approach, sectorial in coverage, and highly centered. Therefore, these programmes have failed to achieve the desired results. The strategy adopted so far has created a wide gap between the provider and beneficiaries, and the lack of involvement of people has led to the failure of the programmes. Thus, there is a growing concern among policy-makers and implimentors that the centralised standardised nature of the schemes gives local programme managers insufficient flexibility to meet varying needs.

There is also an increasing awareness that intra-state variations in terms of language/dialectics, social and religious groupings, distance between settlements, access to services, the health and nutritional status of the local masses, varied levels of education and skills and so on are as significant as variations between states, given the continental nature of the country. There is now a growing consensus that the poverty reduction programmes should as far as possible be tailored to meet the needs of individual regions/district, therefore region/ district should be seen as the basic unit for management of the programme.

As a first step in this direction, there is a need to identify the regions/districts that have large concentration of poor. The selection of such districts should be based on an index constructed by taking into consideration the following indices :

- Asset indices,
- Infrastructure indices,
- Education indices,
- Per capita income,
- Health indices (IMR, MMR, Life Expectancy),
- Nutrition Indices (percentage of under weight children, anaemic mothers and pregnant women),
- Poverty indices (percentage of population BPL),

- Employment indices (unemployment rate), and
- Productivity (land and labour).

In the next step specific projects should be designed for each district/region and local managers should be allowed to play with flexibility within the limits.

It should however, be noted that merely infrastructural facilities and enhancing training of staff will not allow local managers greater flexibility for designing operational strategies to meet local needs that would help improve the income earning capacities of poor unless structural changes are brought about in the programmes. There are long-term causes underlying the poor performance of the poverty alleviation programmes in India, some of which are structural in nature. Almost all the programmes of poverty alleviation have been developed at central level either by Planning Commission or by Ministry of Rural Development/Urban Development. All major decisions and guidelines have been percolated downward from the top with little or no participation of the people for whom the programmes are meant. Therefore, the willingness and commitment of people has not been harnessed. Availability of local resources has not been given due consideration while formulating schemes of poverty reduction. Besides, an area specific approach and marketing strategies have not been adopted, in spite of the fact that in a continental country like India where wide variations exist in terms of population density, degree of development, socio-economic conditions, topography, expectations of the masses, etc., targets have been set and guidelines to achieve these are given by the centre. Because of these strategic lacunas, the success in poverty alleviation is not upto the mark. Given the vast variations that exist in the country, the incidence of poverty has to be treated as a region-specific issue. The overall growth of the economy cannot and should not be directly related to poverty reduction, since it is entirely possible that the growth process may by-pass those regions in which the poor are concentrated.

The present incidence of poverty in some of the regions of the country is still so grim that it requires a specific approach based on local requirements and needs. State institutions are too remote from the ground realities of poor people's lives. These institutions not only ignored the specific needs of the local people but also kept them away from the developmental process. Decentralization, a device of area specific approach of development, is often recommended as a solution. Decentralisation can be powerful tool for achieving development goals in way that respond to the needs of local communities, by assigning control rights to people who have the information and incentives to make decisions best suited to their needs, and who have the responsibility for the political and economic consequences of their decision.[1] It is not in itself a goal of development, but a means of improving public sector efficiency. Decentralisation can make public institutions more responsive to poor people, but only if it allows poor people to hold public servants accountable and ensure their participation in the development process. The pace and design of decentralisation has its impact on efficiency, accountability, participation and ultimately poverty reduction.[2] Local information has many advantages. It can help identify more cost-efficient ways of building infrastructure, providing public services, and organising their operation and maintenance. Moreover, knowing what local needs are more pressing can help the disadvantaged. Local monitoring and supervision for many projects and programmes are more effective and less expensive because of proximity to the point of provision and better interaction at the local level. Social audit under Mahatma Gandhi National Rural Employment Guarantee Programme (MGNREGA) has not only reduced leakages but also improved the effectiveness of the scheme in mitigating the severity of poverty and unemployment.

Decentralisation can greatly enhance the state's capacity to accelerate local development and reduce poverty, but only if it is effectively designed. Local authorities and agencies need considerable autonomy, including on fiscal matters, as well as, considerable support and safeguards from the centre. Moreover, decentralised government needs mechanism to ensure high levels of participation in the design and monitoring of programme and policies by all sections of the population to be served.

The most suitable alternative model of poverty alleviation, in present scenario, must be area specific in nature along with the other aspects of growth and development. Various alternative strategies of poverty alleviation have been discussed in the following paragraphs with the emphasis on their usefulness in the area specific needs and aspirations of the people living Below Poverty Line.

INCLUSIVE GROWTH

Rapid and sustained poverty reduction requires inclusive growth that allows people to contribute to and benefit from economic growth. The term 'inclusive growth' is often used interchangeably with a suite of other terms, such as 'broad-based growth', 'shared growth' and 'pro-poor growth'. Rapid pace of growth of the economy is unquestionably necessary for poverty reduction on sustained basis, but this growth must be sustainable in long-run. It must be broad based across sectors, and inclusive of the large part of the country's population. Inclusiveness a concept that encompasses equity, equality of opportunity; and protection in market and employment transition—is an essential ingredient of any successful growth strategy. Equality of opportunity means the access of poor people to markets, resources and unbiased regulatory environment for business and individual.

The inclusive growth approach takes a longer-term perspective as the focus is on productive employment rather than on direct income redistribution, as a means of increasing income for excluded groups. In majority of countries ruling party adopt short-run approach under which large sums of money from public exchequer is spent on income distribution schemes to attenuate negative impact on the poor of policies intended to jump start growth. It enhances the popularity of ruling class, but for a short span of time. In poor countries/ states such schemes can impose significant burdens on already stretched budgets. It happened in many states in India (especially the poor states such as BIMARU states and Orissa, Jharkhand and Chhattisgarh, etc.). It is theoretically impossible to reduce poverty through redistribution in countries where average income falls below US $ 700 per year. Even in developed countries, redistribution schemes cannot be the only response to rising poverty rates in certain segments of population.[3]

The 'inclusive growth' definition is in line with the 'absolute' definition of 'pro-poor growth', but not the 'relative' definition. In absolute term the growth is pro-poor if poor people are benefited in absolute terms as reflected in some agreed measure of poverty.[4] On the contrary in relative terms, the growth is pro-poor if and only if the incomes of poor people grow faster than those of the population as a whole i.e., inequality of incomes declines. However, while absolute pro-poor growth can be the result of direct income redistribution schemes, for growth to be inclusive, productivity must be improved and new employment opportunities created. Thus, inclusive growth is about raising the pace of growth and enlarging the size of the economy, while leveling the playing field for investment and increasing productive employment scheme. The permanent solution of poverty reduction lies in increase in productivity with additional job opportunities.

By focussing on inequality, relative concept of pro-poor growth could lead to sub-optimal outcomes for the poor and non-poor households. For example, a society attempting to achieve pro-poor growth under relative definition would not relish higher average growth rate of 9 per cent or more, where the income of poor households is growing with 5 per cent. Instead average annual growth rate of 4 per cent would be sufficient if the income of poor households is growing at 7 per cent. While the distributional pattern of growth favours poor household in the second scenario, both poor and non-poor households are better-off in the first scenario. There is broad recognition that when poverty reduction is the objective, then the absolute definition of pro-poor growth is the most relevant.[5] Using the absolute definition, the aim should be to increase the rate of growth to achieve the greatest pace of poverty reduction. Diagramatic representation of inclusive growth is given in Chart 7.1.

Thus, inclusive growth is a better strategy that takes care of those who are struggling hard for their survival and development. As a strategy inclusive growth must emphasise

CHART 7.1
Inclusive Growth

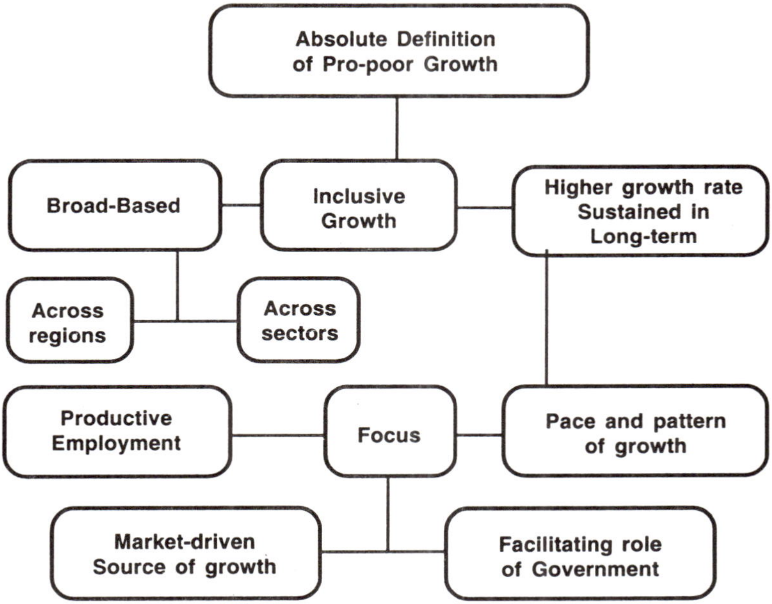

on financial inclusion and social inclusion which are essential for the upliftment of the poor. 'Inclusive growth' can be achieved through financial and social inclusion.

Financial Inclusion

Financial inclusion has a direct link with the poverty reduction. It not only provides financial assistance to the poor in the form of credit for productive purposes, but also enables them to develop thrift habit. The concept of financial inclusion can be understood in a better way by understanding the concept of financial exclusion.

Financial exclusion is the lack of access by certain consumers to appropriate, low cost, fair and safe financial products and services from mainstream providers. Financial exclusion becomes of more concern in the community when it applies to lower income consumers and/or those in financial hardship. There is a large overlap between poverty and permanent financial exclusion. Both poverty and financial exclusion result in a reduction of choices which affects social interaction and leads to reduced participation in society.

Financial illiteracy and discrimination deprive poor people from the mainstream of economic activities of financial institutions. Poor people are often victims of financial exploitation in the hands of local money lenders.

In this manner the poor, socially under-privileged, disabled, old, women, uneducated, ethnic minorities and unemployed are financially excluded. All these sub-sections of the society have limited means for their survival. Consequences of financial exclusion will vary depending on the nature and extent of services denied. It may lead to increased travel requirements, higher incidence of crime, general decline in investment, difficulties in gaining access to credit or getting credit from informal sources at exorbitant rates, and increased unemployment, etc.

Poverty and financial exclusion are closely associated with each other. States, with lack of banking services, have low level of financial inclusion and high level of poverty. Various steps have been taken by the RBI to make the financial inclusion a success. Nationalisation of 14 commercial banks in 1969, creation of Regional Rural Banks (RRBs) in 1975 and the nationalisation of 6 more commercial banks in 1980, mandatory payment, through banks, to beneficiaries of all the programmes of poverty alleviation and employment generation and social assistance and bringing millions of marginalised groups in the credit net are some of the measures adopted during 1970s and onwards for financial inclusion.

It is absolutely beyond any doubt that the financial access to masses has significantly improved in the last three and a half decades but a lot to be done yet. With a view to enhancing the financial inclusion, RBI exhorted the banks, with a view to achieving greater financial inclusion, to make available a basic banking 'no frills' account either with nil or very minimum balances as well as charges that would make such accounts accessible to vast sections of the populations.

Social Inclusion

Social inclusion, can best be understood in terms of social exclusion which is a broader concept. It is a related concept with unemployment and poverty, but not an identical one with them. In general terms social exclusion denotes the following characteristics of a society at large or individuals at least.[6]

(i) Inability to participate effectively in economic, social, political and cultural life;
(ii) Distance and alienation from a so-called mainstream society; and
(iii) Isolation from major societal mechanisms which produce or distributed social resources.

Since majority of poor belong to socially excluded groups such as women, scheduled castes and scheduled tribes, so any scheme of inclusive growth or balanced growth that directly hit the poverty would not succeed unless it includes these groups. Although, the women, SCs and STs have been given due considerations in almost every programme of poverty alleviation and employment generation. For example, it was mandatory that 40 per cent beneficiaries must be women in IRDP and its components. Likewise the MGNREGA had a high workforce participation of marginalised groups like SCs/STs whose participation was 57 per cent in 2007-08 and 55 per cent in 2008-09. Women workforce participation has also surpassed the statuary minimum requirement of 40 per cent. During 2007-08 and 2008-09 the women participation was 43 per cent and 48 per cent respectively. Another ambitious programme of poverty alleviation, the Swarnajayanti Gram Swarozgar Yojna (SGSY) has specific safeguard for socially excluded and marginalised groups. Families below the poverty line in rural areas constitute the target group of the SGSY. Within the target group, special safeguards have been provided to vulnerable sections, by way of reserving 50 per cent benefits for SCs/STs, 40 per cent for women, 15 per cent for minorities and 3 per cent for disabled persons. These types of efforts would certainly help in mitigating the poverty on mass scale.

IMPROVING THE QUALITY OF LIFE THROUGH HEAVY INVESTMENTS IN SOCIAL INFRASTRUCTURES—HEALTH AND EDUCATION

It has been recognised worldwide that improvement in the level of health and education bring the qualitative change in the living standards of the mankind. While a good and sound health makes a person physically fit to perform perfectly, the education improves his mental fitness through upgradation of knowledge and skill. Lack of education robs an individual of a full life. It also robs society of a foundation for sustainable development because education is critical for improving health, nutrition and productivity. 'Achieving universal primary education' has been declared a goal under Millennium Development Goals of United Nations. Achieving Universal primary education and eliminating gender disparities in primary and secondary education require addressing efficiency, equity and resource levels as related problems.[7] Development of educational facilities has been the core agenda of economic planning in India. Five Year Plans place the highest priority on education as a central instrument for achieving rapid and inclusive growth in pursuance to fulfil obligation enshrined in the article 41 under the directive principles of state policy of the Indian constitution. The provision says, "The state shall, within the limits of its economic capacity and development, make effective provision for securing the right to work, to educate and to public assistance in case of unemployment, old age, sickness and disablement, and in other cases of underserved want."

The 86th Constitutional Amendment of 2002 led to inclusion of a new Article 21-A in Part III of the Indian Constitution that made compulsory education to all children of 6 to 14 years of age a Fundamental Right. It is a great and progressive step towards universalisation of elementary education. Finally with the enactment of the Right to Free and Compulsory Education Act, 2008, India joined a select global club setting in motion an ambitious, if much delayed, scheme of providing education to every child in the age bracket of 6-14 years.

Education is a concurrent subject, which means that the Centre and states will have to collaborate. This is a potential minefield, in which we hope the project will not become a casualty. It's time that schools are made more accountable to local civic authorities—including parents via the parent-teacher associations—than being monitored by an opaque bureaucracy. Crucially, greater budgetary allotments must be earmarked for education, much more than the mearly 3 per cent of GDP allocated as of now. This will help sort some of the systemic problems like poor pay for teachers, which in turn feeds absenteeism and indifference on the part of teachers. A country that has great power ambitions must be able to provide basic education and health care to all its citizens.

Since universalization of elementary education has become an important goal, it is also essential to push this vision forward to move towards universalization of secondary education, something which has already been achieved in a large number of developed countries and several developing countries. Not only universal enrolment, but universal retention and satisfactory quality of learning should also be a priority. The major challenge before secondary education is that of meeting the surge in demand due to success of Sarva Shiksha Abhiyan (SSA) whose target is to ensure that all children of elementary school going age enroll by 2010. It has been therefore decided to launch a centrally-sponsored scheme viz., Scheme for Universalization of Access to Secondary Education (SUCCESS) and improvement of quality at secondary stage during the Eleventh Five Year Plan.

Investment in Health

Health is a vital component of an individual's capacity to work. Poor health—poor physical fitness and incapable mental status—leads to poor productivity of an individual and collectively it reduces the productivity of the country. Poor productivity results into slow growth and low per capita income which further prevents a person to improve his health. Income which is considered to be an important determinant of economic growth has a two way relation with health. Whereas, level of income determines good health status, health status also contributes to increase in the level of income, as it is a

CHART 7.2
Investment in Health

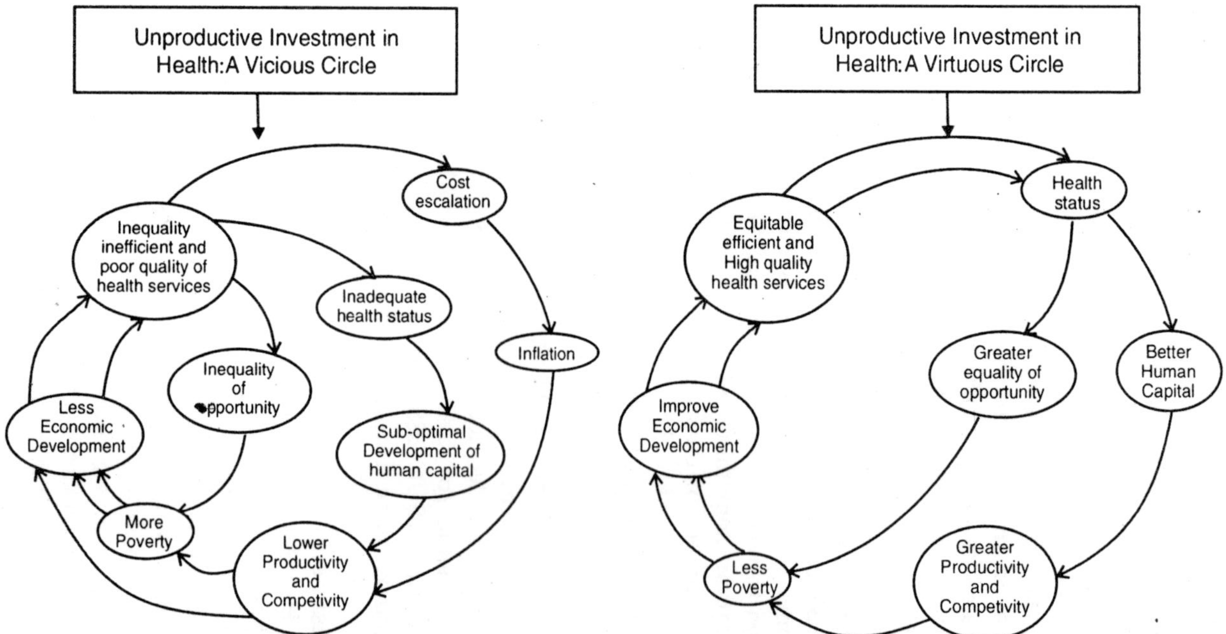

Source : Fundaction Maxicana Para La Salud, 1995.

critical factor for workforce to be productive.[8] Health of an individual is influenced by income of the household, education, food, housing, basic sanitation, social practices, measures to control environmental hazards and communicable diseases. Low level of income, as in the case of poor, prevents a person to acquire desired level of education, food, housing and basic sanitation, which are essential for the betterment of health. Role of state becomes necessary in the society where individuals are not capable enough due to low level of income. Huge public investments are required to provide primary health care facilities to a vast section of the society for the improvement of health. As healthy manpower is a basic pre-requisite for development of the nation, the responsibility of maintaining public health rests with the government of the country. In India, the government providing health services at various levels. Improvement in the health and nutritional status of the population has been one of the major thrust areas for social development programmes of the country. This has been achieved through improving the access to and utilization of health, family welfare and nutrition services with special focus on under-served and under-privileged segments of the population. Over the last six decades, India has built up a vast health infrastructure and manpower at primary, secondary and specialised (tertiary) care in government, voluntary and private sector.[9]

It is also being increasingly realised that merely investing more in health is unlikely to improve the health status of the population. What is required is that policies and strategies are developed to promote equitable access to preventive and curative services so that there is an improvement in health indices, which will have a positive impact on poverty reduction.

Sarva Swasthya Abhiyan

Some innovative measures have been adopted during the Eleventh Five Year Plan with a focus on additional investments in public sector for enabling the existing health infrastructure to be more optimally utilized. Course correlations have also been sought to be made for architecturally correcting primary health care infrastructure, promoting tertiary care and addressing both communicable and non-communicable diseases with greater focus. Sarva Swasthya Abhiyan is an approach in this direction. National Rural Health Mission (NRHM) and National Urban Health Mishan (NRUM) are the parts of Sarva Swasthya Abhiyan.

NRHM was launched to address infirmities and problems across primary health care and bring about improvement in the health system and the health status of those who live in the rural areas. The Mission aims to provide universal access to equitable, affordable, and quality health care that is accountable and at the same time responsive to the needs of the people. The Mission is expected to achieve the goals set under the National Health Policy and the Millennium Development Goals (MDGs).

To achieve these goals, NRHM facilitates increased access and utilization of quality health services by all, forges a partnership between the Central, State and the local governments, sets up a platform for involving the PRIs and the community in the management of primary health programmes and infrastructure, and provides an opportunity for promoting equity and social justice.

The urban poor suffer from poor health status, as per National Family Health Survey III data under 5 Mortality Rate among the urban poor at 72.7, is significantly higher than urban average of 51.9, more than 50 per cent of urban poor children are under weight, and almost 60 per cent of urban poor children miss total immunisation before completing 1 year. Poor environmental condition in the slums along with high population density makes them vulnerable to lung diseases like Asthma, Tuberculosis, etc. Slums also have a high incidence of vector borne diseases and cases of malaria among the urban poor are twice as many than other urbanites.[10] In order to effectively address the health concerns of the urban poor population, the Government of India proposes to launch a National Urban Health Mission which envisaged to meet health needs of the urban poor, particularly the slum-dwellers by making available to them essential primary health care services. This will be done by investing in high caliber health professionals, appropriate technology through public-private-partnership and health insurance to urban poor.

The NUHM would cover all cities (430 in total) with population above one lakh and state capitals during phase I. District Head Quarters towns with population less than one lakh would be covered under phase II of the Mission. The NUHM would have high focus on :

- Urban poor population living in listed and unlisted slums; and
- All other vulnerable population such as homeless, rag-pickers, street children, rickshaw pullers, construction and brick and limeklin workers, sex workers, any other temporary migrants.

ECONOMIC EMPOWERMENT OF POOR—ESPECIALLY WOMEN, DALITS AND TRIBAL PEOPLE

Plathora of studies in India have established that people belonging to scheduled castes, scheduled tribes and other backward castes have the largest share of poor. Women of these vulnerable classes are worst affected segment of the society. Any right-minded strategy of poverty reduction must emphasise on the economic empowerment of women in general and women of SCs, STs and OBCs, in particular.

Empowerment means enhancing the capacity of poor people, especially the women, SCs, STs and other marginalised segments of the population to influence the state institutions that affect their lives, by strengthening their participation in political process and local decision-making. And in more specific terms it means removing the barriers—political, legal and social—that work against particular groups and building the assets of poor people to enable them to engage effectively in markets. Expanding economic opportunities for people indeed contributes to their empowerment. But efforts are needed to make state and social institutions work in the interest of poor people—to make them pro-poor. Formal democratic process are part of empowerment. But sometimes, some specific measures make the system more efficient. Provisions of reservation for Scheduled Castes and Scheduled Tribes in parliament and state legislative assemblies had definitely foster a sense of pride among millions of *Dalits* in

India. Free and fair election process with strong commitments of Election Commission of India allowed the millions of downtrodden to cast their vote according to their choice and finally taste the power, as is the case in Uttar Pradesh. 73rd and 74th amendments of Indian constitution provided a sound platform to women to participate effectively in decision-making at grass-root level. National empowerment of citizens can have important indirect effects on poor people, by influencing the quality and pace of economic and social development. But the outcome for poor people depends on political and social structures within a society.

Economic Empowerment of Women

UN Secretary General Kofi Annan says, "Gender equality is more than a goal in itself. It is a precondition for meeting the challenge of reducing poverty, promoting sustainable development and building good governance". This recognition is currently missing in India, despite the provisions of several fundamental rights in equitable manner as enshrined in the constitution. Looking through the sense of hunger and poverty, women in India are still a deprived lot at least in the following critical areas.[11]

Malnutrition : India has exceptionally high rates of malnutrition, especially among women and girl children, because tradition in India requires that women eat last and the least throughout their lives, even when pregnant and lactating. Malnourished women give birth to malnourished children, perpetuating the cycle. Nutritional deprivation has two major consequences for women, they never reach their full growth potential and anaemia. Both are risk in pregnancy.

Poor Health : Females receive less health care than males. Many women die in childbirth of easily prevented complications. Working conditions and environmental pollution further impairs women's health. Surviving through a normal life-cycle is a resource poor women's greatest challenge.

Lack of Education : Families are far less likely to educate girls than boys, and far more likely to pull them out of school, either to help out at home or from fear to violence. As a result

India has the largest population of non-school-going working girls.

Overwork : Women work longer hours and their work is more arduous than men's, yet their work is unrecognized. Men report that "women, like children, eat and do nothing". Technological progress in agriculture has had a negative impact on women. Although, the women work roughly twice as many hours as men even than their work is not counted in national income.

Unskilled : In women's primary employment sector—agriculture-extension services overlook women. A number of factors perpetuate women's limited job skills. Women have limited or no access to training in modern and advanced manufacturing activities. Unequal access to education and training restricts women's abilities to learn skills that require even functional levels of literacy. In terms of skill development, women are impeded by their lack of mobility, low literacy levels and prejudiced attitudes towards women.

Mistreatment : In recent years, there has been an alarming rise in atrocities against women in India, in terms of rapes, assaults and dowry-related murders. Violence against women and girls is the most pervasive human rights violation in India today. Fear of violence suppresses the aspirations of all women. Female infanticide and sex-selective abortions are additional forms of violence that reflect the devaluing of females in Indian society.

Powerlessness : While women are guaranteed equality under the constitution, legal protection has little effect in the face of prevailing patriarchal traditions. Women lack power to decide who they will marry, and are often married-off as children. Legal loopholes are used to deny women inheritance rights.

India has a long history of activism for women's welfare and rights, which has increasingly focused on women's economic rights. A range of government programmes have been launched to increase economic opportunity for women, although there appear to be no existing programmes to address the cultural and traditional discrimination against women that leads to their abject conditions.

Women represent half of the India's population, and gender inequality exist in every region of the country. To discriminate and prevent half of humanity reaching its full potential is economic folly. Denying women and girls equality and fairness not only hurts them, but also hinders the rest of the society. Economic empowerment of women can be defined in terms of economic independence that gives women the power to think, and act independently in economic matters of the family and the society. Economic empowerment of women results in increase in income. Increased income controlled by women gives them self-confidence which helps them attain a voice and vote in :

- Household decisions such as domestic well-being decisions, for instance women tend to use income clout for more equitable decisions about sons and daughters' diet, education, health and job.
- Economic decisions—acquiring, allocating and selling assets.
- Fertility decisions—economically empowered women tend to have fewer children.
- Land use and conservation decisions; rural women tend to favour sustainable environmental practices since they are usually the ones that collect the families' natural resources such as water, fodder and firewood.

But women's economic empowerment must not be examined in a vacuum. Unfortunately, widespread cultural and economic practices in various parts of the country work to prevent empowerment. Various dimensions of empowerment and their inter-linkages is presdented in Chart 7.3.

World Economic Forum has developed a statistical tool to measure women's empowerment. In its first ever gender gap study covering 58 nations, the World Economic Forum has ranked India at a 114th place in 2007. The report entitled "The Women Empowerment : Measuring the Global Gender Gap" measured the gap between women and men in five critical areas like economic participation, economic opportunities, political empowerment, access in education and access to

CHART 7.3

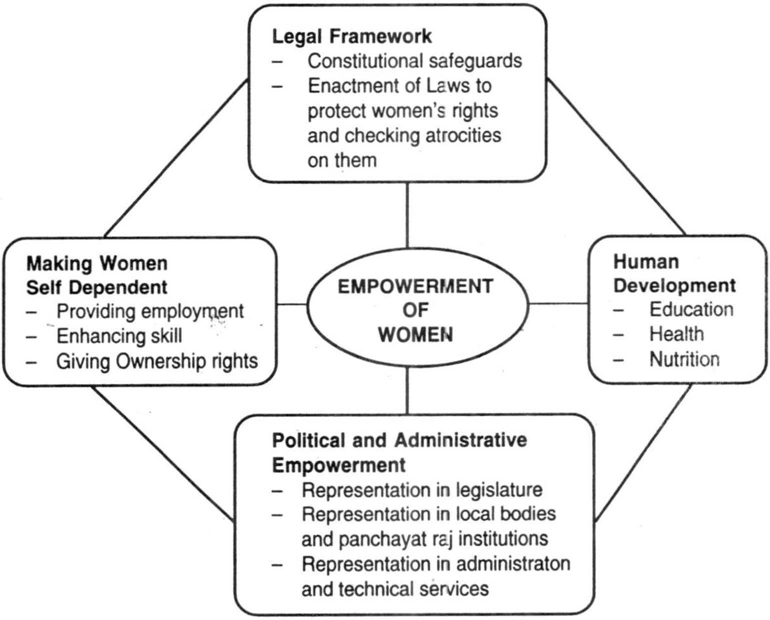

reproductive health care. The report is based on United Nations Development Fund for women's findings on global pattern of inequality between men and women.[12]

Economic Empowerment of Dalits

Inclusive growth demands that all social groups have equal access to the services provided by the state and equal opportunity for upward economic and social mobility. It is also necessary to ensure that there is no discrimination against any section of the society. Despite several constitutional safeguard millions of *dalits* are still facing discrimination in many walks of life. Dalits (scheduled castes) are a deprived lot—economically and socially. Scheduled castes constitute 16.23 per cent of India's population. In the past, they have been socially ostracized, economically exploited and denied human dignity and sense of self-worth. Poverty incidence among SCs is higher as compared to general public. Although the literacy

TABLE 7.1
India's Ranking Global Gender Gap (A Composite Measure of Women's Empowerment)—2007

Indicators	*Global Ranking*	
	Rank	*Value*
1. Global Gender Gap Index	114	0.59
A. Economic Participation and Opportunity	122	0.39
A-1. Labour Force Participation	114	0.43
A-2. Wage Equality for Similar Work	59	0.67
A-3. Per Capita Income	115	0.31
A-4. Legislators, Senior officals, managers	111	0.03
A-5. Profesional and Technical Workers	97	0.27
B. Educational Attainment	116	0.82
B-1. Literacy Rate	117	0.65
B-2. Enrolment in Primary Education	112	0.94
B-3. Enrolment in Secondary Education	114	0.79
B-4. Enrolment in Tertiarry Education	93	0.66
C. Health and Survival	126	0.93
C-1. Sex Ratio at Birth (Female/Male)	125	0.89
C-2. Healthy Life Expectancy	114	1.02
D. Political Empowerment	21	0.23
D-1. Women in Parliament	106	0.09
D-2. Women in Ministerial Position	118	0.04
D-3. Number of Years with a Female Head of State (in last 50 years)	4	0.43

Source : World Economic Forum (2007); Global Gender Gap Report, 2007, p. 8.

rate of SCs has increased considerably, from 10.3 per cent in 1961 to 54.7 per cent in 2001, till recently the gap between literacy rates of the general and SC populations had not reduced. They have limited access to permanent assets such as land. The occupational structure is highly deplorable with more than 52 per cent SCs workers are employed as agricultural labourers in rural areas and only 19.99 per cent are cultivators. Another important dimension of discrimination is the wide gap between the SCs and the rest of the population with respect to the availability of basic amenities such as electricity, banking services, pucca houses, water supply, toilet facilities, drainage and communication facilities.

Due to the lack of access to fixed sources of income and high incidence of wage labour associated with high rate of under employment and low wages, SC households are often faced with low incomes and high incidence of poverty. According to the UNDP India Report (2007) on Human Poverty and Socially Disadvantaged Groups in India, the HDI at all India level for SCs is estimated to be 0.303, which is lower that the HDI for non-SC/ST at 0.393 for the period 1980-2000. HDI for SCs of Bihar is at the minimum (0.195).[13]

Solution of poverty and discrimination of scheduled castes lies in economic empowerment with equal emphasis on capacity enhancing approach. There is a need to provide job-oriented training to SCs to enable them to have better opportunities, financial inclusion, along with skill development will help SCs to improve their income generating capacities. There is a need to complement protective legislation, that is, the Protection of Civil Rights Act, 1955 and Scheduled Castes and Scheduled Tribes (Prevention of Astrocities) Act, 1989 with a promotive legislation which should cover the rights to SCs with respect to education, vocational training, higher education and employment.

Economic Empowerment of Scheduled Tribes

Tribal population in India has different characteristics from the rest of the population. Tribal people have different culture and traditions mode of living. Tribal population in India stood at 84.33 million as per the Census 2001. They constitute 8.2 per cent of the total population of the country with 91.7 per cent of them living in rural areas and remaining 8.3 per cent in urban areas, 68 per cent of the country's tribal population lives in seven states—Madhya Pradesh (14.5%), Maharashtra (10.2%), Orissa (9.7%), Gujarat (8.9%), Rajasthan (8.4%), Jharkhand (8.4%) and Chhattisgarh (7.8%). Highest concentration of tribal population is in the states of Mizoram (94.5% population is STs) followed by Nagaland (89.1%) and

Meghalaya (85.9%). Within the major states, Chhattisgarh (31.8%) has the highest percentage followed by Jharkhand (26.3%) and Orissa (22.1%).[14]

Tribal people are marginalised in every walk of life, despite several constitutional safeguards, the emerging tribal scenario characteristically continues to manifest;

- increasing tribal alienation on account of slipping economic resources like land, forest, common property, resources;
- displacement and dispossession of life-support systems;
- general apathy of official machinery;
- escalating attrocities, at times related to assertion of rights;
- growing clout of market forces;
- meager advancement through planned development efforts;
- higher levels of poverty incidence illiteracy, malnutrition; and
- state sponsored attrocities in the name of curbing naxalites and Maoists activities.

Tribal people have been exploited greatly in economic terms during the process of planned economic development, especially during the era of economic reforms. Large power projects—thermal as well as hydro—displaced many tribal people. Likewise mining projects in minerally rich Orissa, Jharkhand, West Bengal, Chhattisgarh, Madhya Pradesh and Andhra Pradesh ruined the lives of thousands of tribal people.

Land (both owned by community and individual) and the forests are the most important source of livelihood for the tribal people. Despite several laws and regulations to prevent the alienation of tribal land and private grabbing of such land, the practice is widespread. Data of Ministry of Rural Development (GOI) reveals that 3.75 lakh cases of tribal land alienation have been registered covering 8.55 lakh acres of land.

Tribal community has not benefited from the pace and pattern of development during the last decade in the manner non-tribal people have benefited. The tribal economy is still plagued with low growth potential, poor infrastructure, lack of entrepreneurship, inadequate control over natural resources, etc. due to which the growth and development indices of tribal areas continued to be far below the indices for the rest of the country. Majority of tribal people continue to remain vulnerable to deprivation and distress and are subject to insecurity relating to livelihoods, nutrition, health and education.

Despite protective legislation, incidents of atrocities on tribal people, including gang rape and murder, continue to take place in almost all parts of the country. Five states—Madhya Pradesh, Orissa, Rajasthan, Andhra Pradesh and Chhattisgarh—contributed 72 per cent of the total incidents of crimes against scheduled tribes.[15]

Since most of the tribal habitations are located in isolated villages and hamlets in undulating plateau lands coinciding with forest areas, they have limited access to critical infrastructure facilities such as roads, communication, health, education, electricity drinking water and so on. This widen the gap between the quality of their life and the people in the country. The incidence of poverty among STs still continues to be very high at 47.30 per cent in rural areas and 33.30 per cent in urban areas, compared to 28.3 per cent and 25.7 per cent respectively in respect of total population in 2004-05 (old methodology).[16]

A large number of STs who are living below the poverty line are landless, with no productive assets and with no access to sustainable employment and minimum wages. The tribal women suffer even more because of the added disadvantage of being denied equal and minimum wages.

Human Development Index for STs is estimated at 0.270, which is lower than the HDI of SCs and non-SCs/STs for the period 1980-2000. Human Poverty Index for STs is estimated at 47.79, which was higher than SCs and non-SCs/STs for the period 1990-2000.[17]

The above data reveals that unified policies and programmes, developed under centralised planning ignoring the ground realities of tribal areas and without assessing the specific needs and aspirations of tribal people, did little.

Hence, an area specific approach is required for the redressal of problems of development of tribal areas and upliftment of tribal people. In the Eleventh Plan it is being attempted, in a paradigm shift with respect to overall empowerment of the tribal people. The operational comparatives of the Fifth Schedule of the Constitution of India, tribal sub-plan (TSP) 1976, Panchayat Raj Extension in Scheduled Areas (PESA), 1996, RERA, 2006, the desirability of a tribal-centric, tribal participative and tribal managed development process, and the need for a conscious departure from dependence on a largely-under-effective official delivery system required to be kept in view during this shift.

A massive programme of empowerment of tribal people with a special focus on the tribal women through institutional strengthening and capacity building must be aimed at the following critical areas:[18]

- Universal coverage of SHGs focusing on thrift and serving.
- Improvement of social indicators with the active involvement of the women, empowered through SHG network.
- Ending the role of money lenders by making available credit through Mandal Samakhyas, Commercial Banks, Regional Rural Banks and Co-operative credit societies.
- Taking up intensive capacity building activities from habitation level and involving the Panchayati Raj Institutions, so as to enable community-based monitoring of all development programmes.
- Setting up Tribal Project Management Unit (TPMU) for each ITDA.
- Protecting the rights of tribal people on land, especially the forest land.
- Empowering tribal communities to prepare development plans for their habitations duly identifying the untapped potential of the natural resources and critical infrastructure that has to be built-up.

- Intensive capacity building activities must be undertaken for enabling strategic players like ITDAs, PRIs, women groups and USSs for actualising the community-based planning exercise.
- The comprehensive plan for economic development of every household in the TSP area should address issue like sustainable resource management, capacity development, extension and technology support, food processing, marketing and regeneration and value addition of minor forest produce.
- Special focus on employment of tribal youth must be a key factor of development activities in tribal areas so as to alleviate these youth from unlawful activities of naxalites and Maoists. Unemployment and poverty are the two major causes of uprising of extremists activities in tribal areas.
- Good governance for effective delivery of services and financial assistance.
- Specific attention to universalisation of elementary education, primary health care, supply of drinking water for every habitation in tribal areas. Upgrading and strengthening of ashram schools and residential schools with the required staffing, infrastructure and teaching-learning equipment will do more than expected for the development of tribal adolescents.

PEOPLE'S PARTICIPATION IN DECISION-MAKING

Widespread popular participation is vital to successful implementation of poverty alleviation programmes through decentralisation—without it, the potential benefit of local information regarding the needs and aspirations of the people, especially the poor; availability of natural resources, and of course major constraints of growth, etc. can not be realised. Moreover, participation creates a virtuous circle. Participating in local government helps build civil society and ensure that majority needs are heard and goals are achieved. It also helps increase the voice of the poor people in local affairs.

The term 'participation' appeared for the first time in development jargon in the 1950s. In the 1970s, the term was used in development literature and it even became a practice. The term has been used to refer to citizen participation, community participation, public participation, popular participation and people participation, involving renewal or rehabilitation (Soen, 1981).[19] It has also been used in studies on conservation (Curtis and Lockwood, 2000);[20] villages regrouping[21] (Olujini and Egunjobi, 1991), Water supply[22] (Fitzgerald, 1993), housing[23] (Fahui and Van Loo, 1998), Social impact[24] (Durst, 1994), Health promotion (Goddman and Speers, 1998),[25] Community Planning[26] (Berkeley *et al.*, 1995) and also on management of environmental and health riskes[27] (Route and Frewer, 2000).

Participation relates to three concepts, namely, initiative, empowerment and organisation. Initiative is the most important factor in rural development and poverty alleviation. The emergence of indigenous initiatives can come from a mounting need of people caused by pressure of varied needs and problems whereby people are encouraged to change their lives. *Bhoomi Sena* (Land Army) movement in India is an example of indigenous initiative. The *Bhoomi Sena* movement was forging a bond between the *Adivasis* (tribals) and other groups in tribal areas into a united force[28] (Oakly and Marsdon, 1984). Emergence of people's initiative is crucial in people's empowerment as well as rural development in order that people can decide to the maximum possible extent on matters affecting themselves.

Participation is closely related to empowering people because of five reasons[29] (White, 1981).

(i) It has an intrinsic value for participants,
(ii) It encourages a sense of responsibility,
(iii) It uses valuable indigenous knowledge,
(iv) It frees people from dependence on others' skills, and
(v) It makes people more conscious of the causes of their poverty and what they can do about it.

Organisation is an essential requirement to make the participation a success. An organisation is necessary to ensure that participation is fostered on a collective basis such that all members of the community have equal access to the assets and infrastructure of the community and the decision-making rather than the local elites monopolise the benefits or authority and thus reinforce local stratification and cleavages.[30] A strong organisational structure of Panchayati Raj Institutions in India created in 1950s, has further got strength through 73rd amendment of the constitution of India. PRIs have got constitutional status through this amendment. Reservation of a third of seats of all the bodies of PRIs for women of each categories—SCs, STs, OBCs and general, has opened the door of these institutions for women who have been a neglected lot in the society.

Poor people can improve their standard of living through government aided programme provided central and local governments create decentralised mechanisms for broad participation in the delivery of public services and minimise the scope for capture by local elites. Governments generate political support for public action against poverty by creating a climate favourable to pro-poor actions and coalition, facilitating the growth of poor people's associations; and increasing the political capacity of poor people. Political regimes however the rule of law, allow the expression of political voice, and encourage the participation of poor people in political process.[31]

People's participation in governance and developmental activities has gained momentum with the enactment of constitution (73rd Amendment) Act 1992 and constitution (74th Amendment) Act, 1992. Panchayati Raj Institutions, the grass-root bodies of administration, has got constitutional status through 73rd Constitutional Amendment.

Through the experience of the Indian Panchayati Raj Institutions (PRI) 1 million women have actively entered political life in India. The 73rd and 74th Constitutional Amendment Acts, which have spearheaded an unprecedented social experiment which is playing itself out in more than 500,000 villages that are home to more than 600 million people. Since the creation of the quota system, local women—the vast majority of them illiterate and poor—have come to occupy as much as 43 per cent of the seats, spurring the election of increasing number of women at the district, provincial and national levels. Since the onset of PRI, the percentage of women in various levels of political activity have risen from 4-5 per cent to 25-50 per cent.

According to Indian writer and activist Devaki Jain, "the positive discrimination of PRI has initiated a momentum of change. Women's entry into local government in such large numbers, often more than the required 33.3 per cent, and their success in campaigning, including the defeat of male candidates, has shattered the myth that women are not interested in politics, and have no time to go to meatings or to undertake all the other work that is required in political party processes. PRI reminds us of a central truth; power is not something people give away. It has to be negotiated and sometimes wrested from the powerful."[32]

Contrary to fears that the elected women would be rubber stamp leaders, the success stories that have arisen from PRI are impressive. A government financed study, based on field work in 180 villages in the states of Uttar Pradesh, Rajasthan and Madhya Pradesh, and coordinated by the Center for Women's Development Studies in New Delhi, has found that a full two-thirds of elected women leaders are actively engaged in learning the ropes and exercising power. Says Noeleen Heyzer, executive director of UNIFEM, "This is one of the best innovation in grass-roots democracy in the world".[33]

Women leaders in the Panchayati Raj are transforming local governance by sensitizing the State to issues of poverty, inequality and gender injustice. Through the PRI, they are taking issues that had previously gone virtually unacknowledged, including water, alcohol abuse, education, health and domestic violence. According to Sudha Murali, UNICEF Communications Officer in Andhra Pradesh, women are seeing this power as a chance for a real change for them and for their children and are using it to demand basic facilities like primary schools and health care centres.

The PRI has also brought about significant transformations in the lives of women themselves, who have become empowered, and have gained self-confidence, political awareness and affirmation of their own identity. The panchayat villages have become political training grounds to women, many of them illiterate, who are now leaders in the village panchayats. Says Sudha Pillai, Joint Secretary, Ministry for Rural Development, "It has given something to people who were absolute nobodies and had no away of making it on their own. Power has become the source of their growth."

By asserting control over resources and officials and by challenging men, women are discovering a personal and collective power that was previously unimaginable. This includes women who are not themselves panchayat leaders, but who have been inspired by the work of their sisters; "We will not bear it", says one woman. Once we acquire some position and power, we will fight it out... "The fact that the Panchayats will have a minimum number of women (will be used) for mobilizing women at large." It is this critical mass of unified and empowered women which will push forward policies that enforce gender equity into the future.

Another good case of people's participation that achieved success to great extent is the implementation approach of Swarnajayanti Gram Swarozgar Yojna (SCSY).

The objective of Swarnajayanti Gram Swarozgar Yojna (SGSY) is to bring the assisted poor families (Swarozgaris) above the poverty line by ensuring appreciable sustained level of income over a period of time. This objective is to be achieved by *inter alia* organizing the rural poor into Self Help Groups (SHGs) through the process of social mobilization, their training and capacity building and provision of income generating assets.

The SGSY is different from earlier programmes, in terms of the strategy envisaged for its implementation. It has been conceived as a holistic programme of self-employment. It covers all aspects of self-employment of the rural poor viz. organisation of the poor into Self Help Groups (SHGs), their capacity building and training, credit linkages and subsidy, selection of key activities, planning of activity clusters, infrastructure build up, technology and marketing support.

A major shift in the SGSY compared to the erstwhile programmes is in terms of its emphasis on social mobilization of the poor. The programme focuses on organization of the poor at grass-roots level through a process of social mobilization for poverty eradication. Social mobilization enables the poor to build their own organisation, the Self Help Groups (SHGs), in which they participate fully and directly and through internal credit and thrift are able to meet small emergent expenditures through loans from group savings. An SHG may consist of 10-20 persons belonging to families below the Poverty Line. In the case of minor irrigation schemes, disabled persons and in difficult areas, i.e. hills, deserts and sparsely populated areas, the number of persons in a group may range from 5-20. However, if necessary 20 per cent and in exceptional cases upto 30 per cent of the members in a group may be from APL SGSY stress on cluster approach for taking up economic activities. They key activities are to be taken up in clusters. The cluster may not merely be geographic agglomerations but limits where backward and forward linkages can effectively be established. Separate clusters are to be taken up for each activity. More and more Swarozgaris can be added to the cluster each year. The cluster approach in the programmes is adopted to facilitate infrastructure and marketing support to the activity.

Families below the poverty line in rural areas constitute the target group of the SGSY. Within the target group, special safeguards have been provided to vulnerable sections, by way of reserving 50 per cent benefits for SCs/STs, 40 per cent for women, 15 per cent for minorities and 3 per cent for disabled persons.

The SGSY is emerging as a women centric programme. The guideline of the programme stipulates *inter-alia* that at least 40 per cent of the Swarojagaries will be women, and 50 per cent of all SHGs in a district will be women SHGs. During 2008-09 out of the total 18.61 lakh Swarozgaries assisted, about 12.07 lakhs were women Swarozgaris which constitutes around 65 per cent of the total Swarozgaris assisted.[34] With the present experience under the SGSY it has been noticed that the scheme has naturally emerged as women-led programme and in the pockets where the programme has been successfully implemented it has resulted in visible empowerment of women.

The Ministry of Rural Development is in the process of re-designing SGSY to implement it in a mission mode for achieving faster and better results. It is proposed to aim for universalisation of SHGs, i.e. to bring at least one member from each BPL family into the SHG fold in a time bound manner. A dedicated implementation structure is proposed to be put in place with the National Rural Livelihood Mission at the National level supported by similar apex bodies at the state, district and sub-district levels in the states.[35]

In most developing countries, including India, NGOs are central actors in anti-poverty policies and programmes.[36] The social and educational background of many NGO staff enables them to interact easily with the staff of national institutions, outside agencies and grass-root organisations, NGOs can also be very effective in delivering technical assistance to poor people.[37] NGOs in Bangladesh and India are playing a key role in extending micro-credit to rural poor through SHGs.

GOOD GOVERNANCE

Quality of governance is critical to poverty reduction. Since effective and efficient delivery of basic services by the state matters most for the poor, weak governance hurts them disproportionately. Good governance is therefore one of the three pillars of poverty reduction strategy.

- Pro-poor, sustainable Economic Growth
- Social Development

    (i) Human Capital Development
    (ii) Social Capital Development
    (iii) Gender and Development
    (iv) Social Protection

- Good Governance

Good governance facilitates participatory, pro-poor policies as well as sound macro-economic management. It ensures the use of public fund in more transparent manner, encourages growth of the private sector with full of its potential, promotes effective delivery of public goods, and helps to establish the rule of law. A sound macro-economic framework is needed to encourage efficient and production domestic investment and to keep inflationary forces under control to protect real incomes of the poor side by side it helps prevent interest and exchange rate distortions that artificially reduce the cost of capital and discourages the use of labour. An efficient public expenditure management ensures fiscal discipline, economic growth and equity. The equity is achieved through an effective, progressive tax system and adequate allocation of public funds for elementary education, primary health care, drinking water, housing, etc. Effective regulatory and supervisory framework in financial sector not only protects the interests of depositors and borrowers, but also enhance competition, increases efficiency and expands availability of financial resources for all members of the society. As the recent global financial crises has shown, good governance is also essential to avoid, or reduce the severity of economic crises in an era of increasing liberalisation and globalisation. Impact of global financial melt down on Indian economy has been minimal because of highly regulatory framework for the financial sector.

Public sector's inefficiency, corruption, waste and leakages leave insufficient resources to support the requisite level and quality of public services and targeted anti-poverty programmes. However, denial of basic services to the poor is not just a matter of lack of investment. Often, it is the manifestation of:[38]

(i) Institutional structures that lack accountability,
(ii) Domination by local elites,
(iii) Widespread corruption,
(iv) Culturally determined inequality, and
(v) Lack of participation of poor.

Existence of such problems requires systemic change to move from poor governance to government accountable to the poor. A drastic change in the system is rather difficult, since existing arrangements that exclude the poor reflect prevailing economic and power inequalities. Yet unless these issues of inequalities are tackled, it will be difficult to raise living standards of the poor.

Poverty is an outcome not only of economic process—it is an outcome of interacting economic, social, and political forces. In particular, it is an outcome of the accountability and responsiveness of state institutions. Poor people are benefited more if :

- Public administration implement policies efficiently and are accountable and responsive to users, corruption and harassment are curved, and the power of the state is used to redistribute assets and resources for action benefiting poor people.
- Legal system promote legal equity and are accessible to poor people.

Poor women and men stressed in many studies that officials are often unresponsive to them. Poor people shared countless examples of criminality, abuse and corruption in their encounters with public institutions and said they have little resources to justice. In describing the encounters with institutions, poor people also drew attention to the shame and indignity of being treated with arrogance, rudeness, and disdrain.[39]

Corruption takes a toll on economic performance undermines employment opportunities, and clouds prospects for poverty reduction. The burden of petty corruption falls disproportionately on poor people. For those without money and connection, petty corruption in public health or police services can have deliberating consequences. In many parts of India poor people are often denied their fundamental right of legal justice in equitable manner. Their complaints are not registered in the police stations. Corruption affects the lives of poor people through many other channels as well. Widespread corruption in public distribution system in India has marred its desired impact on the reduction of poverty. If IRDP a well designed and articulated programme of poverty alleviation, could not be successful with its full potential than the corruption was one of the most serious bottlenecks in its implementation.

Action for good governance must proceed at two levels :

(i) Public administration and expenditure management at the national level must be strengthened to promote proper growth and social development.

(ii) Responsibility for the delivery of public goods should be devolved to the lowest appropriate level of government such as PRIs and LUBs.

While, designing the strategy for good governance the long-term objective should be empower the poor and develop institutional arrangements that foster participation and accountability at the local level.

Notes and References

1. Bardhan, Pranab K. (1997); *The Role of Governance in Economic Development : A Political Economy Approach.* OECD Development Centre Study, Washington Centre Press, p. 47.
2. Tommari, Mariano and Federico Weischelbaum (1999); "A Principal Agent Building Block for the Study of Decentralisation and Integration", Harward University Press, pp. 117-19.
3. OECD (2008); Growing Unequal Income Distribution and Poverty in OECD Countries, pp. 77-95.
4. Ravallion, Martin and S. Chen (2003); Measuring pro-poor Growth, *Economics Letters,* 78 : pp. 93-99.
5. DFID (2004); "What is pro-poor growth and why do we need to know"? *Pro-poor Growth Briefing Note 1,* Department for International Development, London.
6. Sonowal, C.J. (2008); "Indian Tribes and Issues of Social Inclusion and Eclusion", *Tata Institute of Social Sciences,* Mumbai, p. 126.
7. UNDP (2004); Human Development Report, 2003, Oxford University Press, p. 6.
8. Nabuhide, Hatas (2001); "Health and Economic Development : A Cross-country National Empirical Analysis", *Journal of National Institute of Public Health,* 50(3).
9. Rawat, Deepa, Kalpana Agarwal and Manish Dev (2008); "Status of Public Health and It's Financing in India", In Anil Kumar Thakur and Md. Abdus Salam (eds.), *Economics of Education and Health in India,* Deep and Deep, pp. 170-71.
10. Government of India (2008); National Urban Health Mission (2008-12); Meeting the Health Challenges of Urban Population Especially the Urban Poor (with special focus on urban slums), Ministry of Health and Family Welfare, p. 3.
11. Carol, S. Coonard (1998); "Chronic Hunger and The Status of Women in India", p. 2.
12. Government of India (2009); Eleventh Five Year Plan (2007-12); *Planning Commission,* Vol. 1 : 107.

13. *Ibid.*
14. Government of India (2008); Eleventh Five Year Plan (2007-12), *Planning Commission*, Vol. I, p. 110.
15. *Ibid.*, p. 112.
16. *Ibid.*, p. 114.
17. *Ibid.*, p. 114.
18. *Ibid.*, p. 115.
19. Soen, O. (1981); "Citizen and community participation : Renewal and Rehabilitation—Comments on Theory and Practice", *Community Development Journal*, 16(2) : 107-10.
20. Curtis, A. and M. Lockwood (2000); Land care and catchment management in Australia : Lessons for State-Sponsored Community Participation", *Society and Natural Resources*, 13(1) : 34.
21. Olujini, B. and L. Egunjobi (1991); "Public Participation in Village Regrouping Scheme", *Community Development Journal*, 26(1) : 37-40.
22. Fitzgerald, M. (1993); "Participatory Community Development in Bophythatswana", *Community Development Journal*, 28(1) : 41-43.
23. Fahui, W. and J.A. Van Loo (1998); "Citizen Participation in the North Nelta Mississippi Community Development Block Grants Empowerment Zones and Enterprize Communities", *Planning Practice and Research*, 13(4) : 17-19.
24. Durst, D. (1994); Heavy Sledding, Barriers to Community Participation in Beaufort Sea Hydrocarbon Development. *Community Development Journal*, 29(1) : 37-44.
25. Goddman, R.M. and M.A. Speers (1998); "Identifying and Defining the Dimensions of Community Capacity to Provide a Basis for Measurement", *Health Education and Behaviour*, 25(3) : 96-99.
26. Berkeley, N., G. Goodall, D. Noon and C. Collis (1995); Involving the community in Plan Preparation, *Community Development Journal*, 30(2) : 47-56.
27. Rowe, G. and L.J. Frewer (2000); "Public Participation Methods : A Framework for Evaluation", *Science, Technology and Human Values*, 25(1) : 16-25.
28. Oakly, P. and D. Marsclon (1984); Approach to Participation in Rural Development, Geneva, ILO, Working Paper.
29. White, A. (1981); Community Participation in Water and Sanitation : Concepts, Strategies and Methods"; International Reference Centre for Community Water Supply and Sanitation, Technical Paper, No. 17, The Netherlands.
30. Yusof, K., S. Batumalai, W.Y. Lin and J. Okamura (1989); "The ABC of Community Participation in Primary Health Care : A Manual, Department of Publication, University of Malaysia.

31. World Bank (2001); World Development Report, 2000, Oxford University Press, p. 9.
32. Jain, Devaki (1996); Panchayat Raj : Women Changing Governance, Background Paper Beizing+5 Conference.
33. Carol (1998); *op. cit.*, p. 8.
34. Government of India (2009); Annual Report, 2008-09, Ministry of Rural Development, pp. 21-27.
35. *Ibid.*, pp. 21-27.
36. Riddell, Roger C. and Mark Robinson, John De Conninck, Annu Muir and Sarah White (1995); Non-Government Organisations and Rural Poverty Alleviation, New York, Oxford University Press.
37. Brown, David and Darcy Ashman (1996); Participation and Social Capital and Intersectoral Problem Solving : African and Asian Cases", *World Development*, 24(9) : 1467-79.
38. Asian Development Bank (200..); "Fighting Poverty in Asia and the Pacific : The Poverty Reduction Strategy", p. 13.
39. Narayan, Deepa; Robert Chamber, Meera, K. Shaha and Patti Petesch (2000); "Voice of the Poor : Crying Out for Change", New York, Oxford University Press, p. 117.

CHAPTER

8

Growth and Poverty

Conclusions and Suggestions

CHAPTER

8

Growth and Poverty

Conclusions and Suggestions

The debate over growth and poverty reduction is as old as the emergence of development economics under the shadow of welfare state. Higher levels of growth are considered vital to reduce the poverty incidence as the higher income results into higher levels of living of standard through 'trickle down' effect. However, empirical studies in India could not establish a universal relationship between growth and poverty. What has emerged from the analysis in the present study is that in the initial phases of planned economic development poverty could not be reduced because of slow growth, termed as *Hindu Growth Rate*, during the first three decades. Thereafter, Indian economy witnessed higher growth rate in the era of economic reforms in 1991, but this higher growth rate has also not translated into sharp reduction in poverty. The paradox of high growth and high incidence of poverty has some explanation in the distributional aspect of growing income leading to higher inequalities. The inference is clear. Although overall economic growth is impressive, the composition of growth in recent years has left much to be desired. Growth, unequivocally, is a necessary condition for lifting people out of poverty. But what we see in India is lop-sided growth. While the manufacturing and services sector (together, they employ a third of the country's workforce) record impressive rates of growth of the order of 7-10 per cent and thus enjoyed more than three quarters of the share of GDP, agriculture—on which depends the livelihood of more than two-thirds of the population—has been a laggard. Thus, nearly 70 crore of Indian people are surviving on 17.5 per cent share of GDP.

The gap between the rich and poor has widened in the last 25 years with the widening gap between industrial and services sectors together and agriculture sector. More than three quarters of poor in India are concentrated in ten States—Uttar Pradesh (735.48 million), Bihar (485.60 million), Maharashtra (393.26 million), Madhya Pradesh (316.88 million), West Bengal (289.07 million), Andhra Pradesh (238.76 million), Orissa (220.16 million), Rajasthan (210.31 million), Tamilnadu (186.76 million) and Karnataka (185.69 million). Ironically four states, out of those mentioned above are recognised as developed in terms of per capita income and their contribution in GDP of the country (Maharashtra, Tamilnadu, Gujarat and Karnataka). It is because of intra-state differentials in income and employment generation.

With the rich and the poor gap becoming wider, the overall gains on poverty reduction have not translated into much touted 'inclusive' growth. Planning and economic policies have failed to produce inclusive growth to enable substantial parts of the country to get the benefits of development. The gap between the highest and the lowest per capita income of the states has increased from 2.55 times in 1980-81 to 3.29 times in 1990-91 and further to 7.71 times in 2005-06. In absolute terms, the per capita income gap is Rs. 40,897 during 2005-06. States with low per capita income are Bihar, Uttar Pradesh, Chhattisgarh, Orissa, West Bengal and the whole lot of North-East while those with higher per capita income include Punjab, Haryana, Andhra Pradesh, Kerala, Karnataka and Goa.

Equitable distribution of the dividends of growth is among the most important aspects for poverty reduction and this requires reforms in governance alongwith higher allocations for the development of health and education sectors that are crucial for the enhancement of 'capability' of an individual to work efficiently.

The poor greatly suffer from low human capital. Household size is closely related to both nutrition of adults and children, and to the inter-generatonal transfer of poverty.

Thus, the following areas emerge consensually :

(i) Growth is fundamental for poverty reduction, and in principle growth as such does not seen to affect inequality;

(ii) Growth accompanied by progressive distribution change is better than growth alone;

(iii) High initial inequality is a brake on poverty reduction;

(iv) Poverty itself is also likely to be a barrier for poverty reduction;

(v) Asset inequality seems to predict lower future growth rates;

(vi) Education, health, infrastructure and macro-economic stability seem to positively affect both growth and the distribution of income;

(vii) Unified strategy for poverty reduction programmes and policies has failed in a continental country like India having vast differentials in geo-climatic conditions, availability of natural resources, culture and traditions.

(viii) Gap between rich and poor has widened during the course of time, especially in post-reform period.

(ix) The 'capability enhancing policies' are crucial for alleviating poverty permanently.

(x) Since a unified approach of poverty reduction could not produce desired results, so a combination of growth mediated approach, capability approach, safetynet approach, inclusive growth approach based on area specific needs will be more effective.

(xi) Poverty alleviation strategy needs different policy intervention, to address the problems of different categories of poor of different geographical regions.

Effectiveness of anti-poverty interventions depends upon both design and implementation of policies and capacity, and cohesiveness of institutions. The approach to reducing poverty over the past half century has evolved in response to variety of experience in different parts of the world and deepening of understanding of complexity of development process itself.

Formulation of policies for poverty alleviation, requires the clear-cut understanding of the incidence, depth and severity of poverty in different parts of the world in general and, India, in particular. Different approaches have been used by the planners, policy-makers, individual economists and development institutions to define poverty. Although the poverty has many dimensions, but the main emphasis is on Income poverty and Human poverty. While the income poverty considers the income (or expenditure—alternatively) as the sole criteria to determine an individual's status in economic terms. Whether a person is poor or rich depends upon the level of income he earns. The human poverty, on the other hand captures all those factors of life which affect or may affect, deleteriously, the survival and growth of an individual.

Measurement of poverty is a crucial phenomenon. Various methods have been developed at national and international level to measure the incidence, depth and severity of poverty. Poverty line is the most commonly used concept throughout the world. Poverty line can be defined as an imaginary cut-off line of per capita monthly expenditure (or income) below which the individuals or the households are treated poor.

The Planning Commission, the nodal agency for the implementation of anti-poverty programmes, has adopted the poverty line of Rs. 49.09 per capita monthly expenditure for rural areas and Rs. 56.64 per capita monthly expenditure for urban areas at 1973-74 prices as the poverty lines as recommended by the Expert Group on Estimation of proportion and number of poor headed by Prof. D.T. Lakdawala. These amounts were judged enough to purchase that much of food which contains 2400 calories per person per day in rural areas and 2100 calories per person per day in urban areas. However, the expert group to review the methodology for estimation of poverty, under the chairmanship of Prof. S.D. Tendulkar, moved away from the calorie norms for the estimation of poverty. The Expert Group (2009) recommended Mixed Reference Period equivalent of urban Poverty Line Basket corresponding to 25.7 per cent urban headcount ratio as the new reference poverty line basket to be provided to rural as well as urban population in all the states after adjusting it for within state urban-relative to rural and rural and urban state relative to all India price differentials. In Expert Group's view the estimated urban share of the poor population (described as headcount ratio or poverty ratio) in 2004-05, namely 25.7 per cent at the all India level, is generally accepted as being less controversial than its rural counterpart at 28.3 per cent that has been heavily criticized as being two low. In the interest of continuity as well as in view of the consistency with broad external validity checks with respect to nutritional, educational and health outcomes the expert group adopted new line of thinking. Since the new poverty lines have been arrived at after assessing the adequacy of private household expenditure on education and health, the earlier anchored poverty lines did not explicitly account for these. The proposed poverty lines are in that sense broader in scope. The World Bank developed the poverty line of his own. It is US $ 1 per day per person (PPP terms). The World Bank has also revised its poverty line from US $ 1.0 per day to US $ 1.25 per day per person.

The concept of human poverty has been coined by UNDP which has developed following indicators to measure the human poverty.

Human Development Index (HDI) is a composite index measuring average achievements in three basic dimensions of human development—a long and healthy life, knowledge and a decent standard of living.

Human Poverty Index is measured by UNDP separately for developing countries and developed countries. HPI-I (for developing countries) is a composite index measuring deprivations in three basic dimensions captured in the HDI—a long and healthy life (vulnerability to death at a relatively early age as measured by the probability at birth of not surviving to age 40), knowledge (exclusion from the world of reading and communications, as measured by the adult illiteracy rate) and a decent standard of living (lack of access to overall economic provisioning, as measured by the unweighted average of two indicators—(i) the percentage of the population without sustainable access to an improved water source, and (ii) the percentage of children under weight for age).

HPI-II (for developed countries) put greater emphasis on the survivability up to the age of 60; percentage of adults lacking functional literacy skills; the percentage of population living below poverty line. A fourth dimension, in the form of social exclusion as measured by the rate of long-term unemployment, has been added to HPI-I.

Several agencies, including independent researchers, estimated the incidence of poverty in India. All of them used consumption expenditure data collected by NSSO in its various rounds of surveys and National Account Statistics generated by CSO.

There are conceptual and measurement differences that lead to a discrepancy between per capita income growth rates implied by national account statistics and household level statistics from the NSSO. Changes in the survey methodology in 55th round and in the subsequent rounds of NSSO rendered the latest official poverty estimates not strictly comparable to previous rounds. So far as the incidence and depth of poverty in India is concerned, the estimates may be categorised as under:

1. Official estimates, as are generated by the Planning Commission, Government of India (Prof Y.K. Alagh, Prof. D.T. Lakadwala, A. Dubey, S. Gangopadhyay, Abhijit Sen, Prof. S.D. Tenduklar, etc.).
2. Individual independent economists (Prof. P.D. Ojha, Prof. B.S. Minhas, Prof. S.D. Tendulkar, Prof. L.R. Jain, Prof. S.P. Gupta, Surjeet S. Bhalla, P. Visaria, J. Mehta, S. Venkatraman).
3. Economists associated with the World Bank, UNDP, IMF, etc.—A. Deaton, A. Tarroze, M. Ravallion, etc.

Official estimates and their methodology were often questioned by the individual economists. There are several possible sources of error in the NSS data on consumption and poverty-definition and choice of poverty lines, and price deflators, changes in the distribution of expenditures and inequality, and changes overtime in the completeness of recording of expenditure at high income but also at low income, leading by the 1990s to significant under reporting of both food and non-food expenditure. The statistics of poverty in India are in disarray and it would be good to try to improve them.

Planning Commission claims that incidence of poverty in India declined considerably as a result of launching of various poverty alleviation programmes. Independent economists accepted this claim with caution and they often argued that massive reduction in the incidence of poverty, as reported by the Planning Commission was largely a consequence of the peculiar statistical artifacts used by the commission. These economists are of the view that the Planning Commission has continued to indulge in mindless tinkering with the observed data of NSS regarding NSS size distribution of consumer expenditure.

All the economists associated with World Bank, UNDP, IMF—directly or indirectly are of the view that economic growth has been a leading determinant of poverty reduction. These economists claim that most of the reduction in poverty in the past has been a result of the increase in average consumption driven by economic growth. But, many empirical evidences did not confirm this inference in India. The latest evidences show that higher growth trend in Indian economy has not 'trickled down' in considerable manner. As a result, the gap between rich and poor has increased in post-reforms era.

Leaving the theoretical and/or empirical discussion aside, it is a well known fact that Indian economy has been facing the problem of mass structural poverty in both the rural and urban areas. First two decades saw comparatively a lower growth rate of the order of 0–3.5 per cent per annum. It is often termed as a cause of slow or zero reduction in the incidence of poverty.

The policy-makers attempted to reduce poverty by launching several poverty alleviation programmes since 1971-72. These programmes can be categorised into three categories :

(i) Providing Basic Needs, such as nutritional food, basic education, primary health care, safe and clean drinking water, shelter, roads, etc. The programmes of this category include:

- Minimum Needs Programme
- Integrated Child Development Services
- National Literacy Mission
- Universal Immunisation Programme
- Maternity and Child Health Care

(ii) Income generating direct anti-poverty programmes include—MFAL, SFDA, IRDP, TRYSEM, DWCRA, SITRA, GKY, SGRY, SGSY, PMGY, Antyodaya, SEPUP, PMIUPEP, UBSP, etc.

(iii) Employment generating or indirect, anti-poverty programmes include: PMCP, Food for Work Programme, NREP, RLEGP, EAS, JRY, NRY, Million Wells Scheme, Indira Awas Yojna, NREGA, etc.

The concept of IRDP and its sub-programmes—TRYSEM, DWCRA, SITRA, GKY as well as its earlier versions—SFDA/MFAL, was based on 'cluster approach' to assist rural people living BPL to derive economic benefits from the development assets of each area. BPL Households were given soft-loans and subsidies too to develop their own income generating asset. Improper implementation and leakages of funds made these programmes less effective. Planning Commission accepted that the IRDP and its sub-components had been successful in providing incremental income to the poor families, but in most cases the incremental income had not been adequate to enable the beneficiaries to cross the poverty line on a sustained basis mainly because of a low per household investment. The major constraint in the implementation of these programmes has been sub-critical investments which have adversely affected the Incremental Capital Output Ratio (ICOR) levels and thereby undermined the viability of the projects. In addition to this, inadequate development of infrastructure and insufficient forward and backward linkages and market facilities had been an area of concern of these programmes.

IRDP and its allied programmes (TRYSEM, DWCRA, SITRA and GKY), and Million Wells Programme were merged into a single programme known as Swarnajayanti Gram Swarozgar Yojna (SGRY), which was conceived as a holistic programme of micro-enterprise development in rural areas with emphasis on organising the rural poor into SHGs, capacity building, planning of activity clusters, infrastructure support, technological upgradation, credit and market linkages.

Self-employment programmes (SEEUYS, SEPUP, PMIUPEP and UBSP) have also been started in urban areas for the upliftment of urban poor above the poverty line. The latest data of poverty incidence (2004-05) show that urban poverty alleviation programmes could not control the spread of poverty in urban areas. As per Planning Commission's latest estimates number of poor in urban areas were 80.7 million in 2004-05 (25.7%), while in 1993-94 the 76.3 million people were living BPL in urban areas (32.4%).

The third set of anti-poverty programmes consists of employment generation programmes mainly: PMCP, Food for Work Programme, NREP, RLGP, EAS, SGSY, NREGS, JRY, NRY, etc. The core issue of these programmes was to create employment opportunities for rural/or urban poor during lean season and developing community assets of permanent nature.

Although the employment generation target under these programmes had been achieved. However, it was not known as to how much of that had been directed towards those who were landless and the poorest among the poor. To this extent these programmes apparently lacked a direct focus on the target-group population, however, they had a substantial impact in terms of stabilisation of wages in rural areas, containing prices of foodgrains and the creation of a wide variety of community assets which could be expected to help in raising the levels of living of the rural population.

Employment generation programmes could not produce desired result because of the following reasons:

- Presence of middle men (contractor) on a large scale.
- Leakage of funds through bureaucracy and local politicians.
- Black marketing of foodgrains allotted under these programmes.
- No provision for the maintenance of assets created through these programmes.

India has had 60 years of economic planning and programmes to promote development and eradicate poverty. India has many achievement to her credit from food sufficiency to eradication of mass killer diseases like cholera, small pox etc. So far as the incidence of poverty in India is concern, the problem is still unsolved. The share of people in income poverty has fluctuated widely in the past but the trend is downwards. In 1951, the proportion of the rural population living below the poverty line was 47 per cent. It rose to 61 per cent in 1954-55, fell to 45 per cent in 1960-61, then rose again to 56.4 in 1973-74. During 1973-74 to 1993-94 rural poverty declined from 56.4 to 37.3 per cent (19.1 percentage point decline in 20 years of period). The decline in rural poverty remains rather slow during 1993-94 to 2004-05, where the incidence of poverty in rural areas could come down 11.0 percentage point in 11 years (from 37.3% in 1993-94 to 28.3 per cent in 2004-05). The data of 2004-05 (URP) is somewhat comparable with 1993-94.

So far as the incidence of poverty in urban areas is concerned, it was 49.2 per cent in 1973-74, which came down to 32.4 per cent (16.8 percentage point decline in twenty years). Again the declining trend in urban poverty continued, but with a slow pace. It came down from 32.4 per cent in 1993-94 to 25.7 per cent (URP) in 2004-05 (6.7 percentage point in 11 years). What is significant here? In absolute figures the number of poor in rural areas declined from 244 million in 1993-94 to 220.9 million in 2004-05, in contrast to this the number of poor in urban areas increased from 76.3 million in 1993-94 to 80.7 million in 2004-05. These figures are based on Expert Group's

(1993) methodology. Poverty data further swelled up in the new methodology suggested by Expert Group (2009) (Tendulkar Committee). Poverty HCRs for 1993-94 are 50.1 per cent, 31.8 per cent and 45.3 per cent in rural areas, urban areas and combined respectively. For 2004-05 these figures are 41.8 per cent, 25.7 per cent and 37.2 per cent respectively. However, percentage point decline in poverty HCR between 1993-94 to 2004-05 is almost the same under both methodologies.

Thus, more than 300 million people (440 million as per new methodology) in India are still living below the poverty line (27.5%). There has been a divergence in poverty reduction across Indian states. Poorer northern states (BIMARU and Orissa) have lagged behind the others major states in lowering poverty incidences over the last three decades. The states with the poorest initial conditions grew more slowly than the rest, resulting is an increase in inequality across regions. Regional economic growth has been slower in the poorer northern states, leading to an increased concentration of poverty in the north. High Economic growth has not been a sole criteria for the greater impact on poverty reduction. Had it been a case then one of the high performing states, Maharasthra, would not have the high incidence of poverty of the order of 30.7 per cent in 2004-05. Kerala's success in poverty reduction is spectacular even with a slow growth rate of SGDP. The incidence of poverty in Kerala is 15 per cent in 2004-05, which was more than 55 per cent in 1973-74.

Reasons or the causes of poverty, its various dimensions and their measurement might have several controversies, but unanimously it is regarded a curse on the life of an individual. It is obligatory on the part of government in a 'welfare state' that none of its citizen remains entrapped under the poverty-income or human.

Breaking out of poverty traps requires a multifaceted approach—one that goes beyond the usual sound commandments of good economic and political governance. For a country like India, trapped in poverty, the following six policy clusters are crucial :

(i) Investing in human development—nutrition, health, primary health care and reproductive health, education, skill development, water and sanitation—to foster productive labour force that can participate effectively in the national economy.

(ii) Helping small and marginal farmers increase productivity and breakout of subsistence farming and chronic hunger—especially in BIMARU States and Orissa.

(iii) Investing in infrastructure—roads, power, ports, communications, warehousing—to attract new investments in non-traditional areas.

(iv) Developing industrial policies that bolster non-traditional private sector activities, with special attention to small and medium-size enterprises.

(v) Emphasizing human rights and social equity to promote the well-being of all people and to ensure that poor and marginalised people—including girls and women—have the freedom and voice to influence decisions that affect their lives.

(vi) Promoting environmental sustainability and improving urban management, especially the development of slums. There is a greater need to protect biodiversity and ecosystem that support life.

A comprehensive anti-poverty strategy encompasses not just policies intended to create self-employment and wage-employment opportunities to the poor and marginalised nor is it limited to merely accelerating growth of the economy. While both sets of policies are necessary and complementary to each other, they are not sufficient. It should also include the third element—politics to improve the quality of life of the poor and those directed to expand their ability to shape their own future. This calls for not just accelerating growth but improving the quality of growth itself.

What needs to be done to ensure that the benefits of growth go more to the poor? In India, recent pro-poor initiatives include legislation that ensures the right to work (in the form of NREGA, which guarantees 100 days of work in a year at minimum wages to at least one member of each poor rural family), the right to education (free and compulsory education up to the school-leaving stage), the right to information (to enforce transparency in government and reduce corruption), the right to food (entitling each BPL family to 25 kg of foodgrains per month at Rs. 3 a kg) and financial inclusion (greater flow of credit from the banks to the poor entreprenures through self-help groups).

The following measures, if adopted with good intention and political will may be path breaking for eradicating poverty and hunger:

- ❖ The current methodology of identification of poor in the society is full of controversies, hence it requires reforms. Instead of putting greater emphasis on the consumption of expenditure of the households, a more comprehensive poverty index should be developed by taking into consideration the following indicators :

    - Family belonging to scheduled caste or scheduled tribe.
    - Number of children under five years old.
    - Having even one illiterate.
    - With only one or no adult employed
    - Living in *kutch* house or *jhonpadi.*
    - Have no clean source of water.
    - Without a household sanitary latrine.
    - Consuming only two or less meals per day.
    - The meals short of required calorie per person per day (2400 kcl per person per day for rural areas and 2100 kcl per person per day for urban areas).

    If four or more of the conditions are present in a family, it should be put in the high risk poverty group.
- ❖ Area specific approach should be adopted to deal with the poor in order to put greater emphasis on the locally available resources which have to be tapped for the advantage of the poor.
- ❖ Knowledge and skill of the poor should be enhanced in such a manner that they are capable enough to start own micro-enterprises.

- Greater emphasis should be given to make the poor self-reliant.
- Dependency on public fund such as subsidy should be minimised. Such funds should be diverted to the creation of income generating assets for poor.
- Efficiency and growth must be enhanced by the unfinished economic reforms. This would amount to a successful implementation of the 'indirect' anti-poverty, 'pull-up' strategy that relieves poverty by providing gainful employment. It would also generate resources that must then be increasingly used to sustain, even enhance, the social expenditures, thus supporting the 'direct' anti-poverty strategy.
- Need-based projects should be allowed to be prepared by the households living below the poverty line. The government functionaries should then assist the household to generate resources for the successful implementation of these projects.
- A shared partnership with NGOs will definitely boost functioning of anti-poverty programme because the NGOs have the commitment and the micro-knowledge, and government have the resources. By involving NGOs in anti-poverty programmes, the development efforts would rest on the two legs of the 'indirect' or 'pull-up' growth strategy and the 'direct' social expenditure and social engineering strategy, while resting the later in turn on two other legs: governmental resources in symbiotic partnership with NGO activity.
- Higher growth may, however, be important for the reduction of poverty in India, need-based anti-poverty programmes will play an important role in poverty reduction, so poverty alleviation programmes should be continued with highest priority.
- Almost all the poverty alleviation programmes were sound in objectives, but their implementation was the victim of bureaucratic and political interference

and thus, they resulted into high leakage of funds. Leakages, if stopped, would give better results.

- A strategic policy framework for pro-poor growth can be built upon the twin pillars of improving the investment climate to accelerate growth and empowering poor people to contribute to and benefit from this growth.
- The investment climate is concerned with the factors that determine :

  - The level of current investment,
  - Productivity of existing investment, and
  - Stability of returns over the medium term on sustainable basis.

- Within the realm of the investment climate, the policies and programmes, as well as, institutional arrangements should be organised around three broad categories :

  - Macro-economic stability and openness,
  - Economic governance and institutions, including both the implementation of efficiency—enhancing regulation and the elimination of regulations that lead to waste and rent-seeking behaviour.
  - Development of infrastructure.

- Empowerment of poor-people will enhance their ability so that they will be shaping their own lives in their own ways. Empowerment is the process that enables people to contribute to, and participate in, economic growth.
- The fight against poverty in India cannot be waged through an improved investment climate alone. Growth will be more pro-poor, if poor people have a higher level of human capital and an opportunity to shape the decisions that shape their lives.
- India's citizens, especially the poor, remain handicapped by low average levels of education and

a poor health status. Overcoming this handicap is a critical challenge for the planners and policy makers.

- Concrete efforts should be made, with public and private partnership and active involvement of NGOs, wherever, it is possible to enhance educational facilities in an affordable manner to include the previously excluded segments of society, women, religious and ethnic minorities, and those in the less favoured castes categories.
- In addition, improving educational levels, health status, and participation in decision-making bodies-political, social, economic, will enhance poor people's opportunities to control their destiny. This increased opportunity is an end in itself, while the human capital development will also improve income-generating potential (a means).
- Mechanism for public accountability should be improved because it will empower the poor to demand the quality and mix of public services that they need.
- Public policies directed to reduce poverty should contain an optimal mix of 'capacity improving' and 'safety net' policies, or 'growth meditated' and 'support-led' security.
- Planning and implementation of anti-poverty programmes should be decentralised to a structure called the community development society, which can be a registered society of women from poor families within the limits of nagarpalikas/town areas/panchayats.

Annexure 4.1

Percentage of People Below the Poverty Line : Total

Sl. No.	*State/U.T.'s*	*1973-74 (URP)*	*1977-78 (URP)*	*1983-84 (URP)*	*1987-88 (URP)*	*1993-94 (URP)*	*1999-2000 (MRP)*	*2004-05 (MRP)*	*2004-05 (URP)*
(1)	*(2)*	*(3)*	*(4)*	*(5)*	*(6)*	*(7)*	*(8)*	*(9)*	*(10)*
1.	Andhra Pradesh	48.86	39.31	28.91	25.86	22.19	15.77	11.1	15.8
2.	Arunachal Pradesh	51.93	58.32	40.88	36.22	39.35	33.47	13.4	17.6
3.	Assam	51.21	57.15	40.47	36.21	40.86	36.09	15.0	19.7
4.	Bihar	61.91	61.55	62.22	52.13	54.96	42.60	32.5	41.4
5.	Chhattisgarh	—	—	—	—	—	—	32.0	40.9
6.	Goa	44.26	37.23	18.90	24.52	14.92	4.40	12.0	13.8
7.	Gujarat	48.15	41.23	32.79	31,54	24.21	14.07	12.5	16.8
8.	Haryana	36.36	29.55	21.37	16.64	25.05	8.74	9.9	14.0
9.	Himachal Pradesh	26.39	32.45	16.40	15.45	28.44	7.63	6.7	10.0
10.	Jammu & Kashmir	40.83	38.97	24.24	23.82	25.17	3.48	4.2	5.4
11.	Jharkhand	—	—	—	—	—	—	34.8	40.3
12.	Karnataka	54.47	48.78	38.24	37.53	33.16	20.04	17.4	25.0
13.	Kerala	59.79	52.22	40.42	31.79	25.43	12.72	11.4	15.0

(Contd.)

ANNEXURE 4.1 (Contd.)

(1)	(2)	(3)	(4)	(5)	(6)	(7)	(8)	(9)	(10)
14.	Madhya Pradesh	61.78	61.78	49.78	43.07	42.52	37.43	32.4	38.3
15.	Maharashtra	53.24	55.88	43.44	40.41	36.86	35.02	25.2	30.7
16.	Manipur	49.96	53.72	37.02	31.35	33.78	38.54	13.2	17.3
17.	Meghalaya	50.20	55.19	38.81	33.92	37.92	33.87	14.1	18.5
18.	Mizoram	50.32	54.38	36.00	27.52	25.66	19.47	9.5	12.6
19.	Nagaland	50.81	56.04	39.25	34.43	37.92	32.67	14.5	19.0
20.	Orissa	66.18	70.07	65.29	55.58	48.56	47.15	39.9	46.4
21.	Punjab	28.15	19.27	16.18	13.20	11.77	6.16	5.2	8.4
22.	Rajasthan	46.14	37.42	34.46	35.15	27.41	15.28	17.5	22.1
23.	Sikkim	50.86	55.89	39.71	36.06	41.43	36.55	15.2	20.1
24.	Tamil Nadu	54.94	54.79	51.66	43.39	35.03	21.12	17.8	22.5
25.	Tripura	51.00	56.88	40.03	35.23	39.01	34.42	14.4	18.0
26.	Uttar Pradesh	57.07	49.05	47.07	41.46	40.85	31.15	25.5	32.8
27.	Uttarakhand	—	—	—	—	—	—	31.8	39.6
28.	West Bengal	63.43	60.52	54.85	44.72	35.66	27.02	20.6	24.7
29.	Andaman & Nicobar	55.56	55.42	52.13	43.89	34.47	20.99	17.6	22.6
30.	Chandigarh	27.96	27.32	23.79	44.67	11.35	5.75	3.8	7.1
31.	Dadra & Nagar Haveli	46.55	37.20	15.67	67.11	50.84	17.14	30.6	33.2

32.	Daman & Diu	—	—	—	—	15.80	4.44	8.0	10.5
33.	Delhi	49.61	33.23	26.22	12.41	14.69	8.23	10.2	14.7
34.	Lakshadweep	59.68	52.79	42.36	34.95	25.04	15.60	12.3	16.0
35.	Pondicherry	53.82	53.25	50.06	41.46	37.40	21.67	18.2	22.4
	All India	54.88	51.32	44.48	38.86	35.97	26.10	21.8	27.5

Based on URP—Consumption.

Based on MRP—Consumption.

Hence the data of 1999-2000 and 2004-05 are not comparable, but the data of 1993-94 and 2004-05 are roughly comparable.

Source : GOI, Tenth Five Year Plan (2002-07) and http://pib.nic.in.

ANNEXURE 4.2
Percentage of People Below the Poverty Line : Rural Areas

Sl. No.	State/U.T.'s	1973-74 (URP)	1977-78 (URP)	1983-84 (URP)	1987-88 (URP)	1993-94 (URP)	1999-2000 (MRP)	2004-05 (MRP)	2004-05 (URP)
(1)	(2)	(3)	(4)	(5)	(6)	(7)	(8)	(9)	(10)
1.	Andhra Pradesh	48.41	38.11	26.53	20.92	15.92	11.05	7.5	11.2
2.	Arunachal Pradesh	52.68	59.82	42.60	39.35	45.01	40.04	17.0	22.3
3.	Assam	52.68	59.62	24.60	39.25	45.01	40.04	17.0	22.3
4.	Bihar	62.99	63.25	64.37	52.63	58.21	44.30	32.9	42.1
5.	Chhattisgarh	—	—	—	—	—	—	31.2	40.8
6.	Goa	46.85	37.64	14.82	17.64	5.34	1.35	1.9	5.4
7.	Gujarat	46.35	41.76	29.80	28.67	22.18	13.17	13.9	19.1
8.	Haryana	34.23	27.73	20.56	16.22	28.02	8.27	9.2	13.6
9.	Himachal Pradesh	27.42	33.49	17.00	16.28	30.34	7.94	7.2	10.7
10.	Jammu & Kashmir	45.51	42.86	26.04	25.70	30.34	3.97	2.7	4.6
11.	Jharkhand	—	—	—	—	—	—	40.2	46.3
12.	Karnataka	55.14	48.18	36.33	32.82	29.88	17.38	12.0	20.8
13.	Kerala	59.19	51.48	39.03	29.10	25.76	9.38	9.6	13.2

14.	Madhya Pradesh	62.66	62.52	48.90	41.92	40.64	37.06	29.8	36.9
15.	Maharashtra	57.71	62.97	45.23	40.78	37.93	23.72	22.2	29.6
16.	Manipur	52.67	59.82	42.60	39.35	45.01	40.04	17.0	22.3
17.	Meghalaya	52.67	59.82	42.60	39.35	45.01	40.04	17.0	22.3
18.	Mizoram	52.67	59.82	42.60	39.35	45.01	40.04	17.0	22.3
19.	Nagaland	52.67	59.82	42.60	39.25	45.01	40.04	17.0	22.3
20.	Orissa	67.28	72.38	67.53	57.64	49.72	48.01	39.8	46.8
21.	Punjab	28.21	16.37	13.20	12.60	11.95	6.35	5.9	9.1
22.	Rajasthan	44.76	35.89	33.50	33.21	26.46	13.74	14.3	18.7
23.	Sikkim	52.67	59.82	42.60	39.35	45.01	40.04	17.0	22.3
24.	Tamil Nadu	57.23	57.68	53.99	45.80	32.48	20.55	16.9	22.8
25.	Tripura	52.67	59.82	42.60	39.35	45.01	40.04	17.0	22.3
26.	Uttar Pradesh	56.53	47.60	46.45	14.10	42.28	31.22	25.3	33.4
27.	Uttarakhand	—	—	—	—	—	—	31.7	40.8
28.	West Bengal	73.16	68.34	63.05	43.30	40.80	31.85	24.2	28.6
29.	Andaman & Nicobar	57.43	57.68	53.99	45.80	32.48	20.55	16.9	22.9
30.	Chandigarh	27.96	27.32	23.79	14.67	11.35	5.75	3.8	7.1
31.	Dadra & Nagar Haveli	46.85	37.64	14.81	67.11	51.95	17.57	36.0	39.8

(*Contd.*)

ANNEXURE 4.2 (Contd.)

(1)	(2)	(3)	(4)	(5)	(6)	(7)	(8)	(9)	(10)
32.	Daman & Diu	—	—	—	—	5.34	1.35	1.0	5.4
33.	Delhi	24.44	30.91	7.66	1.29	1.90	0.40	0.1	6.9
34.	Lakshadweep	59.19	51.48	39.03	29.10	25.76	9.38	9.6	13.3
35.	Pondicherry	57.43	57.68	53.99	45.80	32.48	20.55	16.9	22.9
	All India	56.44	53.07	45.65	39.09	37.27	27.09	21.8	28.3

Based on URP—Consumption.
Based on MRP—Consumption.
Hence the data of 1999-2000 and 2004-05 are not comparable, but the data of 1993-94 and 2004-05 are roughly comparable.
Source : GOI, Tenth Five Year Plan (2002-07) and http://pib.nic.in.

ANNEXURE 4.3

Percentage of People Below the Poverty Line : Urban Areas

Sl. No.	State/U.T.'s	1973-74 (URP)	1977-78 (URP)	1983-84 (URP)	1987-88 (URP)	1993-94 (URP)	1999-2000 (MRP)	2004-05 (MRP)	2004-05 (URP)
(1)	(2)	(3)	(4)	(5)	(6)	(7)	(8)	(9)	(10)
1.	Andhra Pradesh	50.61	43.55	36.30	40.11	38.33	26.63	20.7	28.0
2.	Arunachal Pradesh	36.92	32.71	21.73	9.94	7.73	7.47	2.4	3.3
3.	Assam	36.92	32.71	21.73	9.94	7.73	7.47	2.4	3.3
4.	Bihar	52.96	48.76	47.33	48.73	34.50	32.91	28.9	34.6
5.	Chhattisgarh	—	—	—	—	—	—	34.7	41.2
6.	Goa	37.69	36.31	27.00	35.48	27.03	7.52	20.9	21.3
7.	Gujarat	52.57	40.02	39.14	37.26	27.89	15.59	10.1	13.0
8.	Haryana	40.18	36.57	24.15	17.99	16.38	9.99	11.3	15.1
9.	Himachal Pradesh	13.17	19.44	9.43	6.29	9.18	4.63	2.6	3.4
10.	Jammu & Kashmir	21.32	23.71	17.76	17.47	9.18	1.98	8.5	7.9
11.	Jharkhand	—	—	—	—	—	—	16.3	20.2
12.	Karnataka	52.53	50.36	42.82	48.42	40.14	25.25	27.2	32.6
13.	Kerala	62.74	55.36	45.68	40.33	24.55	20.27	16.4	20.2

(Contd.)

ANNEXURE 4.3 (Contd.)

(1)	(2)	(3)	(4)	(5)	(6)	(7)	(8)	(9)	(10)
14.	Madhya Pradesh	57.65	58.66	53.06	47.09	48.38	38.44	39.3	42.1
15.	Maharashtra	43.87	40.09	40.26	39.78	35.15	26.81	29.0	32.2
16.	Manipur	36.92	32.71	21.73	9.94	7.73	7.47	2.4	3.3
17.	Meghalaya	36.92	32.71	21.73	9.94	7.73	7.47	2.4	3.3
18.	Mizoram	36.92	32.71	2173	9.94	7.73	7.47	2.4	3.3
19.	Nagaland	36.92	32.71	21.73	9.94	7.73	7.47	2.4	3.3
20.	Orissa	55.62	50.92	49.15	41.63	41.64	42.83	40.3	44.3
21.	Punjab	27.96	27.32	23.79	14.67	11.35	5.75	3.8	7.1
22.	Rajasthan	52.13	43.53	37.94	41.92	30.49	19.85	28.1	32.9
23.	Sikkim	36.92	32.71	21.73	9.94	7.73	7.47	2.4	3.3
24.	Tamil Nadu	49.40	48.69	46.96	38.64	39.77	22.11	18.8	22.2
25.	Tripura	36.92	32.71	21.73	9.94	7.73	7.47	2.4	3.3
26.	Uttar Pradesh	60.09	56.23	49.82	42.96	35.39	30.89	26.3	30.6
27.	Uttarakhand	—	—	—	—	—	—	32.0	36.5
28.	West Bengal	34.67	38.20	32.32	35.08	22.41	14.86	32.0	36.5
29.	Andaman & Nicobar	49.40	48.69	46.96	38.64	39.77	22.11	18.8	22.2
30.	Chandigarh	27.96	27.32	23.79	14.67	11.32	5.75	3.8	7.1

31.	Dadra & Nagar Haveli	37.69	36.31	27.00	—	39.93	13.52	19.2	19.1
32.	Daman & Diu	—	—	—	—	27.03	7.52	20.8	21.2
33.	Delhi	52.23	33.51	27.89	13.56	16.03	9.42	10.8	15.2
34.	Lakshadweep	62.74	55.62	45.68	40.33	24.55	20.27	16.4	20.2
35.	Pondicherry	49.40	48.69	46.96	38.64	39.77	22.11	18.8	22.2
	All India	49.01	45.24	40.79	38.20	32.36	23.62	21.7	25.7

Based on URP—Consumption.

Based on MRP—Consumption.

Hence the data of 1999-2000 and 2004-05 are not comparable, but the data of 1993-94 and 2004-05 are roughly comparable.

Source : GOI, Tenth Five Year Plan (2002-07) and http://pib.nic.in.

Annexure 4.4
Number and Percentage of Population Below Poverty Line by States—2004-05 (Based on URP—Consumption)

Sl. No.	State/U.T.'s	Rural		Urban		Combined	
		Percenage of persons	*No. of persons (lakhs)*	*Percenage of persons*	*No. of persons (lakhs)*	*Percenage of persons*	*No.of persons (lakhs)*
(1)	(2)	(3)	(4)	(5)	(6)	(7)	(8)
1.	Andhra Pradesh	11.2	64.70	28.0	61.40	15.8	126.10
2.	Arunachal Pradesh	22.3	1.94	3.3	0.09	17.6	2.03
3.	Assam	22.3	54.50	3.3	1.28	19.7	55.77
4.	Bihar	42.1	336.72	34.6	32.42	41.4	369.15
5.	Chhattisgarh	40.8	71.50	41.2	19.47	40.9	90.96
6.	Goa	5.4	0.36	21.3	1.64	13.8	2.01
7.	Gujarat	19.1	63.49	13.0	27.19	16.8	90.69
8.	Haryana	13.6	21.49	15.1	10.60	14.0	32.10
9.	Himachal Pradesh	10.7	6.14	3.4	0.22	10.0	6.36
10.	Jammu & Kashmir	4.6	3.66	7.9	2.19	5.4	5.85
11.	Jharkhand	46.3	103.19	20.2	13.20	40.3	116.39
12.	Karnataka	20.8	75.05	32.6	63.83	25.0	138.89

13.	Kerala	13.2	32.43	20.2	17.17	15.0	49.60
14.	Madhya Pradesh	36.9	175.65	42.1	74.03	38.3	249.68
15.	Maharashtra	29.6	171.13	32.2	146.25	30.7	317.38
16.	Manipur	22.3	3.76	3.3	0.20	17.3	3.95
17.	Meghalaya	22.3	4.36	3.3	0.16	18.5	4.52
18.	Mizoram	22.3	1.02	3.3	0.16	1.6	1.18
19.	Nagaland	22.3	3.87	3.3	0.12	19.0	3.99
20.	Orissa	46.8	151.75	44.3	26.74	46.4	178.49
21.	Punjab	9.1	15.12	7.1	6.50	8.4	21.63
22.	Rajasthan	18.7	87.38	32.9	47.51	22.1	134.89
23.	Sikkim	22.3	1.12	3.3	0.02	20.1	1.14
24.	Tamil Nadu	22.8	76.50	22.2	69.13	22.5	145.62
25.	Tripura	22.3	6.18	3.3	0.20	18.9	6.38
26.	Uttar Pradesh	33.4	773.00	30.6	117.03	32.8	590.03
27.	Uttarakhand	40.8	27.11	36.5	8.85	39.6	35.96
28.	West Bengal	28.6	173.22	14.8	35.14	24.7	208.36
29.	Andaman & Nicobar	22.9	0.60	22.2	0.32	22.6	0.92
30.	Chandigarh	7.1	0.08	7.1	0.67	7.1	0.74
31.	Dadra & Nagar Haveli	39.8	0.68	19.1	0.15	33.2	0.84
32.	Daman & Diu	5.4	0.07	21.2	0.14	10.5	0.21

(Contd.)

ANNEXURE 4.4 (Contd.)

(1)	(2)	(3)	(4)	(5)	(6)	(7)	(8)
33.	Delhi	6.9	0.63	15.2	22.30	14.7	22.93
34.	Lakshadweep	13.3	0.06	20.2	0.06	16.0	0.11
35.	Pondicherry	22.9	0.78	22.2	1.59	22.4	2.37
	All India	28.3	2209.24	25.7	807.96	27.5	3017.20

Notes : (1) Poverty Ratio of Assam is ued for Sikkim, Arunachal Pradesh, Meghalaya, Mizoram, Manipur, Nagaland and Tripura. (2) Poverty Line of Maharashtra and expenditure distribution of Goa is used to estimate poverty ratio of Goa. (3) Poverty Ratio of Tamil Nadu is used for Pondicherry and A & N Islands. (4) Urban Poverty Ratio of Punjab used for both rural and urban poverty of Chandigarh. (5) Poverty Line of Maharashtra and expenditure distribution of Dadra & Nagar Haveli is used to estimate poverty ratio of Dadra & Nagar Haveli. (6) Poverty Ratio of Goa is used for Daman & Diu. (7) Poverty Ratio of Kerala is used for Lakshadweep.

URP consumption = Uniform Recall Period consumption in which the consumer expenditure data for all the items are collected from 30-day recall period.

Source : http://pib.nic.in.

Annexure 4.5

Number and Percentage of Population Below Poverty Line by States—2004-05 (Based on MRP—Consumption)

Sl. No.	State/U.T.'s	Rural		Urban		Combined	
		Percenage of persons	No. of persons (lakhs)	Percenage of persons	No. of persons (lakhs)	Percenage of persons	No.of persons (lakhs)
(1)	(2)	(3)	(4)	(5)	(6)	(7)	(8)
1.	Andhra Pradesh	7.5	43.21	20.7	45.50	11.1	88.71
2.	Arunachal Pradesh	17.0	1.47	2.4	0.07	13.4	1.54
3.	Assam	17.0	41.46	2.4	093	15.0	42.39
4.	Bihar	32.9	262.92	28.9	27.09	32.5	290.01
5.	Chhattisgarh	31.2	54.72	34.7	16.39	32.0	7.11
6.	Goa	1.9	0.13	20.9	1.62	12.0	1.74
7.	Gujarat	13.9	46.25	10.1	21.18	12.5	67.43
8.	Haryana	9.2	14.57	11.3	7.99	9.9	22.56
9.	Himachal Pradesh	7.2	4.10	2.6	0.17	6.7	4.27
10.	Jammu & Kashmir	2.7	2.20	8.5	2.34	4.2	4.54
11.	Jharkhand	40.2	89.76	16.3	10.63	34.8	100.39

(Contd.)

ANNEXURE 4.5 (Contd.)

(1)	(2)	(3)	(4)	(5)	(6)	(7)	(8)
12.	Karnataka	12.0	43.33	27.2	53.28	17.4	96.60
13.	Kerala	9.6	23.59	16.4	13.92	11.4	37.51
14.	Madhya Pradesh	29.8	141.99	39.3	68.97	32.4	210.97
15.	Maharashtra	22.2	128.43	29.0	131.40	25.2	259.83
16.	Manipur	17.0	2.86	2.4	0.14	13.2	3.00
17.	Meghalaya	17.0	3.32	2.4	0.12	14.1	3.43
18.	Mizoram	17.0	0.78	2.4	0.11	9.5	0.89
19.	Nagaland	17.0	2.94	2.4	0.09	14.5	3.03
20.	Orissa	39.8	129.29	40.3	24.30	39.9	153.59
21.	Punjab	5.9	9.78	3.8	3.52	5.2	13.30
22.	Rajasthan	14.3	66.69	28.1	40.50	17.5	107.18
23.	Sikkim	17.0	0.85	2.4	0.02	15.2	0.87
24.	Tamil Nadu	16.9	56.51	18.8	58.59	17.8	115.10
25.	Tripura	17.0	4.70	2.4	0.14	14.4	4.85
26.	Uttar Pradesh	25.3	357.68	26.3	100.47	25.5	458.15
27.	Uttarakhand	31.7	21.11	32.0	7.75	31.8	28.86
28.	West Bengal	24.2	146.59	11.2	26.64	20.6	173.23
29.	Andaman & Nicobar	16.9	0.44	18.8	0.27	17.6	0.71

30.	Chandigarh	3.8	0.04	3.8	0.36	3.8	0.40
31.	Dadra & Nagar Haveli	36.0	0.62	19.2	0.16	30.6	0.77
32.	Daman & Diu	1.9	0.03	20.8	0.14	8.0	0.16
33.	Delhi	0.1	0.01	10.8	15.83	10.2	15.83
34.	Lakshadweep	9.6	0.04	16.4	0.05	12.3	0.09
35.	Pondicherry	16.9	0.58	18.8	1.34	18.2	1.92
	All India	21.8	1702.99	21.7	682.00	21.8	2384.99

Notes : Same as Table No. 4.13.

MRP consumption = Mixed Recall Period consumption in which the consumer expenditure data for five non-food items, namely, clothing, footwear, durable goods, education and institutional medical expenses are collected from 365-day recall period and the consumption data for the remaining items are collected from 30-day recall period.

Source : http://pib.nic.in.

Bibliography

Agarwal, Meenu (2008); Education in Third World Countries, Kanishka, New Delhi.

Ahluwalia and I.M.D. Little (ed.) (2006); *India's Economic Reforms and Development*, Oxford University Press, New Delhi.

Bhalla, Surjit S. (2002) : *Imagine There's No. Country : Poverty, Inequality and Growth in the Era of Globalisation*, Institute for International Economics, Washington D.C.

Basu Kaushik (ed.) (2006); *India's Emerging Economy : Performance and Prospects in 1990s and Beyond*, Oxford University Press, New Delhi.

Dandekar, V.M. and Neelkanth Rath (1971); *Poverty in India*, Indian School of Political Economy, Lonavala.

Deaton, A. and Dreze (2008); *Nutrition in India : Facts and Interpretations*, Princeton University.

Deaton, A. and A. Tarrozi (1999); Price and Poverty in India, Prince.

Dhingra, I.C. (2004); *Indian Economy*, Sultan Chand & Sons, New Delhi.

FAO (2008); *The State of Food Insecurity in the World*, Rome.

Government of India (1991); Economic Survey, 1990-91, Minsitry of Finance, New Delhi.

———, (1992); Economic Survey 1991-92, Minsitry of Finance, New Delhi.

Government of India (1993); Economic Survey, 1992-93, Minsitry of Finance, New Delhi.

———, (1996); Economic Survey, 1995-96, Minsitry of Finance, New Delhi.

———, (2002); Economic Survey, 2001-02, Minsitry of Finance, New Delhi.

———, (2006); Economic Survey, 2005-06, Minsitry of Finance, New Delhi.

———, (1952); First Five Year Plan (1951-56), Planning Commission, New Delhi.

———, (1957); Second Five Year Plan (1956-51), Planning Commission, New Delhi.

———, (1961); Third Five Year Plan (1961-66), Planning Commission, New Delhi.

———, (1969); Fourth Five Year Plan (1969-74), Planning Commission, New Delhi.

———, (1974); Fifth Five Year Plan (1974-79), Planning Commission, New Delhi.

———, (1980); Sixth Five Year Plan (1980-85), Planning Commission, New Delhi.

———, (1985); Seventh Five Year Plan (1985-90), Planning Commission, New Delhi.

———, (1992); Eighth Five Year Plan (1992-97), Planning Commission, New Delhi.

———, (1997); Ninth Five Year Plan (1997-2002), Planning Commission, New Delhi.

———, (2002); Tenth Five Year Plan (2002-07), Planning Commission, New Delhi.

———, (2007); Approach Paper to Eleventh Five Year Plan, Planning Commission, New Delhi.

———, Annual Reports—1990-91, 1993-94, 1997-98, 2002-03, 2005-06, Ministry of Rural Development.

———, Annual Reports—1990-91, 1993-94, 1997-98, 2002-03, 2005-06, Ministry of Urban Development.

Heller, Peter S. and M. Govind Rao (ed.) (2006); *A Sustainable Fiscal Policy for India : An International Perspective*, Oxford University Press, New Delhi.

Iliffe, J. (1987); The Agrican Poor, Cambridge University Press.

Jalan, Bimal (ed.) (1992); *The Indian Economy : Problems and Prospects,* Oxford University Press, New Delhi.

Kapila, Uma (ed.), (1998-99); *Indian Economy Since Independence,* Academic Foundation, New Delhi.

Lal, Deepak and H. Myint (1996); "The Political Economy of Poverty, Equity and Growth", Oxford, Clarendon Press.

Mahal, A. and Others (2001); *Who Benefits from Public Health Spending in India : Health Nutrition and Population,* Working Paper, World Bank, Washington D.C.

Maxwell, Simon (2001); The Meaning and Measurement of Poverty, Overseas Development Institute.

Mishra, G.P. (ed.) (1985); *Regional Structure of Growth and Development in India,* Ashish Publishing House, New Delhi.

Mishra, S.K. and V.K. Puri (2003); *Indian Economy,* Himalaya Publishing House, New Delhi.

Narayan, Deepa; Robert Chambers, Meera K. Shah and Patesh (2000); "Voices of the Poor : Crying and One for the Change", Oxford University Press, New York.

Nehru, Jawahar Lal (1946); *The Discovery of India,* The John Day Company, New York.

Peters, D.; A. Yazbeek, R. Sharma *et al.* (2002); *Better Health System for India's Poor*; World Bank, Washington D.C.

Rudra Datta and Sunderm, K.P.M. (2002); *Indian Economy,* S. Chand & Co., New Delhi.

Rao, K. Nageshwar (ed.) (2005); *Poverty in India : Global and Regional Dimensions,* Deep and Deep Publications, New Delhi.

Rao, M. Govind (2006); *Development, Poverty and Fiscal Policy : Decentralisation of Institutions,* Oxford University Press, New Delhi.

Ravallion, M. (1994); "Poverty Comparisons", Chur, Harward Academy.

Sachs, Jeffery, Nirupam Bajpai and Ashutosh Varshney (1999); *India in the Era of Economic Reforms,* Oxford University Press, New Delhi.

Sen, Amartya (1981); *Poverty and Farmers : An Essay on Entitlement and Deprivation*, Oxford University Press.

———, (ed.) (1984); Resources, Values and Development, Basil Blackwell, New York.

Shariff, Abuodeh, Prabir Ghosh and Samir Mondal (2002); *Indian Public Expenditure on Social Sector and Poverty Alleviation Programmes during in 1990s*, ODI Working Paper 169, Overseas Development Institute, London.

Srinivasan, T.N. and P.K. Bardhan (eds.) (1974); *Poverty and Income Distribution in India*, Statistical Publishing Society, Kolkatta.

Sukhatme, P.V. (1965); *Feeding Indian Growing Millions*, Asia Publishing House, New York.

Thakur, Anil Kumar and Chauhan, Shyam Sunder Singh (2009); Inter-regional disparities in India, Deep and Deep, New Delhi.

Thakur, Anil Kumar and Md. Abdus Salam (eds.) (2008); Economics of Education and Health in India, Deep and Deep, New Delhi.

Thakur, Anil Kumar and M.S. Kallur (eds.) (2008); Growth Theory and Globalisation of India, Deep and Deep, New Delhi.

Thakur, Anil Kumar and Dalip Kumar (eds.) (2007); Gender Empowerment and Development, Deep and Deep, New Delhi.

Tim Calle *et al.* (2001) : *India at the Cross Roads Sustaining Growth and Reducing Poverty*, International Monitary Fund, Washington D.C.

World Bank (1990); *World Development Report*, 1990, Oxford University Press, New York.

World Bank (1991); *World Development Report*, 1891, Oxford University Press, New Delhi.

World Bank (1995); *World Development Report*, 1995, Oxford University Press, New York.

World Bank (1998); *Reducing Poverty in India : Options for more Effective Public Services*, World Bank Country Report, Washington DC.

World Bank (2001); *World Development Report 2000/2001*, Oxford University Press, New York.

World Bank (2002); *India-Fiscal Policies to Accelerate Economic Growth*, Green Cover Report 2473-IN, South Asia Region, Poverty Reduction and Economic Management Unit, Washington D.C.

World Bank (2003); *India : Sustaining Reforms, Reducing Poverty*, Oxford University Press, New York.

World Bank (2005); *World Development Report, 2004*, Oxford University Press.

World Bank (2006); *World Development Report, 2006*, Oxford University Press, New Delhi.

UNDP (1997); *Human Development Report, 1997*, Oxford University Press, New York.

———, (2001); *Human Development Report, 2001*, Oxford University Press, New Delhi.

———, (2002); *Human Development Report, 2002*, Oxford University Press, New Delhi.

———, (2003); *Human Development Report, 2003*, Oxford University Press, New Delhi.

———, (2004); *Human Development Report, 2004*, Oxford University Press, New Delhi.

———, (2005); *Human Development Report, 2005*, Oxford University Press, New Delhi.

———, (2006); *Human Development Report, 2006*, Oxford University Press, New Delhi.

Journals and Periodicals

Asian Development Review

Economic Journal

Economic and Political Weekly

Indian Economic Journal

Journal of Development Studies

Journal of Economic Growth

Journal of Development Economics

Kurukshtra
Samaj Kalyan
Social Welfare
The American Economic Review
Yojana

Newspapers

Economic Trimes
The Hindu Business Line
Business Standard
Financial Express

Index